THE APPEARANCE OF EVIL

THE APPEARANCE OF EVIL

Apparitions of Spirits in Wales

EDMUND JONES

EDITED WITH AN INTRODUCTION BY JOHN HARVEY

UNIVERSITY OF WALES PRESS

CARDIFF

2003

British Library Cataloguing-in-Publication Data.
A catalogue record for this book is available from the British Library.

ISBN 0–7083–1854–1 paperback
    0–7083–1855–X hardback

Published with the financial support of the University of Wales, Aberystwyth

Typeset at University of Wales Press
Printed in Great Britain by Henry Ling Limited, Dorchester

For Jacqueline

Many devils are in woods, in waters, in wildernesses, and in dark pooly places, ready to hurt and prejudice people; some are in the thick black clouds, which cause hail, lightnings, and thunderings, and poison the air, the pastures and grounds. When these things happen, then the philosophers and physicians say, it is natural, ascribing it to the planets, and showing I know not what reasons for such misfortunes and plagues as ensue.

Martin Luther, *Table Talk* (1566)

Contents

List of Illustrations

Preface

Edmund Jones was born in Penllwyn near Nant-y-glo in Monmouthshire (a few hundred yards from the place where I entered the world). He first came to my attention during the late 1970s, when I lived in Abertillery in the Ebbw Fach valley. The local chapel deacons spoke reverently of him as a shadowy prophet-like chronicler from over the mountain on the east side of town. My introduction to his writings on the occult came, again, through an oral tradition. Several accounts recorded in his books endured, in some form or other, as local folklore. I heard tales of events that had supposedly taken place on and around the Arail (the mountain on the west side of Abertillery) several centuries earlier: how, on one occasion, a company of mischievous fairies had carried away travellers on the summit; on another occasion, they had been witnessed flying in formation along the mountainside, weaving an undulating path through the sky from Blaina down towards Hafod-y-dafol (59). For me, these tales transformed the valley into a preternatural and disquieting place in a time before industry, wherein wandered foul forces.

Today one can still take an imaginative leap across the centuries and return to this lost world. From the top of the Arail, the valley below appears silent and invisible. The only signifiers of mining and modernity are the rusting remains of pit-frames, the fissures filled with abandoned refrigerators, and the derelict motorcars, wedged amid the creaking firs, which appear to have dropped out of the clouds like apports (material objects that appear – supernaturally, it is supposed – out of thin air). Elsewhere are grassland, bleached bones, drystone walls, and sheep – a barren and undistinguished landscape, much like that encountered by the abducted travellers. The summit is an eerie place: natural phenomena conspire to unnerve the solitary walker. There are strange sounds: the disembodied bleating of a lamb carried on the breeze, heard one moment as though from a great distance and the next, close at hand; the unearthly whirring of the wind through the telegraph wires or drawing breath along the long grass; and an unfathomable dull thud underfoot, like some great door slamming shut inside the mountain. Thus, far from the reassuring glow of sulphurous street-lights, terraces, and traffic, the idea that dark and extraordinary events once took place on the mountain seems less remote.

Like an inscription on an old gravestone, the source of these stories, together with their dates and the names of witnesses, had long since worn away. They came to light again some years ago, when I discovered Jones's book on apparitions along with Edgar Phillips's biography of Jones (published in the year I was born) while I was researching Protestant visions. Like the visions of Christ, the devil, and angelic beings which Welsh Nonconformists claimed to have seen, apparitions represent a visualization of spiritual ideas and entities; their accounts provide a tantalizing glimpse into how the lower orders of Welsh society conceived of the invisible agencies of evil and good. In this respect, the preparation of this new edition of Jones's book represents a further contribution to my studies on ephemeral and intangible forms of working-class visual culture and religious experience.

Dimensions (where known) are in centimetres, height × width.

All biblical quotations are from the Authorized (King James) Version (1611), to which Edmund Jones referred in his preaching and publications.

The county names given in this book are those of the pre-1974 counties, by which the counties were known during the historical period to which this book refers.

The numbers in parentheses in the preface, introduction, epilogue, and notes refer to individual accounts in this edition of Jones's work. The numbers in parentheses and printed bold in the preface and introduction refer to illustrations.

John Harvey
Centre for Studies in the Visual Culture of Religion
School of Art, University of Wales, Aberystwyth

Acknowledgements

I would like to thank David C. Jones and Ann Parry Owen of the Centre for Advanced Welsh and Celtic Studies, University of Wales; Alan Gauld of the School of Psychology, University of Nottingham; Richard E. Huws, Head of Services and Training, Charles Parry, Assistant Librarian, and Mervyn Wyn Tomos, Assistant Archivist at the National Library of Wales, Aberystwyth; the staff of the British Library, London; and the Society of Psychical Research, London. I would also like to acknowledge the financial assistance received from the Sir David Hughes Parry Award and the University of Wales, Aberystwyth.

All reasonable steps have been taken to trace the copyright holder of NLW MS 16161B held in the National Library of Wales, Aberystwyth, part of which has been reproduced here. The publishers would be glad to hear from the copyright holder.

Acknowledgement for permission to reproduce images and photographic credits are due to: British Library, London, for Illustration 13; Fortean Picture Library for Illustration 18; National Library of Wales, Aberystwyth, for Illustrations 1, 2, 3, 4, 5, 6, 7, 8, 9, 10, 11, 12, 14, 15, 16, 17, and Plate 4; National Museum and Galleries of Wales, Cardiff, for Illustration 20 and Plate 2; National Museum of Western Art, Tokyo, for Plate 1; Tate Gallery, London, for Plate 3; and the Royal Commission on the Ancient and Historical Monuments of Wales for Illustration 19.

Introduction

There is not a single portrait of Edmund Jones (1702–93) among the innumerable extant drawings, engravings, and paintings depicting notable eighteenth-century Welsh Dissenting ministers. Yet he left a far more significant visual legacy. It comprises lucid personal observations on the geography and geology of his native parish of Aberystruth and county of Monmouthshire, together with copious accounts that give unprecedented definition to the frequently worrisome supernatural beings that inhabited these and other places in Wales. Jones rendered the shape and context of these creatures with a descriptive prowess that far surpassed his gift for preaching, but which, like his preaching, reflected a compulsively emblematic outlook on life.[1] In collecting and publishing these relations, Jones, like Luke the Evangelist, determined: 'to set forth in order a declaration of those things most surely believed among us, even as they delivered them unto us, which from the beginning were eyewitnesses, and ministers of the word' (Luke 1:1–2). In so doing, he knit together the beliefs and imaginings of hundreds of people (whose experience of the supernatural was typical of considerably more), otherwise separated by many mountains and miles. They were the witnesses, and their accounts the evidence, in his prosecution on behalf of the afterlife and against the denial of such by eighteenth-century materialism. Jones's collection of spirit narratives, together with his other writings, also provides an insight into the consciousness and convictions of a man who, while characteristic of Welsh ministers of his age in many aspects of doctrine and practice, was in other respects uniquely idiosyncratic. As such, Jones's works render in words a portrait more vivid than most other preachers received in pencil, print, or paint.

Jones was an Independent minister associated with the vicinity of Pontypool in the county of Monmouthshire, where he preached regularly during the 1730s, and where he gathered a congregation and established a meeting-house at the village of Pontnewynydd in 1741.[2] He sustained a punishing itinerant ministry too, travelling (on horseback and on foot, throughout Wales and his seventy years of service) across, what he considered, a cursed and pestilent landscape, infested with the emissaries of darkness.[3] Jones's thumbnail autobiography, written by his pseudonymous alter ego Solomon Owen Caradoc (S.O.C.), reveals a man of modesty and candour – an autodidact, for the most part, whose life was rooted in a pastoral setting redolent of biblical times and places: 'He hath been bred up only to Husbandry and looking after Cattle and Sheep, and although He was not in any University, or Academy; nor was instructed in any Liberal Sciences: Yet was a great Lover of Books, buying and borrowing as much as he could come at.'[4] Jones published as much as he could, too, at least eleven works: eight chiefly comprising sermons on doctrine, one on geography and religious history, and two on the occult (the collections of spirit narratives) of which the second of the two was titled *A Relation of Apparitions of Spirits, in the Principality of Wales; to which is Added the Remarkable Account of the Apparition in Sunderland* (1780) (1).

The books consist of accounts of ghosts, devils, fairies, witches, evil and disembodied spirits, and what today is termed poltergeist activity, most of which Jones collected by word of mouth from people he met during his itinerancy around the parishes and counties of Wales.[5] The credibility of his accounts was founded on the moral rectitude of the witnesses and relaters, the majority of whom were either ministers or clergymen, and godly and honest believers – people who (he was sure) did not engage in, or have reason to profit from, lies.[6] He received many of their relations at first or second hand. However, a large number of other accounts have no known or stated pedigree. Uncommonly for this type of collection, the witnesses and relaters were representative of broad social strata. There were professionals such as a soldier, a scientist, a doctor, a schoolmaster and scholars; artisans, including a blacksmith, a gunsmith, a farrier, a turner, and tailors; and – the vast majority – members of the servile and labouring classes (farm workers and maidservants, for instance). Thus, whereas collected accounts of ghosts usually reflect the experience of the gentry, Jones's work, uniquely, described the religious imagination of predominantly the lower orders, many of whom were (like himself) Dissenters. The narratives are vignettes of their habitual way of life at home and in the field, eating, journeying, working, worshipping, conjuring, resting, sleeping, dying, and burying.

A Relation of Apparitions of Spirits, the historian Thomas Rees (1815–85) wrote, is 'a very curious production, full of strange ghost-stories, such as no nervous person should read in the night'.[7] They are not, however, ghost-stories in the nineteenth-century sense of the genre – imaginary tales contrived to satisfy a craving to be scared – but a collection of testimonies, describing allegedly genuine encounters with spiritual entities, designed to convince of a truth and convict of a heresy. In these respects, Jones's work belongs to a tradition of histories of spirits, written mostly by Dissenting ministers and Protestant and Roman Catholic clergymen, which marshalled accounts of ghosts, demons, fairies, and witches to vindicate revealed religion, prove post-mortem life, and administer (to invoke the title of Henry More's 1653 book) an 'antidote against atheism'.

While there has been no common Protestant view on apparitions, two discernible and contrasting tendencies emerged at the outset of the Reformation, typified by its principal architects: Martin Luther (1483–1546) and John Calvin (1509–64). Both believed in the scriptural doctrine of spirits (good and bad) and in their continued operation in human affairs. Luther retained the monastic belief that demons inhabited the natural world and could assume visible form, appearing as people or weird and terrifying creatures. Abiding by the principle of *sola Scriptura*, Calvin ignored the medieval accretions and encouraged a

A

R E L A T I O N

O F

APPARITIONS

O F

S P I R I T S,

I N T H E

PRINCIPALITY OF *WALES;*

T O W H I C H I S A D D E D

THE REMARKABLE ACCOUNT

O F T H E

APPARITION IN *SUNDERLAND,*

with other

NOTABLE RELATIONS FROM *ENGLAND;*

T O G E T H E R W I T H

OBSERVATIONS ABOUT THEM, AND

INSTRUCTIONS FROM THEM:

Defigned

TO CONFUTE AND TO PREVENT THE INFIDELITY OF DENYING

THE BEING AND APPARITION OF SPIRITS; WHICH TENDS TO

IRRELIGION AND ATHEISM.

Nam Sadducæi quidem dicunt non effe refurrectionem, neque
angelum, neque fpiritum. —— Acta xxiii. 8.

PRINTED IN THE YEAR, M,DCC,LXXX.

1. Title-page of *A Relation of Apparitions of Spirits, in the Principality of Wales; to which is Added the Remarkable Account of the Apparition in Sunderland* (1780).

A RELATION OF

APPARITIONS

OF

SPIRITS,

In the County of Monmouth,

AND THE PRINCIPALITY OF

WALES:

With other notable relations from England ; together
with observations about them, and instructions
from them : designed to confute and to
prevent the infidelity of denying
the being and Apparition
of Spirits ; which

Tends to Irreligion and Atheism.

By the late Rev. EDMUND JONES,

of the *Tranch.*

Nam Sadducæi quidem dicunt non esse resurrectionem,
neque angelum, neque spiritum.—Acta xxiii. 8.

NEWPORT,

MONMOUTHSHIRE:

PRINTED AND SOLD BY E. LEWIS,
BOOKSELLER, STATIONER, AND BOOKBINDER;
ETHERIDGE AND TIBBINS:
SOLD ALSO BY CROSBY AND CO. STATIONER'S-
COURT, LONDON; C. FROST, BROAD-STREET,
BRISTOL; AND MOST BOOKSELLERS
IN TOWN AND COUNTRY.

1813.

2. Title-page of *A Relation of Apparitions of Spirits, in the County of Monmouth, and the
Principality of Wales* (1813).

conception of demonic activity, the ministration of angels, and spectral appearances which was influenced almost entirely by the New Testament.

Nowhere does the New Testament suggest that the devil and his associates took on visible semblance or corporality: Christ and the Apostles portray the devil solely through verbal metaphors illuminating his character and devices (1 Peter 5:8); the Evangelists' only reference to Satan's presence, at Christ's temptation in the wilderness, depicts the adversary as a disembodied voice. Demoniacal opposition to his ministry is elsewhere evident in possessions: demons speaking through their hosts and making people blind, violent, dumb, and prone to fits (Matthew 4:1–11; Luke 8:27–8). Likewise, the New Testament represents angels merely by what they say and do. On only one occasion, where two angels appear at the tomb after Christ's resurrection, is a visual attribute mentioned (John 20:12). Ghosts, the Reformers and Puritans believed, were either the ministering spirits of the redeemed or, more probably, demon impersonators (such as the spirit of Samuel, invoked by the witch of Endor in 1 Samuel 28:7, was understood to be).[8] In the New Testament references to a ghost (in Greek, *phantasma*) concern the disciples' misinterpretation of Christ's appearance when he walked on the water and after the resurrection (Matthew 14:26; Mark 6:49; Luke 24:37).[9] In mistaking Christ for 'a deceitful vision, as if it had been a vaine Ghost', Calvin judged, they exhibited a 'grosse and blockish . . . infirmitie' resulting from fear, tiredness, and sorrow. He held this opinion of all who similarly countenanced such 'delusions'.[10] As the Reformer banished spirits into biblically sanctioned obscurity, Protestant accounts of apparitions greatly diminished.[11]

Luther and Calvin's respective emphases on the visualization and conceptualization of spirits echoed their theological differences regarding tangible spiritual images. Luther encouraged the setting-up of representations of God and holy persons in churches to serve as books for the illiterate; Calvin forbade them, believing that pictures and sculptures were impious lies, a snare to the superstitious and (like visible spirits) lacking biblical warrant.[12] The Puritans and early Dissenters, equally convinced that the unseen things of the spirit should remain so, implemented Calvin's ban. Yet many also adopted Luther's demonology, believing that apparitions were not, like icons and dumb idols, the fabrication of man's art and vain imaginings, but visible and sentient self-representations: true likenesses, verified by many sightings. They regarded apparitions, as Roman Catholics had used holy relics and miraculous pictures and statues, as the perceptible evidence of religious realities, serving to confirm believers in the faith and, as importantly, to challenge scepticism: 'the consideration of the Devil's power, in those wonderful effects we call *supernatural operations*, if well proved and attested; must needs be of great weight . . . with a rational man.'[13] In the same vein, the Puritan divine Richard Baxter (1615–91) reflected: 'Apparitions, and other sensible Manifestations of the certain existence of Spirits of themselves Invisible, was a means that might do much with such as are prone to judge by Sense.'[14]

Edmund Jones believed that his own history of spirits could serve the same purpose. Belief in ghosts and fairies in Wales, as elsewhere, had fallen out of favour among educated people in general by the mid-eighteenth century. This followed the development, during the Enlightenment, of a critical attitude to supernatural revelation, the spread of materialism and the growth of liberal Christianity. In a scientifically enlightened but spiritually dark age, wherein 'Sense' was the principal agent of experience and verification, *A Relation of Apparitions of Spirits* had a deeply religious objective: it aimed to arrest the progress of scepticism and provide proof of the life to come, and thereby to confute the fashionable infidelity of denying the soul's immortality and the existence of the occult. Failure to believe such doctrines, Protestants and Roman Catholics warned, would lead to a renunciation of the reality of the soul and eternity and, inevitably, to Atheism; for, as Joseph Glanvill (1636–80) argued in *Saducismus Triumphatus* (1661), 'these things hang together in a Chain of connexion'.[15] The result would be an erosion of moral idealism and aspirations, and the eventual collapse of society.[16]

The title of Glanvill's book refers to 'Sadducism', the doctrine of the Sadducees in the New Testament, who denied the resurrection of the body (Mark 12:18). 'Sadducism' was commonly used as a derogatory synonym for Deism, a movement (whose clarion call was the title of John Toland's (1670–1722) work *Christianity Not Mysterious* (1695)) which repudiated apparitions, the necessity of biblical revelation, and God's supernatural intervention in the natural world through angels.[17] Jones also directed the charge at Protestants who believed in spirits but denied that they appeared. Intolerant of superstitious beliefs in general and apparitions in particular, many Protestants maintained that, after the completion of the canon of Scripture, God no longer employed supernatural intermediaries to communicate with mankind, since everything he wished them to know was contained therein.[18] For this reason, they interpreted apparitions not as divine messengers, redeemed returnees, or the spirits of the purgatorial dead (as the Roman Catholic Church supposed), but as demons, deceptions, or delusions (in keeping with Calvin's judgement), whose purpose was to draw people away from the word of truth.

In arguing for the existence of apparitions, Jones, along with Dissenting and Anglican advocates, was mindful not to encourage either Popish abuses or, as one writer put it, the fanciful excesses found 'even amongst *Protestants*, [for whom] abundance of these Apparitions have been mere Banter and Collusion, or the Impressions of Fear, and Melancholy Imagination'.[19] To this end, they developed criteria to distinguish between authentic sightings and those that were inventions of deceit or mania, and a demonology which identified the nature, province, and characteristics of apparitions.[20] The proof and verification of apparitions was established, on the basis of precedent, using accounts of various manifestations in the Scriptures, extra-biblical texts, and contemporary narratives. Such evidences, George Sinclair (d. 1696) asserted confidently, 'leave a deeper impression upon minds and more lasting, than thousands of subtle

Metaphysical Arguments'.[21] Nevertheless, Protestants, too, sought a philosophical credibility for apparitions deploying citations to works by ancient
scholars (for even the heathen 'believe and tremble') and sympathetic Enlightenment thinkers, such as John Locke's (1632–1704) *The Reasonableness of
Christianity* (1695), sprinkled liberally, if superficially, in prefatory treatises and
vindications.[22]

Jones also had an antiquarian purpose in publishing his book. He regarded it
as a providential response to a call by the Honourable Society of Cymmrodorion
for an account of apparitions in Wales:

> And who will blame the Honourable Cymmrodorion Society in London, composed of some
> Nobility, members of Parliament, great numbers of Gentry, many Clergymen, in all, several
> Hundreds, who, among other Curious parts of knowledge from Wales, desire the account of
> Apparitions, in the Printed account of this great, and Honourable Society: for here is a fair
> call of providence for this kind of work for the Press.[23]

The Society's constitutions ('the Printed account'), published in 1754, included
among the general headings 'Of Subjects to be occasionally considered and
treated (among others) in the Correspondence of the Society':

> Queries of the Invisible World, whether it be true or false what is reported of 1. Apparitions
> and Dreams. 2. Haunted Houses, and Treasures discover'd by that Means. 3. Knockers in
> Mines, a kind of beneficent Spirits. 4. Appearances in Day-time of Funerals, followed soon
> after by real Funerals; the same with Psalm-singing heard in the Night. 5. Corps Candles.[24]

Before the publication of Jones's accounts, apparitions in Wales received scant
attention either in books dealing mainly with historical and topographical topics
or in histories of spirits in Great Britain and Europe. Most notably, the *Itinera-
rium Cambriae* by Giraldus Cambrensis (*c*.1147–1223) mentioned apparitions of
demons and spirits, and even of buildings, orchards, and pastures.[25] These were
only some of the accounts of extraordinary phenomena occurring in Wales,
including an animal that was half stag and half horse, a soldier who secreted a
calf, pygmies from the underworld, and a run-of-the-mill batch of possessions,
exorcisms, and non-sensible, stone-throwing spirits. Several accounts of
apparitions in Wales were included in Baxter's *The Certainty of the Worlds of
Spirits* (1691), *The History of The Principality of Wales* (1730) by Robert Burton,
and an anonymous eighteenth-century compilation entitled *Fair and Fatal
Warnings*. Baxter mentioned knockers (to which the Society's constitutions
refer) – subterranean spirits often encountered in Cornish metal mines whose
presence, in the form of supernatural knockings, whistles, footsteps, and sometimes appearances of diminutive people, helped miners in trouble. Accounts of
'knockers in mines' in Wales were interpreted, along with sightings of the ghosts
of miners killed underground, as portents of disaster.[26]

Among the most conspicuous omens of death in Wales, which Baxter, Burton, and the constitutions mention, were corpse-candles (*cannwyll y corph*).[27] Jones included four accounts in the 1780 edition. In one, the characteristic lambent, bluish flame emerges from the nostrils of a dead body at night; in another account, it floats above the ground along the route where a funeral cortège would later travel. Sometimes, witnesses observed the ghost of the deceased holding the flame; others noted that the flame vanished or retaliated when struck (18, 19).[28] A large flame was said to anticipate the death of an adult, and a small one that of an infant or an abortion.[29] (Marie Trevelyan records that, in the nineteenth century, corpse-candles sometimes also appeared before a colliery explosion.[30]) Those who looked for a scientific rationalization interpreted the phenomenon associated with corpses as an electrical discharge or effluvium from 'a body already in an incipient state of putrescence'. Will-o'-the-wisp (a phosphorescent light caused by the combustion of methane) was cited as the most likely explanation for flames seen on marshy ground or down mines.[31] The audible equivalent of corpse-candle was the *cyhyraeth*: 'a doleful foreboding noise heard before death' resembling the voice of 'the groaning sick persons who are to die', often heard in the middle of Carmarthenshire and before foul weather. In some cases, the course of the noise, like that of the candle, anticipated the path afterwards travelled by the burial party (14, 15, 16, 108).[32]

    The other classes of death portents listed in the constitutions were ghostly nocturnal psalm-singing and premonitory funerals. There are two accounts of the former and four accounts of the latter among Jones's collection (22, 24, 25, 60).[33] The agents of these phenomena were disembodied voices (in one example, a kind of singing *cyhyraeth*), fairies, and spirits. In the case of prophetic, apparitional cortèges, these spirits either were or could seem palpably real. Jones includes fourteen accounts of houses that spirits occasionally troubled rather than haunted (strictly speaking).[34] Their nuisance took the form of poltergeist activity (such as moving furniture and throwing objects), apparitions, and animal-like noises (11, 32, 45, 85, 98, 102, 121, 133).[35] While there are no accounts of treasure found in connection with haunted houses in *A Relation of Apparitions of Spirits*, Jones does include several testimonies by witnesses to recovering money and other concealed items guided by an apparition (2, 3, 41, 42, 49).[36]

    The Society's constitutions gave Jones an agenda for collecting.[37] Thus, with the exception of accounts of knockers and dreams (which were too subjective a phenomenon for Jones's purpose), *A Relation of Apparitions of Spirits* encompassed, to a greater or lesser degree, all the classes of apparition mentioned in the constitutions. As such, Jones was the first author to give Wales an extensive and representative account of its strange and supernatural underbelly, the like of which England and some European countries had possessed for many years.[38]

    For Wales, however, the timing of the book's publication was entirely appropriate. Jones wrote the original book (now lost) and its sequel during a century which saw the rise of Evangelical religion and a succession of local revivals nurtured by the ministry of Methodist preachers like Howel Harris

(1714–73) and Daniel Rowland (1713–90).[39] The Methodist leaders preached a
vital and experiential Christianity in order to raise the Old Dissent (the Baptists,
Independents and other Nonconformist bodies) and the Established Church
Lazarus-like from the tomb of religious lassitude and indifference. Glanmor
Williams succinctly describes the condition of the old denominations prior to
Methodism's incursion into Wales: they were

> shrunken in numbers, withered in zeal, tending to exclude newcomers and to turn inwards
> on themselves, with much of their energy being absorbed by sterile theological disputes
> within their own ranks. Moreover, Dissenters and churchmen alike seemed to have allowed
> the rationalism of the age, and even deism, to spread too widely among them. Such
> intellectual attitudes deplored religious enthusiasm, encouraged prudential morality,
> nurtured enlightened self-interest, and, most damaging of all, emptied religion of all its
> emotional appeal.[40]

Methodism sought to reawaken conscience, to promote an emotional, heartfelt
religion, to encourage a passion for souls, and to emphasize the ordinary, and
sometimes extraordinary, work of the Holy Spirit.[41]

While Jones remained ardently Independent, he embraced the new enthusiasm, thus bridging the Old Dissent and New Dissent. In Methodism, he found
support for the cause of infant baptism (for which he campaigned tirelessly
throughout his life), and a theological outlook that, in contrast to Deism and
Rationalism (the twin targets of his books), stressed the supernatural operations
of God. Besides powerful preaching, unusual spiritual phenomena were a
hallmark of the revivals. In a climate of heightened religious emotion and
susceptibility, testimonies to curious providences, divine retribution, and
dreams and visions abounded. Adjectives such as 'astonishing', 'surprising',
'extraordinary' and 'wonderful' were commonplace descriptions of these experiences. Pamphlets such as *An Account of the Most Remarkable Particulars Relating
to the Present Progress of the Gospel* (1743) disseminated these accounts and, in
turn, cultivated a longing in others for the same experiences. *A Relation of
Apparitions of Spirits* was not, therefore, out of tune with either the general tenor
or the excesses of its age, simply one among a variety of numerous proofs of
spiritual activity.

Eighteenth-century accounts of revivals, anxious not to diminish the glory of
or to deflect from the attention due to God, emphasized the work of the Holy
Spirit in conviction and conversion rather than the machinations of the devil. In
his influential treatise, *Some Thoughts Concerning the Present Revival of Religion
in New England*, the philosopher-theologian Jonathan Edwards (1703–58)
conceived of the latter merely in terms of Satan's hindrance to the Great
Awakening through its detractors, and of the indiscreet, imprudent, and
excessive behaviour of revival enthusiasts.[42] Jones's book provided a counter-
poise to this approach, describing instead the sensible or spectacular activities of
the devil. For Jones, demonology was a sphere of study as legitimate and God-

honouring as theology: 'there is nothing so bad either on Earth or in Hell but some fearful instruction can be deduced from it, by an ingenious Spiritual mind . . . Since all scripture was given for our profitable instruction, then so also the knowledge of spirits.'[43] His book, like many Protestant works on the subject, was precautionary and didactic, aiming to vanquish ignorance of Satan's wiles and devices, to alarm the unconverted, and to equip believers for spiritual warfare[44] by making visible the evil from which revivals sought to liberate sinners. From the circumstances surrounding apparitions, he readily deduced the sins that had solicited them, thereby denouncing card-playing, Sabbath-breaking, fornication, the heinous sin of suicide, and conjuring.[45] Thus, in the tradition of the medieval *exemplum* (a short, moralizing essay written by clergymen), Jones's accounts were also didactic in intent – written to exemplify theological points, and as cautionary tales to illustrate the dangers of transgression and meddling with evil, and the torments of unrepentant souls after death. Following the pattern of medieval spirit narratives, Jones also records that witnesses frequently fell ill and died shortly after seeing the apparition (62, 101, 105).[46]

Jones's book shared with earlier Protestant histories of spirits, such as R. B.'s *The Kingdom of Darkness; or, The History of Daemons, Specters, Witches, Apparitions, Possessions, Disturbances* (1688), a general classification of apparitions into those that were visible, invisible or unseen, perceptual or auditory, evil or good. Jones described their purpose (where known) as variously: mischievous or portentous; retributive or restorative; to dispose or receive recompense, to warn or reprove; to prove or prevent. There are accounts of ghosts returning from the afterlife to attend to unfinished business, rectify an injustice, or seek release from their torments (1, 112). In some cases, they compelled witnesses to uncover money, clothes, or tools (which they had holed up in walls or buried while on the earth), and cast them into deep waters (3).[47] However, their reasons for so doing remained concealed: 'That the spirits of men are troubled after death for hiding iron instruments and tools is fact proved by numerous instances, but there is a mystery in it that cannot be understood by men upon earth. The spirits who are troubled have never revealed it.'[48] Nevertheless, Jones speculated 'that partly the spirits of the dead do it out of envy that others do enjoy what they are deprived of'.[49] Other apparitions returned to minister mercy: consoling grief-stricken loved ones, lifting the spirit of a saint at worship or in extremis, and preventing sin (9, 30, 31, 96).[50] Yet others appeared as the harbinger of some dreadful discovery or death, to enact future events, or to punish the witness's misdemeanour and dispatch the soul of the damned to hell (10, 17, 28, 54, 56).[51] There were, too, the 'unholy walkers to and fro through the earth', as Jones called them. Their mission was merely malice: to confute and confound, let and hinder, or simply scare the witness witless (32, 33, 39, 40, 63, 67, 88, 92, 113).[52] Not all apparitions had some purposeful appointment with the witness. As often, witnesses were reluctant spectators, observing the spirit going about its business, pursuing its quarry, malingering, traversing the landscape, or travelling to the kingdom of darkness (57, 64, 79, 94, 114, 115).[53]

In contrast to his predecessors, Jones includes few accounts describing an apparition of *the* devil (Satan, as distinct from lesser devils) and none of the sensual concomitants, like the foul, sulphurous smell of brimstone often said to accompany demonic presence.[54] Absent, too, is any reference to individual possessions (commonly reported in seventeenth-century accounts) and the more unsavoury manifestations associated with it, such as individuals vomiting substantial quantities of pins, nails, spoons, handles, glass, hair, or lumps of meat.[55] Nor does Jones include accounts of sexual fraternization between devils and young girls; or the base, if picturesque, practice of 'kissing Satan's arse' (**16**); or the shocking bodily contortions and vexations attributed to witches who, as Francis Hutchinson observed, 'can turn their Eyes inward, swallow their Tongues, foam at the Mouth, and put their own Arms, or Legs, or Back-bones out of Joint' – the damning evidence of their contrariness to nature.[56] The witches mentioned in Jones's book confine their craft to telekinesis, transmuting dairy products and transforming themselves into animals (53).

Jones's sanitized and non-forensic accounts of apparitions reflected as much the limits of his own experience as the sensibilities and proprieties of his age and intended readership. Reaching that readership was largely a private enterprise. He procured the funds for printing the sequel from Dissenters he met in the course of his ministry. His diary for 1780 (the year of publication) records that, for example, William Powel and Thomas Parry each contributed five shillings, and Gheziah Powel donated ten shillings and sixpence, 'to help printing'.[57] (These were considerable sums of money, relative to the annual wages earned by rural workers at the time.[58]) Later, Jones 'paid at Trefeca 3 Guineas for 6 sheaths of paper to print 200 of the account of Apparitions in Wales: and 16 shillings for marble paper to cover them & 5 shillings for the carriage of the paper.'[59] He bought the materials from Trefeca, the home of Howel Harris's Methodist printing and bookbinding trade. Though there are no publication details on the title-page, it is likely that the press at Trefeca printed the sequel, as it had almost all of Jones's earlier and subsequent works.[60] The press had already had a foretaste of the proposed book from his *Geographical, Historical, and Religious Account of the Parish of Aberystruth*, published a year earlier. It comprised topographical, geographical, geological, theological, doxological, historical, and biographical observations, together with a section on apparitions. In the opinion of the Revd John Evans (thirty years later), the latter was the book's only redeeming feature:

> What gives his work the most interesting trait, as indicative of the mental imbecility of the author, and the credulous state of the country, is the description 'on Apparitions, Fairies, and other Spirits of Hell' . . . This extraordinary publication and author would have been totally unworthy of notice, had not the farrago of its contents demonstrated, how ill qualified such men are to direct the spiritual concerns of others, who are themselves so totally unacquainted with the spiritual world.[61]

The yoking together of Jones and the publication, though unfeeling, was not unwarranted. The author was indeed as strange as the book. From an early age, he demonstrated a propensity to see apparitions and visions which remained with him all his life. As a young boy Jones saw, while walking with his aunt early one morning, a company of fairies in a field between Hafod-y-dafol and Penllwyn, and, as a young man, confronted the spectral hag on Llanhilleth mountain (57, 90) (3).[62] Towards the latter part of his life, he experienced vivid religious dreams, some of which were significant enough to record in his diary. Not surprisingly, given the nature and intensity of his vocation, several dreams concerned preaching.[63] For instance, in 1789 he noted: 'The night of the 18th. I dreamed I saw an old book the life of some very bad man & in it a sermon of some good man upon Psalm 41:11.' The same year, he confessed to being 'Disturbed by a girl spirit in bed 12 day twixt 10 and 11 at night'.[64] In 1740, Jones and his wife, May Jones (1696–1770) – who was of one mind with her husband in her convictions about the supernatural world – moved into an empty house called the 'Transh' (where they lived for the remainder of their lives). The house, situated near Pontypool in the parish of Trevethin, 'was troubled by an evil spirit' that manifested itself in knocks and various animal-like sounds, and, on one occasion, as a light (121–4).[65]

Jones also claimed the gift of prophecy,[66] which was evident in his ability to interpret, among other things, natural phenomena as divine omens. On several occasions, including one Sunday evening after preaching at Tŷ'n-y-fyd in the Ebbw Fawr valley, he saw:

> a white Cloud in the clear sky, and a perfectly calm evening, in the form of a Bow, of an equal breadth, reaching over the middle of the Valley, from one Mountain to another, from East, to West, which continued visible for some time; and it was a notable sight to look upon.

Its colour and appearance suggested to him 'Peace and felicity', more particularly a promise of 'God's Peace and Favour to his Church', as evidenced by the current success of the Gospel in those parts.[67]

His sensibility for signs and portents derived in part from an interest in astrology. Jones collected books on the subject, and charted his horoscope on the blank pages of popular English almanacs. The *Merlinus Liberatus* (which included the 'Protestant Remembrancer') and *Coelestial Atlas* contained astro-nomical information, forecasts about the weather and world events, and a calendar of months and days. It was not uncommon for Protestants to consult the stars about the future. After all, they argued, did not God decide the course both of the affairs of men and of the heavenly bodies, and had he not guided the wise men to the Christ-child using a star?[68] Jones was also interested in the much grander predictions of biblical prophecy and typology (a system of biblical interpretation by which incidents, people, and objects in the Old Testament are seen as shadows prefiguring the same in the New Testament).[69] Jones published five sermons on typological subjects, including *The Leaves of the Tree of Life; or, The Nations Healed by the Gospel of Jesus Christ* (1745), under his pseudonym

3. T. H. Thomas, 'The Old Woman of the Mountain',
engraving, 11.1 × 7.1, *British Goblins* (1880).

Solomon Owen Caradoc, the headings of which sermon, Jones claimed, Caradoc
had received supernaturally (as John Bunyan (1628–88) had his *Pilgrim's
Progress* (1678)) in a dream.[70]

If typology established the union of the Old and New Testaments, the
'analogy of faith' established the union of the natural and spiritual worlds. This
was a theological principle, propounded by Ambrose (*c.*339–97) and popularized
in the early eighteenth century in *The Analogy of Religion* (1726) by the anti-
Deist and natural theologian Joseph Butler (1692–1752), in which God's work in
Creation was seen, as Jones put it, as the 'representation of the things of the
spiritual world'.[71] (The bow of white cloud was a sign of divine goodwill.)
The principle of typological correspondence could also apply in the realm of
spirit apparitions: 'For I have observed that the very circumstances of some
apparitions bore a resemblance of the circumstances of the evils to come.' 'Two

brands of fire striking against each other (a double sign of evil to come)' he saw as prescient of 'two wicked men [who, later] quarrelled and one murdered another in that place' (128).[72]

The analogical union of the physical and the spiritual was one expression of a much broader concept of their connectedness. In the Bible there is no duality (as in Greek metaphysics) between either the physical and the spiritual, or the natural and the supernatural (a term foreign to Scripture). All that is physical originated spiritually, *ex nihilo*, at the Creation by the will of God who, afterwards, remained immanent (Genesis 1–2; Acts 17:28). As John Wood Oman concluded: 'The two are not in opposition, but are so constantly interwoven that nothing may be wholly natural or wholly supernatural.'[73] The only distinction the New Testament draws between the physical and the spiritual is in terms of things that are seen and temporal, and things that are unseen and eternal (2 Corinthians 4:18). Historians of spirits frequently alluded to the distinction in the metaphor of the visible and invisible worlds. There was considerable latitude of opinion regarding how the one related to the other metaphysically. Andrew Moreton (the pseudonym of Daniel Defoe (?1660–1731)) maintained that the properties of each world (and their inhabitants) were immiscible. Spirits, therefore, did not possess physical bodies but 'Bodies without Body', made of spiritual, invisible substance suitable for the regions of the invisible world.[74] On the contrary, the artist and poet William Blake (1757–1827) insisted that 'spirits are not . . . a cloudy vapour or a nothing: they are organised and articulated beyond all that mortal and perishing nature can produce'.[75] Moreover, spirits (as distinct from ghosts, which were evident to the 'gross bodily eye') were perceptible only with heightened vision.[76] Giraldus held that both ghosts and spirits could 'be discerned by the eyes of mortals' and assumed 'corporeal substance'.[77] Glanvill conceded the same, but limited corporeity to evil spirits chiefly which, being '*more foeculent and gross*, [were] nearer allied to *palpable constancies*.'[78] For his part, Jones tentatively suggested that since God (who is spirit) took on human form in the incarnation, other immaterial beings might do so too. Indeed, he speculated that some spirits require material form in order to expedite their purpose.[79] A number of accounts in *A Relation of Apparitions of Spirits* strongly suggest that both evil spirits and ghosts had solidity and mass, sufficient to make the ground on which they walked reverberate, and to be able to strike or shake hands with witnesses. One Margaret Richard, for example, testified that her ghostly former sweetheart's hand felt 'like moist moss' (106).[80]

Eighteenth-century paintings and woodblock engravings of apparitions endorsed the concept of them as physical entities, if inadvertently so in some cases. In Henry Füseli's (1741–1825) *Theodore Meets in the Wood the Spectre of his Ancestor Guido Cavalcanti* (c. 1783) (a work which draws its inspiration from John Dryden's (1631–1700) 'fable' *Theodore and Honoria*, itself an adaptation of a story from Boccaccio's (1313–75) *Decameron* (1348–58)), the spectre and horse of the suicide Cavalcanti are painted as palpably as the terrified young man from

4. 'The Phantom Drummer of Tedworth', engraving, 4.6 × 4.8,
Saducismus Triumphatus (1661).

Ravenna (whose naked lover is being set upon viciously by a pack of mastiffs)
(Plate 1). Only Cavalcanti's grotesque skeletal features and fiery hand, along with
the conflagration in the middle ground, signify his supernatural essence. The
illustration of 'The Phantom Drummer of Tedworth', in Glanvill's *Saducismus
Triumphatus*, portrays the apparition of demons as solidly as the flesh and blood
witnesses (**4**).[81] The economy and stylization of the pictorial language, the raw-
ness of the medium, coupled with the absence of rendered shadow (which would
otherwise have helped to distinguish solid and immaterial objects), made it
extremely difficult for artists to suggest even major distinctions of substance.[82]
Instead, engravings of this period differentiated between spirits and mortals by
reference either to the sense of the narrative they illustrated or to iconographic
devices used in Christian art to signify spiritual creatures. Illustrations show
apparitions framed by flames or a luminescence (a convention adapted from the
aureole) (**5**), or borne aloft (like angels and the Virgin Mary in Renaissance art)
on clouds, separated from the world of normal appearances.

Artists also suggested the apparition's otherness by obscuring part of its
figure. In an illustration from Moreton's *The Secrets of the Invisible World
Disclosed* (1729) a very low cloud covers the apparition's head. In another
illustration, the head only (carried on a cloud) is visible to just one person in
the picture (**6**). (Jones describes a similar motif in his account of an apparition
seen in Mynyddislwyn, Monmouthshire (101).[83]) Sometimes the apparition is
wholly obscured, as it were, by being placed outside the composition; in this way,
the object of fear is present only to the witness (within), whose terrified
expression alone conveys the horror of the visitation. As John Alderson noted

regarding the staging of ghosts in theatre, apparitions often exert a more dreadful influence on the imagination when placed off-stage.[84]

In the eighteenth century, obscurity, in its fullest and sublime sense, also implied lack of distinctness and clarity. This quality, argued the philosopher Edmund Burke (1729–97), when an attribute of objects (such as supernatural creatures) seen in the context of danger, enhanced their terror: 'how much the notions of ghosts and goblins, of which none can form clear ideas, affect minds, which give credit to the popular tales concerning such sorts of being'.[85] Moreover, Burke believed, words were better than pictures at conveying the affections of the mind, and a lively and spirited verbal description of apparitions could raise an obscure and imperfect idea of such objects, with the power to provoke a stronger emotion than could the best painting.[86] Words conjure mental images without clear lineaments or fixity (couched in uncertainty), free of the cloying materiality of medium and the strictures of the artist's imagination. Jones maintained the obscurity of apparitions in his accounts by using an economy of description. ('Truth is not the worse for being in plain dress', he insisted.[87]) Often, he conveyed only their most rudimentary features – shape, colour, and bearing. At other times, his verbal description followed pictorial conventions of representation, and portrayed not so much the object of terror as the witness's fearful disposition of mind. The witnesses' intensely emotional and physiological responses usually found expression in crying, fainting, or dumbness, although some, like Lewis Thomas from the parish of Aberystruth, experienced many bodily symptoms simultaneously: 'Lewis's hair moved upon his head, his heart panted and beat violently, his flesh trembled, he felt not his clothes about him, and felt himself heavy and weak' (52).[88]

Jones's vernacular, plain style of writing was, like the bare-walled austerity of a Dissenting meeting-house, devoid of sensationalism and elaboration. He described these 'wonderful extranatural thing[s]' (as he called apparitions) in the same matter-of-fact way as he did the backdrop to their appearance, in the majority of cases, a landscape. The insistent presence of rural scenery dis-tinguished Jones's collection among histories of spirits, and from the traditional eighteenth-century pictorial representations of ghosts, angels, and demons. In paintings by Blake and Füseli, the setting of the apparition is often Romantic, visionary, otherworldly, or otherwise fantastic. In contrast, Jones strove to suggest not the transcendence of the witness's experience but the plausibility of the apparition's presence by association with an actual place. The account of John ab John of Cwm-celyn, Aberystruth, is a good example. While walking before sunrise on Milfraen mountain towards Caerleon, he encountered a sudden and unpredictable movement of a supernatural cry from one part of the landscape to another. One of the notable features of the narrative is the extraordinary transition at the end of the encounter, at daybreak. At that moment, the dark, frightening supernatural event fades and is replaced by tranquil pastoralism – birdsong and sheep. Its prosaic detail, coupled with the precision with which Jones describes the traveller's orientation within the landscape, imparts a veracity

5. 'And Saul perceived that it was Samuel, and he stouped with his face to the ground, and bowed himself. 1st Samuel. Chap: 28: v: 14', engraving, 14.3 × 9.6, *Saducismus Triumphatus* (1661).

6. 'The Murtherer sees the murther'd Innocent plainly before his eyes', engraved
by I. V. Gucht, 14.7 × 8.7, *The Secrets of the Invisible World Disclosed; or,
An Universal History of Apparitions* (1729).

to the supernatural creature which is the more terrifying by contrast (55).[89] In this way, Jones's descriptions of landscape make the spiritual figures that inhabit it the more believable, which was the chief end of his book.

A century earlier, religious painting in Italy and the Netherlands had achieved the same effect by using landscapes as the setting for spiritual beings, characters, and stories from the Bible. Even though the setting was an imaginary and Arcadian fantasy, the appearances and forms derived sufficiently from the contemporary and local world to be intelligible and real. The amalgamation of the artist's perceptions of the visible world with the biblical world was not a product of technical innovation alone but also an expression of theological conviction: the more familiar and comprehensible the appearance, garb, and surroundings of supernatural entities and biblical characters, the more they pressed home the enduring relevance of the ideas they embodied. With the development of a naturalistic depiction of landscape in the Dutch tradition, indigenous and allusive religious symbols, such as trees, churches, and windmills, replaced representations of supernatural beings, in keeping with Calvin's ban on traditional Roman Catholic images. By populating a rural genre scene with clearly visible incarnations of spirits, Jones brought together this naturalistic conception of landscape with an eighteenth-century, Blakean vision of the supernatural in a manner rare in either histories of spirits or of fine art.

Jones's fascination with the physical characteristics of landscape, and his facility in conveying their palpable presence, were developed in no small way by his collecting and studying books on the geography and geology of foreign countries, like the West Indies, Egypt, and Italy. These books influenced the writing of his more modest *Geographical, Historical, and Religious Account of the Parish of Aberystruth*. Aberystruth was an ecclesiastical region in Monmouthshire bounded by the Ebbw Fawr river on its west, by the Ebbw Fach on the east and the south, and by disputed landmarks that divided it from the parishes of Llangattock and Llanelli in Breconshire in the north.[90] In the tradition of seventeenth-century chorography, he defined the proportion, shape, relation, and orientation of the parish's valleys, the surface of the mountains, the course of the rivers, sun and shadows, and the grandeur of a prospect. He did so, however, with the deftness of a picturesque watercolourist, and with a sense of terror that anticipates the romantic sublime.[91] He had an eye not only for the broader picture but also for the landscape's particular curiosities. For instance, Jones described a remarkable sight witnessed on the Ebbw Fawr, the river which divides the Ebbw and Sirhowy valleys. During times of heavy rain, the ferocious floods so beat upon the stones, 'that sparks of fire are sometimes seen in the night to rise up from them; for I have seen it myself'.[92] One wonders whether he saw in this unusual elemental spectacle an intimation of the hellish fireballs which he recounts rising up within the forests, hills, fields, and lanes of the parish to stalk terrified travellers (99).

Jones concentrated on describing the geological and geographical features of Aberystruth in the absence of anything else of note: 'There is neither Town nor Village in the Parish. Nor ruins of any Castle, Tower, or Monastery, there never

7. Detail from a map of Monmouthshire (1724) by Herman Moll, National Library of
Wales, Aberystwyth.

having been such things in it.'[93] Over twenty years later, Archdeacon William
Coxe (1747–1828), in *An Historical Tour of Monmouthshire*, concurred: the
parish, which was 'supposed to be barren of objects, either interesting or
picturesque, is therefore called the *Wilds* of Monmouthshire, and seldom
travelled by the gentry, except for grouse shooting'.[94] Maps of Monmouthshire
from the first half of the eighteenth century illustrate just how desolate
these *Wilds* were. North of Llanhilleth (Llanhithel), at the base of the parish,
there was only one village recorded – Blaenau Gwent (Blanagwent), also called
Aberystruth (7).[95] (Less than a century later, this most sparsely populated area
would form part of Wales's industrial centre.[96]) Blaenau Gwent marked the site
of the parish church of St Peter. In the whole of the *Geographical Account*, Jones
mentions only two other buildings in Aberystruth: the Beacon House, at the top
of the parish, and the Baptist meeting-house situated at Cwmtyleri, as it is
known today.[97] It was a far cry from the cornucopian supply of Roman and
Saxon remains which distinguished the landscape in the south of the county,
around the villages of Caerleon and Risca (8).

1. Henry Füseli, *Theodore Meets in the Wood the Spectre of his Ancestor Guido Cavalcanti* (c.1783), oil on canvas, 276 x 317, National Museum of Western Art, Tokyo.

2. Richard Wilson, *Dolbadarn Castle* (early 1760s), oil on canvas, 92.7 x 125.7, National Museums and Galleries of Wales, Cardiff.

3. William Blake, *Nebuchadnezzar* (1795), engraving with watercolour and ink, 44.6 x 62, Tate Gallery, London.

4. 'Fairies', engraved by I. Havell, 14.3 x 9.6, *The Cambrian Popular Antiquities of Wales* (1815).

Thomas Pennant's (1726–98) *A Tour in Wales* (1770) wholly circumvented Monmouthshire's antiquarian wilderness, as did almost every picturesque and topographical artist. Without the requisite motifs with which to organize perception, they simply could not 'see' the landscape there. One rare, un-attributed engraving shows, not surprisingly, the parish church set in the middle distance of a standard Claudian composition (**9**).[98] With this exception, it seems that Aberystruth was essentially invisible to the outside world, neither tamed nor made polite by art. Quite apart from their potential to make a landscape as interesting as a painting, castles, abbeys, churches, manors, and gardens were emblems of civilization and cultivation (in both the mental and physical senses).[99] They signified learning, discrimination, reason, faith, and power – values which preserved the people from anarchy, depravity, and superstition. In the absence of these reminders and controls, and due to their remoteness from centres of culture, one writer concluded that:

> The Welsh peasantry are highly superstitious; living, as they do, in so rude and secluded a country, and amidst scenery so wild and imposing, their very being is incorporated with divers strange fantasies, handed down from father to son, and influencing their imagination, more or less, according to the intensity of impression produced upon their minds. The inhabitants, indeed, of all pastoral and mountainous countries are generally [more] affected with superstition, than those who dwell in plains, and well-cultivated regions.[100]

In Coxe's view, Jones's book of apparitions was worthy of note only insofar as it provided proof of this observation. The parish was, thus, to those who described (but had clearly never visited) it 'a sequestered region' which proved deleterious to credulous minds.[101] Jones would not have condoned this caricature of the lower orders. If, indeed, they were 'incorporated with divers strange fantasies', it was because the region was incorporated with divers strange phantasms. Like Luther, Jones believed that the physical world (and Aberystruth in particular), while created by God, shared in the fatal consequences of Adam's fall and was the habitat of dead and apostate spirits as seen in balls of fire, dogs from hell, corpse-candles, and doleful voices.[102] Antiquaries and artists, too, pictured a landscape of the dead. Their dead were ancient peoples, English royalty, nobles, gentry, and the victims of battle, represented by the artefacts they left behind: their monuments and effigies, coffin lids and genealogies, inscriptions and ruins (**10**). These two melancholic landscapes shared one common feature: the fragment from antiquity and the ghost from the afterlife were both vestigial tokens of a more substantial whole. The activities of spirits and demons had been most prevalent in the time before the spread of the gospel began casting out evil and malevolent forces in Wales. Those that stalked the landscape in Jones's day were but a remnant still fleeing from the light.

This conception of the world stood in stark contrast to the essentially classicist sensibility espoused by the picturesque and antiquarian traditions. Jones's con-temporary, the Welsh landscape painter Richard Wilson (1714–82), deployed

MONMOUTHSHIRE.

8. 'Panoramic View of the County', engraving, 9.2 × 14.7, *A Curious Collection of Bird's-eye Views of Several Counties in England and Wales* (1796).

9. 'Aberystwith, or Blaenau Gwent, Monmouthshire', engraving, 9.2 × 14.4, *A Topographical and Historical Description of the County of Monmouth* (1810).

Claude Lorrain's (1600–82) stock-in-trade *repoussoire*, serpentine composition, graduated atmospheric perspective, cumulus clouds, and ethereal air to evoke an orderly landscape pervaded by an aura of goodness and well-being (Plate 2). Jones's depiction of the Welsh landscape offered no such consoling vision. The world, for him, was not some latter-day Arcadia or fantasy idyll. Granted, there had been Paradise, but it was real not mythic, Eden not Arcadia – and Eden had fallen. The consequences of the fall were evident throughout the parish. Jones considered that its mountains and valleys clearly showed the Creation in decline – dying (or 'groaning', as the Apostle Paul declared), under the curse of sin (Romans 8:22).

Jones's outlook was influenced by not only a biblical world-view but also natural theology, a blend of pseudo-scientific and religious thought, typified by John Ray's *Wisdom of God Manifested in the Works of the Creation* (1691) and William Derham's *Physico-Theology* (1713). These writers appropriated geology and geography (as Jones did apparitions of spirits) to demonstrate the truth of the biblical record, and the continuity between the spiritual and physical domains. The geology of the parish, Jones interpreted, demonstrated the effects of earthquakes, excessive rain and the universal flood, which were the result of the curse; its displaced boulders, rude outcrops of rock and irregular outlines of mountains were, for him, not picturesque motifs but evidence of 'the hurts ... and everlasting deformities of the earth' and signs of God's wrath. 'Here then', he asserted, 'we have in Geography one of the greatest proofs of Original Sin.'[103]

Though scarred and reduced to rubble, the world was nevertheless a magnificent ruin in Jones's view. Its remains still declared the wisdom, glory,

10. Monument to Giraldus Cambrensis, designed by John Carter, engraved by James Basire,
14.1 × 19.1, *A Tour Through Monmouthshire and Wales* (1781).

design, and beneficence of a mighty Creator, and were redolent with biblical
associations. For these reasons, he praised the parish with a psalmodic rhapsody
which recalled passages from John Speed and Peter Koerius's *Description of
Great Britain: Wales and Monmouth* (1627):

> Rivulets, Brooks, Springs, and Fountains of water within the bounds of the Parish are a 1000
> in number. All of them springing from the sides of the Mountains, so that what is said of the
> Land of Canaan, that it was a Land of Hills and Valleys, of Rivers and Fountains of Water
> . . . may be applied to the Hilly parts of this County.[104]

Here, too, he saw vestiges and recollections of biblical stories and events. Jones
seriously countenanced the legend, local to Abergavenny, that the rent in the
Skirrid mountain was caused, as Wyndam H. Penruddocke explained, by 'the
miraculous effects of the convulsions of nature, on the day of the crucifixion'
(Matthew 27:54).[105] A natural phenomenon (also observed by other geographical
writers) common to several parts of Wales, in which clouds were seen to rack
much lower than the tops of the mountains was, for Jones, a potent reminder of
that most catastrophic of natural convulsions mentioned in the Bible:[106]

> once going over the *Beacon Mountain*, the Valley of *Ebbw Fawr* was filled very high up the
> Mountain sides with dark Clouds, whose Surface was like Waves, perfectly immovable, thro'
> which I could see nothing in the Valley, either Land, Trees, or Houses; tho' all was clear

upon the Mountain about me. I never saw the like, either before or after; and it may be that few besides me have seen the like. It was Wonderful to look upon, and it brought to my mind that then I saw a resemblance of *Noah's* Flood, which very likely reached this Valley, tho' not strong enough to bring up the Sea-sand and Shells of Fishes, as in grounds nearer to and more level to the Sea.[107]

Most Evangelicals believed that the earth was no more than about 4,000 years old. (The *Merlinus Liberatus* almanac posited that the Deluge had taken place precisely 1,657 years after the creation of the world and 2,351 years before Christ.[108]) The relative proximity of the event, chronologically (and, Jones believed, geographically), heightened the sense of continuity between the present day and the biblical era.

For Jones, particular objects in the landscape also had a deeply biblical resonance. He found a stone pillar set up at Bwlch y Llwyn on the east side of Milfraen mountain in the north of the parish:

At the foot of which there is a small Stone in which is deeply impressed a perfect resemblance of a young lamb's foot . . . by whom, or by what it was made is to me not intelligible; For it cannot be thought that any Man should spend his time in doing such a thing, and indeed it was scarce possible for any Man to do it naturally.[109]

Jones suspected it was an *acheiropoeitus* – an image, like the Veronica Veil, believed to have been made not by human hands but by God. The emblem of a lamb's foot (the lamb being an antitype for Christ) intimated its maker's identity. It was as though the stone had been precipitated into this world from another – like the phantoms that plagued the landscape of his parish.

On another occasion, he discovered in Ebbw Fawr a pair of stones of unknown origin, purpose, and antiquity, though undoubtedly of no historical value, inscribed with a text that might have summed up his fundamental outlook on life. Within Jones's intensely biblical mindset, these stones would probably have summoned associations with the two tablets of stone on which Moses received the Ten Commandments (Exodus 24:12):

That no stones with ancient Character have been found in this Parish, yet many years ago, I have seen upon an old Wall, deeply sunk into the ground, two Stones with their faces downward, with the figures of two Notable Texts of Scriptures Ingraved on them. The one a pretty large Stone of the Tile kind with a smooth surface, upon which was Ingraved with some tool, 2 *Cor.* iv. 18. which contains the following remarkable words. WHILE WE LOOK NOT AT THE THINGS WHICH ARE SEEN, BUT THE THINGS THAT ARE NOT SEEN, FOR THE THINGS THAT ARE SEEN ARE TEMPORAL, BUT THE THINGS THAT ARE NOT SEEN ARE ETERNAL.[110]

The idea of two parallel, coexistent domains – the one visible and temporal, and the other unseen and eternal – had a physical counterpart in the geographical relationship of the parish of Aberystruth and the county of Monmouthshire. Aberystruth was in shape, Jones surmised, 'about 12 or 13 Miles compass . . . somewhat of a four-square form, not very different from the County [of Monmouthshire] itself, of which it is a part'.[111] Curiously, this motif of a square within a square is like a diagram he often drew on the pages of his diaries.[112] It was an astrological chart in which the lesser square signified the earth and the greater square the heavens (**11, 12**). The heavens divide into twelve compartments (or houses) to represent the lunar months. Within this frame-work, Jones charted the positions of constellations and planets, and their procession (and thus the progress of his life). A square within a square, a world within a world, bodies in the heavens interfering with those on earth: in essence, this was how he conceived of the communication between the spiritual and the material worlds in his cosmology of apparitions.

The majority of communications between humans and apparitions mentioned in Jones's accounts involve adult males of the lower orders, travelling in the landscape at night. The inclusion of comparatively fewer accounts of adult female experiences may simply reflect the paucity of such accounts that he received. However, vindicators of Jones's 1780 edition believed that women 'chiefly speak against the account of Spirits and Apparitions', and possess an aversion to seeing apparitions due to 'a certain proud fineness, excessive delicacy, and a superfine disposition, which cannot bear to be disturbed with what is strange and disagreeable to a pleasant vain mind'.[113] In popular Protestant misogyny, women were considered the weaker vessel – more gullible, frail of strength, faith and mind, and vainer than men; it was believed to be a disposition inherited from Eve, the first to succumb to Satan's deception and the seducer of Adam (Genesis 3:1–6).[114]

Apparitions were seen mostly by the lower orders while travelling at night because, Jones judged, 'the gentry . . . do not travel so much alone and by night as others do'.[115] The image of a traveller encountering supernatural entities was familiar to the Nonconformist imagination, popularized by Bunyan's protagon-ist Christian who, similarly, journeyed through a landscape filled with mani-festations of evil and good spirits (**13**). Protestant emblem books (devotional aids, popular in the eighteenth century, comprising engravings adjacent to quotes, epigraphs, and moralizing maxims) frequently deployed this motif. Francis Quarles's (1592–1644) *Emblemes* (1635) included figures of fantastic and devilish characters engaging human beings in a landscape, symbolizing the battle between the forces of darkness and Christians in this world (**14, 15**). For some Protestants, though, such images were not just emblems but the visualiz-ation of distressingly real experiences.

Night-time was a period of fear and foreboding for the lower orders in the eighteenth century. The association of darkness with ghosts made it terrible and, thus, a fit scene for ghosts, wrote Burke.[116] Evil spirits, Jones deduced, 'chose the greatest darkness of the night, and avoided the light of the day and of the Sun; which shews plainly that they belonged . . . to the kingdom of darkness'.[117]

Darkness was, furthermore, in the analogy of faith, 'the diabolical image, and the hellish form which the evil spirit impressed on the mind of man when he fell from his primitive integrity'.[118] In Burke's scheme of things, darkness was a further condition of obscurity which prevented knowledge of the full extent of danger, and thereby exacerbated the sense of terror.

Darkness (and its synonyms), when not an attribute of the time of day, sometimes described the apparition itself. A young woman, walking her cow through a wood in the parish of Trevethin during the daytime, met a 'black man . . . [who] stretched out his black tongue'; he was 'very big in the middle and narrow at both ends – going before, treading very heavily . . . [and] whistled so exceeding strong that . . . the narrow valley echoed it back' (115).[119] The black man was a common motif in European folklore, usually associated with the devil.[120] (In the accounts of Baxter, Glanvill, and Sinclair, he appears either intrinsically black, or wearing black clothes, or both.[121]) In Jones's analogical view, black 'after the Fall, was proper to represent, and is in Scripture often made to represent the Sin and Misery of fallen Nature'.[122] Lamentably, the pejorative connotations of black, and of the black man in particular, spawned an erroneous theological interpretation of racial colour. Darker-skinned races bore

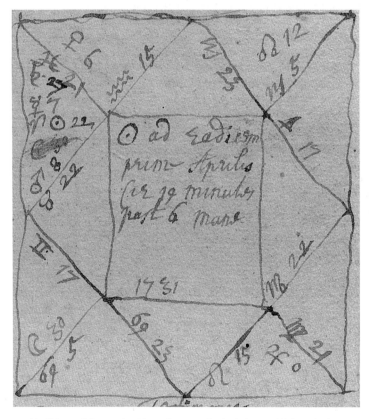

11. Edmund Jones, drawing of an astrological chart with inscription (1731), pen and ink, 14.6 × 8.6, National Library of Wales MS 7022A.

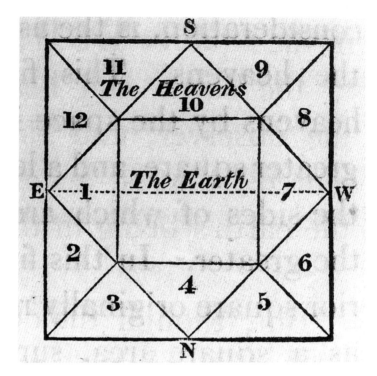

12. Diagram of an astrological chart,
The Cambrian Popular Antiquities of Wales (1815).

in their external aspect, as the landscape in its craggy despoliation, the effects of
the fall: 'We see how the Curse of Sin hath reached the human Complection in
the *Indians* and *Africans*', Jones concluded.[123] Conversely, paler-skinned races
were regarded as closer to the ideal condition of humankind in its state of
innocence.

Ugliness was a further sign of sin's corruption that was attributed to apparitions. The uncommon shape of the black man in the previous account implied
deviation from the norms of beauty and proportion – an externalization of his
inner, spiritual deformation. Medieval artists pictorialized the association between
evil and physical deviance using the conventions of the grotesque, partial-
ness, and human and animal syntheses or associations. They predicated the
iconography of demons, satyrs, hobgoblins, and gargoyles upon the intentional
perversion of the divine image and chain of being – rupturing the whole ('to
spoil' or 'to smash in pieces' are root meanings of the Hebrew word for evil, *ra*),
transgressing boundaries, and confusing types (**16**). The most swarthy and
obscenely emaciated or corpulent examples of the human frame, with disfigured
or absent limbs, distended mouths and tormented physiognomies, were hybrid-
ized with horns, tails, cloven feet, serpentine tongues, pointed ears, and claws.[124]

Apparitions possessed these characteristics in some cases.[125] A tailor in
Cardiganshire met a man whose feet 'were not like a man's but like a horse's'

13. William Blake, 'The Traveller Hasteneth in the Evening',
engraving with etching, 5.2 × 4.2, *For Children: The Gates of
Paradise* (1793).

(12).[126] In the parish of Bedwas, a traveller coming home at night saw 'the likeness of a big man . . . it was a dark thing without regular members' (73).[127] In identical circumstances, in Pembrokeshire, Mr D. W. observed 'the likeness of a man but could not see his arms and [the witness judged equally remarkable] he was without a hat' (130).[128] Similarly, Thomas Andrew, in the parish of Llanhilleth, was frightened by 'the similitude of a dark man creeping on all fours – scraping the ground and looking aside (this way and that way, and aside backward) and also making some dreadful noises' (92).[129] The image anticipated Blake's painting of *Nebuchadnezzar* (1795), condemned by God to dwell 'with the beasts of the field' in a state of madness reflected in his animal-like appearance (Daniel 4:32–3) (Plate 3).[130] One wonders whether such semi-human apparitions were, in reality, all-too-human beings suffering from the most appalling physical handicaps or insanity, unsequestered from society.[131] Before institutionalization, Roy Porter remarks, lunatics 'were looked after (or neglected) within the family, kept under the watch of the village community, or simply allowed to wander'.[132] Female gypsies (as the account of Lewis Thomas and his wife of Bedwellty parish demonstrates) were often identified with witches (53).[133] They were itinerants and outsiders without a bond or

14. Book 1, Emblem 11, engraving, 9.2 × 5.7, *Emblems, Divine and
Moral* (1736).

commitment to the community – strangers whose strangeness, villagers considered, was a sufficient cause for any mystifying occurrence and misfortune.

The occult notion of the changeling may have derived from like mis-
construction. Fairies, it was thought, stealthily substituted 'children while their
parents slept leaving in their stead such as were of no growth, good appearance,
or sense' (17). In the parish of Aberystruth, Jones recorded, they exchanged the
son of Edmund John William for an 'Ideot . . . There was something diabolical in
his aspect, but more in his motion than in his voice; For his motions were mad,
and he made very disagreeable screaming sounds . . . His complexion was a dark
tawny colour.'[134] Apparently healthy babies could develop, in later infancy, severe
illness, the symptoms of which included uncoordinated behaviour and a stunted
development and lifespan. For parents from the lower orders, demonic
substitution was, perhaps, a consoling explanation for an otherwise inexplicable
transformation. Here, as elsewhere in Jones's accounts, dark skin-tone, absence
of control, unnaturally frenetic movements, and unwholesome noise were
among the salient signifiers of diabolism.

15. Book 3, Emblem 15, engraving, 9.2 × 5.7,
Emblems, Divine and Moral (1736).

Protestant historians of spirits conceived of fairies as exhibiting these traits too. Like Jones, Cotton Mather (1663–1728), the theologian of the Salem witch-trials, believed fairies to be the embodiment of either evil spirits or the dis-possessed souls of the dead, intent on deception and mischief. Mather recounted that they were 'of a tawny *colour* [and] of a little *stature*'.[135] Extremes of size were a further indicator of fearful alterity. Fairies (and, conversely, giants, such as 'a woman so prodigiously tall as to be about half as high as the tall beech trees') transgressed social expectations regarding physical (and, by inference, spiritual) normalcy (50).[136] Their physical abnormality also included a power (shared by witches) to assume the shape and substance of animals and human beings. In the

16. Kissing Satan's arse, woodcut, 6.1 × 7.5, *Compendium Maleficarum* (1608).

latter semblance, fairies conducted wild dancing and music-making, wearing gaily coloured jackets, aprons, and headscarves with striped and spotted designs reminiscent of those worn variously by gypsies, morris dancers, and soldiers (a far cry from the winged sylphs of nineteenth-century art (Plate 4)) (34, 57, 87) (18).[137] Protestants probably interpreted such sights and sounds of dreadful intensity, which defied accepted norms of Christian decorum (in both dress and behaviour), as further evidence of the fairies' demonic nature.

Marginalized and foreign members of communities shared some of the characteristics commonly attributed to apparitions. Arguably, apparitions were thus, in some cases, a projection of social fears and prejudices regarding people who were different for reasons of race, colour, or deformity.[138]

The interpretation of apparitions within social, historical, cultural, and medical rather than strictly theological frameworks developed apace in the nineteenth century, alongside increasing psychoanalytic, psychiatric, and sceptical repudiations of the supernatural hypothesis. Apparitions were considered to be well-founded phenomena but to have arisen from secondary physical causes – illusions of the mind produced by lack of sleep, illness, partial insanity, delirium, hallucinations, and chemicals (a view not unlike that proposed earlier by more rationalistic Protestants).[139] The raw materials for such illusions, the philosopher James Frederick Ferrier believed, derived 'from the imagination of ecclesiastical writers; from the stone or carved images of saints and angels, which have adorned the walls of religious edifices; or from emblematic pictures or portraits, which might have otherwise met with popular diffusion'.[140] Quite how such ideas and images influenced the 'appearance of evil' (to adapt a Pauline expression) and other manifestations of the spirit in eighteenth-century Wales is hard to determine.

The despoliation wrought by the sixteenth-century Puritan iconoclasts eradicated almost all, and certainly the best, examples of Wales's heritage of medieval religious imagery. As Madeline Gray laments: 'A few battered and faded wall paintings, some stained glass in the north, much of it fragmented and of a poor quality, and a few carvings are all we have left.'[141] The even fewer images of demons and angels that survive represent a traditional medieval iconography. For example, the crudely drawn demon heads painted on the domestic interior wall at Beaumaris, Anglesey are complete with the horns and menacing eyes commonly attributed to their type (19). These features are conspicuously absent from the descriptions of the same in Jones's accounts,

17. T. H. Thomas, 'Jennet Francis Struggles with the Fairies for her Baby', engraving, 9.5 × 9, *British Goblins* (1880).

which would suggest that customary modes of representing evil beings had little if any influence on the popular imagination.

The visualization of the atrocities that confronted the lower orders has more in common with the few battered, faded, and fragmented remains of the paintings and carvings of Christ, the Virgin Mary, and saints. The iconoclasts neither removed nor totally obliterated all (what they considered to be) offending images. Untouched, damaged, and severely mutilated remnants of statues and pictures either remained standing or lay where they fell. Thus, while their capacity to promote false notions of God and worship was curtailed, such images remained visible and not without influence. As the hammer, torch, brush, and sword of zealotry scarred these sacred figures, once whole and holy images of Christ, Mary, martyrs, saints, and angels were variously dissected, dismembered, defaced, decapitated, scorched by fire, and obscured by limewash (**20**). Thereafter, their represented figures, in some cases, resembled no longer the

18. Fairies dancing, woodcut, English chapbook (sixteenth century).

bodies of the blessed, but the torsos of the tormented. Such figures looked, too, fortuitously like the blackened, misshapen, faceless, and otherwise diminished creatures that loitered in the landscape of Jones's accounts. Thus, the iconoclasts, if unintentionally, in breaking holy images extended the iconography of profanity, creating a radically new vision of evil predicated on corrupted images of the great and divine, a vision that (perhaps) influenced some witnesses' conceptions of evil spiritual entities far more than traditional pictures of devils and spirits in their undamaged state.

In view of the extremely limited availability of religious imagery and the low level of English literacy in the seventeenth and early eighteenth centuries (among the lower orders especially) in Wales, the popular imagery of apparitions would have been diffused, for the most part, through stories told for entertainment (rather than for spiritual edification) at the fireside and public house.[142] The conception of such imagery, however, was not dependent on the influence of pictorial precedents. Arguably, had the lower orders had access to ready-made types, their imaginings of ghosts and spirits would have been derivative rather than inventive.

The lower orders envisioned these fearful presences, as the Dissenters conceived and constructed their meeting-houses, on the plan and using the raw materials of the local, familiar, and everyday. In the majority of accounts, the sensible forms of apparitions were not, like Füseli's *The Nightmare* (1782), exotic monstrosities which required an exceptional imagination and craft to envisage and depict them. Instead, they were part of a tradition of folk art, well within the capacity of most people to perform, which deployed simple but nonetheless effective permutations, collagings, distortions, or incomplete renderings of everyday people, things, and natural elements, made terrifying by the primal fear of darkness, marauding animals, fire, and pursuit.

Indeed, apparitions in several accounts reflect very little imaginative creativity, assuming rudimentary, almost abstract forms – such as a white pyramid and a dark roller (119, 83).[143] Henry Lewelin, for instance, coming home at night towards Mynyddislwyn, saw 'a living thing, round like a bowl, rolling from the

19. Wall painting of demon heads inside roundel (*c.*1610),
George and Dragon Inn, Beaumaris, Anglesey.

right hand to the left, crossing the lane, moving sometimes slowly, sometimes very swiftly (swifter than any creature on earth could, if not swifter than a bird flying, tho' it had neither wings nor feet). It altered, also, its size . . . It seemed to be of a reddish colour, with some mixture of an ash colour' (100).[144] Edward Frank, of the parish of Llanfihangel Llantarnam, Monmouthshire, travelling at night, witnessed both 'a dark thing, without any regular shape' and, shortly after, 'on the way before him, and between him and the hedge, two dun-coloured things (like posts)' (86).[145] Both witnesses comprehended the unusual entity by comparison with an ordinary object or thing and, strangely, singled out the attribute of colour as noteworthy. Many of the accounts suggest that the witness's imaginative faculty was in complete abeyance – the apparition being either invisible or unseen. In others, it is not the form but the operation that defines the apparition's contrariness. For instance, an inversion of the customary experience of sound occurs in this encounter with an audition (as distinct from an apparition) of hunting sky-hounds (*cŵn wybr*), a death omen, by Thomas Andrew (mentioned above): 'When they came near him, their voices were but small, but increasing as they went from him' (93). The disembodied 'deep, hollow voice' of these supernatural hounds was heard often in the night sky and, sometimes, 'to pass by the eves of some houses before the death of some in the family' (26, 93).[146] A profound disparity with the limits and laws of the physical world was also expressed in abrupt and radical transformations of human, animal, and elemental apparitions, one into the other, and the instantaneous transmigrations of spirits and their abductees from one place to another (4, 67).[147]

20. Figure of Christ from the Mochdre Rood (sixteenth century), Mochdre church, Powys

 The majority of people from the lower orders were familiar with the Bible; therefore, it is not surprising that Old and New Testament visualizations of the supernatural shaped their own. A pillar of fire seen in an apparition sent to prevent a young man debauching his sweetheart recalls that which went before the Israelites in the wilderness to lead them at night (Exodus 13:21). A cloud, like that which appeared at Christ's baptism, and out of which proceeded the benediction, comes across the field in Mynyddislwyn to ask a young man of which of three diseases he would prefer to die (Matthew 17:5). The dove alighting on the bier of a pious Christian evokes the dove which descended on Christ after his baptism (Matthew 3:16). The mastiff dog that terrorized travellers in fields and forests was, for Jones, the enduring embodiment of the powerful dog from which the psalmist prayed for deliverance (Psalms 22:20); while the journey of 'three days and three nights', by a young man from the parish of Ystradgynlais who was transmigrated by a spirit, evokes the period of Jonah's confinement in the belly of the whale, and (typologically) of Christ's descent into 'the heart of the earth' (Jonah 1:17; Matthew 12:40) (96, 101, 31, 129, 4).[148] The language and phraseology Jones used to describe these accounts, in some instances, reflected the mind of a minister immersed in the Scriptures. He referred to one witness approaching a 'marriage company' of fairies in Aberystruth as the 'chief servant of the house coming through the fields' – images which cast upon the scene the shadow of Christ's parables (69).[149] Thus, Jones rendered the geography of mind as well as place.

While Jones's chief objective had been to prove the existence of spirits, ultimately this was neither the achievement nor the enduring legacy of his writing on the occult. His collections of spirit narratives are a repository of supernatural folklore equal, in clarity of description and intent, to the best examples published in the seventeenth and eighteenth centuries. Furthermore, the narratives turn out to have been (as Edgar Phillips pointed out) the source of many fictional ghost stories written since then,[150] as well as containing precedents for apparitions commonly sighted elsewhere during that period (and today), while some reveal remarkable atypical examples. However, the most significant and lasting value of the collections is as a biography of ordinary country folk, whose outlook had more in common with the medieval than with the scientific age; who understood, as did W. B. Yeats (1865–1939), that 'this world and the world we go to after death are not far apart', and that there is a traffic of spirits in both directions.[151] Unlike more educated and theologically sophisticated Protestants, these country people did not consider Christianity and occultism as separate; consequently, they were able to reconcile the realms of God and ghosts, providence and prodigies, and to conceive of apparitions as other than necessarily demonic or dangerous.[152] They were people for whom, too, the afterlife and evil were more than notions, who considered themselves co-habitants on earth with the representatives of hell and heaven, and believed that neither the 'Hobgoblin, nor foul Fiend' of Bunyan's hymn were metaphors.[153] As importantly, Jones's collections preserve the iconography of colloquial imagery, the endeavours of ordinary folk to visualize extraordinary things.

A Note on the Text

Jones published his first book on apparitions, of which there appears to be no surviving copy, in 1767. In 1780, he published a sequel called *A Relation of Apparitions of Spirits in the Principality of Wales; to which is Added the Remarkable Account of the Apparition in Sunderland*, and this is the basis of my edition, for the most part. H. Lewis printed a second edition of the sequel entitled *A Relation of Apparitions of Spirits, In The County of Monmouth, and the Principality of Wales* in 1813, probably to commemorate the twentieth anniversary of Jones's death (2).[1] Lewis bowdlerized the text, deleting names and dates, and depriving the accounts of their specificity and concreteness thereby. He also confused the 1600s with the sixteenth century and, in so doing, backdated a number of accounts by a hundred years. Moreover, in a well-intended endeavour to edit for repetition and resolve ambiguous pronouns, Lewis sacrificed too much of Jones's authorial voice and the substance of his narratives.

My edition follows Lewis's best practice, but restores both sense and presence. The aim is to present Jones's narratives to a broad and contemporary readership. In an attempt to clarify meaning and ease reading, overlong sentences have been repunctuated, the syntax modified in order to resolve sentences grammatically, stylistic conventions regularized, and a few additional words (consistent with Jones's vocabulary and usage) inserted. I have modernized Welsh phrases and their English translation, as well as spelling and capitalization in general, and, as far as possible, brought the orthography of place-names in line with *Rhestr o Enwau Lleoedd/A Gazetteer of Welsh Place-Names* (1958), *A List of Welsh Place-Names* (1968), and *Welsh Administrative and Territorial Units* (1969). Where no alternative is available, I have retained Jones's spelling (see appendix).[2] Thus, this edition constitutes something approaching a translation rather more than a direct transcription of the source texts. However, Jones's charmingly idiosyncratic, formulaic, and characteristically eighteenth-century prose style remains intact.

The aim, also, is to allow the general reader immediate and uninterrupted access to the accounts. To this end, my edition omits, along with Jones's discursive footnotes included in the original accounts, testimonies to apparitions seen in England (these were too long, reiterated examples of types of apparition mentioned in accounts from Wales, and were not original).[3] I have also interspersed narratives of good and evil spirits (the former represented in this, as in the 1780 and 1813 editions, by two accounts only), placed the accounts in alphabetical order of county and parish and, as far as possible, grouped them according to type. This is in contrast to their rather haphazard arrangement in the previous editions in all these respects.[4] As a result, the reader can either dip into the book or read it from beginning to end with some sense of narrative continuity.

Uniquely, this new edition also includes what Edward Ifor Williams (1885–1957) claimed to be the unpublished remainder of a holograph entitled 'A Relation of Apparitions. Collected by Edmund Jones'.[5] Williams's careful transcription of Jones's manuscript consists of forty-three accounts – about a third of the whole – which he intended to print. (He got only as far as the galley proof for one account, it appears.) The other two-thirds of the holograph, Williams implied, comprised the 1780 collection. I demur, and suggest that in all likelihood Williams copied not a remnant of relations but the source and substance of Jones's 1767 book on apparitions. In other words, Jones had split up and published the holograph as two separate books. This is why Jones refers to the 1780 publication, at the very opening of its preface, as the sequel to rather than (as many previous writers on Jones's works have interpreted, erroneously) as a new or revised edition of the earlier collection.[6] The quality of this 'remnant' and its serviceability to Jones's cause is equal to that of the collection in print: it would have been clearly disadvantageous for him – as for me, also – not to publish them.

I have interleaved accounts taken from the sequel with those from Williams's transcript, along with several illuminating testimonies, chiefly to fairies seen in the parish of Aberystruth in Monmouthshire, which appeared in Jones's *A Geographical, Historical, and Religious Account of the Parish of Aberystruth* (1779). Together they represent the most comprehensive compilation of Jones's accounts of apparitions ever before published. The accounts here can be identified with their original sources as follows: *A Relation of Apparitions of Spirits in the Principality of Wales* (1780) for: 1, 2, 3, 4, 10, 11, 12, 13, 14, 15, 16, 17, 18, 19, 20, 21, 22, 23, 24, 25, 26, 27, 28, 29, 30, 31, 33, 34, 35, 41, 45, 47, 48, 49, 50, 51, 52, 53, 54, 55, 63, 68, 69, 72, 74, 76, 77, 78, 80, 81, 85, 86, 87, 88, 89, 90, 91, 92, 93, 95, 98, 99, 100, 101, 103, 104, 105, 106, 107, 108, 110, 111, 114, 115, 116, 123, 124, 125, 126, 127, 129, 130, 133, and 134; Edward Ifor Williams transcript for: 5, 6, 7, 8, 9, 32, 36, 37, 38, 39, 40, 42, 43, 44, 46, 57, 61, 70, 71, 73, 75, 79, 82, 83, 84, 94, 96, 97, 102, 109, 112, 113, 117, 118, 119, 120, 121, 122, 128, 131, and 132; and *A Geographical, Historical, and Religious Account* for: 56, 58, 59, 60, 62, 64, 65, 66, and 67.

Apparitions of Spirits in Wales

Apparitions of Spirits in Wales

ANGLESEY

1. I received the following account on December 28, 1771, (which I hope is authentic) from a young gentleman of Anglesey, concerning the Revd Mr Hughes, a clergyman of the Church of England, who was counted the most popular preacher and, therefore, the most followed in the county; and upon this account envied by the rest of the clergy, which occasioned his becoming a field preacher for a time (though he was received into the Church again).

At one time, going by night to preach, he went by an artificial circle (said to be haunted by an evil spirit) upon the ground between Amlwch village and St Eilian church. When he came near or entered into the circle, the similitude of a greyhound came against him. He was presently pulled off his horse and beaten. The next night, having occasion to go that way, he went with an intention to speak to the spirit. He went, but was beaten again. It did not avail that he was a big, strong, and courageous man (and such he was), for who could fight with a spirit? He did indeed speak to him, but had no answer. Another time (for it was still in his way), he passed by without a horse. Then, he saw (I suppose in the eyes of his mind) that the spirit was chained, and also saw how far his chain reached. Standing out of the reach of the chain, he questioned the spirit about why he troubled those who passed by. Mr Hughes received for answer that, going with a company when he was alive to offer a silver groat (which is expected and received at Eilian church for some parish use), he had hid it under a stone and said he had lost it, to be excused from payment.[1] He told Mr Hughes where it was (who found and paid it), and the trouble ceased. There is something odd in the relation, but I deliver it as I had it from a person who I am sure would not knowingly tell an untruth or otherwise than as he had it.

BRECONSHIRE

2. This is an account of another very remarkable apparition (in the valley of Towy, above Ystradgynlais) I had from Thomas Lewis, a very godly substantial man of this valley, many years ago, who knew the man who saw the apparition and was with him when he died. As it is long ago since I heard the account (which was very particular and large), I choose not to be very particular for fear of mistaking; I shall only relate some parts of it, which I best remembered.

The man was employed by some spirits to throw away hidden things in two or three places. There appeared to him (as he thought) a clergyman in black clothes with a band and white wig, on horseback. I choose not to name him lest there should be a mistake in it (it being a very sinful thing to wrong the dead), though the man who saw the apparition named him; (the person named was a great clergyman, and of a great family). Once, when the man was at an alehouse late in the evening, he saw the clergyman near the alehouse door, on horseback. He went out to him, and the clergyman was seen pulling off his hat, bowing, offering drink, and saying to him: 'Atoch chwi, Syr' ('Towards you, Sir'), the word formerly used when one man drank to another before the fashion of drinking healths took place. But the people could see nothing. Whether it were then or some other time, the spectre strictly charged him to go to some castle in Radnorshire (which he named) and take out of it some money concealed, and throw it into the river. The clergyman threatened him severely if he did not do it, and that he should have no rest. He was allowed to take a friend along with him as far as the castle, but only he himself was to enter into it. He must make no stay with the money in his hand, but to run with it to the river. When they came near the castle, it became very dark upon them. But he must go into some dark place underground, and was either lighted or guided by some spirit to where the money was. He brought it out in haste (and a blow given him to mend his pace), and he ran and cast it to the river.

3. Another notable apparition, and of great effect, came to pass in the parish of Ystradgynlais (which lies in the extreme corner of Breconshire, which stands between Glamorganshire and Carmarthenshire), as follows:

A. D—l, after being in great trouble of mind for a long time, at last (alas, that it was done) hanged herself, about the year 1769.[2] Not long after, a young man from Llywel parish came to see a young woman whom he courted, who lodged at the house of Thomas Richard (who was not then at home). He stayed a while there till it was somewhat far in the night, and then would go to an alehouse not far off (though he was persuaded to stay). Going towards the alehouse, in a field not far from it he could see fire by a smith's shop on the other side of the river. Presently, he could see the fire in the field hard by the way he was to pass, and he was greatly afraid and turned out of the way to avoid it. Presently, he could see this woman before him, whose shape and clothes he well remembered – although he had seen her but once; (he had travelled with her from the market at Neath). Upon which he was exceedingly terrified, and went to the alehouse faint and indisposed. The woman of the house made him welcome and put him to bed, suspecting he had seen an apparition (and asked him about it), which he owned he had.

Next day he went, ill, towards home. Being gone home, and out late at night, he saw her, but came in and went to bed. There he saw her by the bedside. A cousin of his (a young man) came to see him, and thinking his illness to be nothing but disappointment in his love affair began to rally upon it, merrily asking him: 'Has she refused thee?' To which his cousin soberly replied and told him how it was. This cousin replied: 'Thou must speak to her.' He being loath to do, his cousin said to him: 'But thou must do it, or thou shalt have no quiet. I will come with thee and see thou shalt have no harm.' They went out, and called at Tafarn-y-garreg (an inn, so called), but he could not drink and often looked towards the door. Some who were in the house took notice and asked what ailed the man. He was uneasy to go out. But when he went out, his cousin followed him.

And as soon as he was out in the yard, he saw her – very little in size, but still the same – the woman who had hanged herself, who was now in the kingdom of darkness (for no eternal life is promised to self-murderers (1 John 3:15)). As soon as he saw her he said: 'O God, here she is!' Upon which his cousin said: 'This is a sad thing; I don't know what to think about thee. But come, I will go with thee – go where thou wilt.' Both went into the alehouse where he had been at first, not far from the house where the unhappy woman had hanged herself. When he was in the house, and it was late at night, he began again to be uneasy to go out, and showed them he must go out. His cousin said he would go with him, but the young man said: 'No. Thou shalt not.' Others also offered to go with him, but he said that none of them should go with him. He went out, and she appeared to him. She bid him not fear, but said that he must follow her. When he offered to go the other side of the lane they were going through, she said: 'Come this way.' She led him to the back side of the house where she had lived, and bid him raise up his hand and take from the wall a linen small bag. This he did. It was a thin one (such as they turn about their cheese), and in it a great sum of money – supposed to be large pieces of gold (but it may be they were large pieces of silver) – as he guessed, about 200 pounds. He was in too much fear to look what they were. She bid him go and cast it into the river – which he did. Some persons who heard of this went to the river to see for the money, but could find none. We have several instances of money cast into the water at the request of disembodied spirits (but the money could never be found).

The Revd Mr Thomas Lewis, who related to me this passage, saw the place where the money was hid. He wondered how the man could reach it, it being so high. It is likely, therefore, that he was helped by the spirit. Mr Lewis, the Dissenting minister in those parts, asked the young man what sort of voice she had, and whether it was not terrible. He said it was a sound as if it were out of a drum, but not so terrible. The man, Mr Lewis said, was not well when he saw him.

4. In the parish of Ystradgynlais came to pass the following remarkable occurrence, which I had from under the hand of the Revd Mr T.L., who then lived in that neighbourhood:

A young man (son to an innkeeper) was often troubled by supernatural odd sights – sometimes of light, sometimes of darkness, and of dark misshapen things in the night – for some years. At last, a spirit appeared to him in the shape of a well-dressed woman (whose clothes he described), who stood before him in a narrow lane. He strove to pass by her, and did so in much fear, as doubting what she might be. Some time after, having occasion to pass that way at night, he saw her in the same shape and in the same dress, and he failed to pass by her. He, then, strove to take heart and asked her what she wanted with him, as he was not without fear (and fearfully looked upon her). She bid him not fear: she would do him no hurt, for she had looked often in his face in the space of eight years' time. The woman told him he must go to Philadelphia in Pennsylvania, and take a box from a house there (which she described) in which was 200 pounds in half-crowns, and charged him to meet her again next Friday night.

He having declared this to some neighbours, the news went to the ears of the curate of the parish (who is a good man). He sent for this young man to come to his house. There they appointed a prayer-meeting to be that Friday evening in some house in the neighbourhood, to which they desired the young man to come. The meeting continued till midnight, in which he was observed to be very uneasy to go out. When the meeting ended, he went out with the parson's servants to the horses. Coming back from the stable door, he was taken from among them and they lost him, and knew not how (at which they were greatly amazed, not knowing what to think of it). The apparition carried him away to a river hard by, threw him into it, and wetted him. She did chide him for telling the people of the appointed meeting, and not coming to meet her according to promise. Yet, she bid him not fear – that she would not hurt him.[3]

'And now', said she, 'we begin the journey.' And he was lifted up and carried away (he knew not how) without seeing sun and moon in all the journey. When he came to the place, he saw light, and was carried into a house (he knew not how) and into a fine room, but saw no man. When he was come into that room, the spirit bid him lift up a board – which he did. He saw the box, and took it. Then the spirit said, he must go three miles and cast it into the black sea. They went (as he thought) to some lake of clear water, where he was commanded to throw the box into it. When he did, there was such a noise as if all about was going to pieces. From thence, he was taken up and brought to the place where he was taken up. He then asked her whether he was free now. She said he was, and told him some secret thing, and strictly charged him to tell no person. He was three days and three nights in this mysterious journey (from Friday night to Monday night), which only they in the other world fully understand. When he came home he could hardly speak, and his skin was somewhat like leather. He can hardly look in another man's face and looks rather sickly (for he is still alive, or lately was so). As to her person: she was largely made, looked pale, her looks severe and her voice hollow (different from a human voice). He was not in great dread while she spoke, but in great dread before she spoke and when she parted from him. A woman in the neighbourhood remembered, lately, that (about eighty years ago) one Elizabeth Gething went from this neighbourhood into Pennsylvania; most likely, it was her spirit (which, perhaps, she told the young man).

Some will object (or at least will wonder), how a spirit should be able to carry a man in the air over land and sea about 4000 miles, forward and backward. But, let it be remembered, that an evil spirit carried the body of our Saviour in the day that he was suffered to tempt him through the air to Jerusalem and the pinnacle of the temple (Matthew 4:5). This was uphill indeed, and more difficult than to carry him either downward or onward (unless spirits are not subject to the pressure of the atmosphere as bodies are and, therefore, inconceivably stronger to carry burdens than if they were subject to the pressure of the air). Besides, disembodied spirits are vastly stronger out of the body than they can possibly be in it, because it is a load about the spirit, which greatly hinders its operation. This takes off the difficulty to believe that the spirit of this woman was able (who also might be helped by another spirit) to carry this young man to and from Philadelphia over the vast Atlantic sea and much land.

The difficulty is: What end could be answered by the destruction of so much money as was done here, and in diverse other places in the same manner, and even in this parish, as shall presently be related? My answer is: that we know little of the manner of the world of spirits, and there are many instances in the apparitions of spirits of eternity that they were very short in giving account of the other world. Good spirits will not, and evil spirits durst not, give a large or larger account. And why? Because the strong human corruption, which corrupts everything, would be sure to make some ill use of a larger and more particular knowledge of the things of the other world, as it doth of this.

Thus, I have (as well as I could) given account of this wonderful apparition and transaction, according as I have received it. There seems, indeed, some defective circumstances in the relation, which make it liable to objections, which the relater (a man of undoubted verity) either forgot or did not particularly enquire into. But the substance of it may be depended upon.

Only one gentleman in the parish objected against it and (as was said) threatened to punish the harmless undesigning young man for telling lies. But the gentleman had not then, and maybe not afterwards, condescended to examine the young man about it. But why is it that so many of the gentry affect to deny these important matters of fact? Is it not because they are farther alienated from God and spiritual things than others in common. They were poor that received the Gospel in the days of Jesus Christ, not the Sadducees –who denied the being of spirits: 'For the Sadducees say that there is no resurrection, neither angel, nor spirit' (Acts 23:8). Here, they deny the very being of God and eternity, etc. And the self-righteous Pharisees did not receive the Gospel. A minute after death will convince them of their obstinate, unreasonable infidelity. And hell must do it for many, and it will be a home conviction.

5. This account I had from T.F. (one of the schoolmasters of the circulating Welsh charity schools), a good man of undoubted veracity and born in the neighbourhood:

A young man in this county, after the death of a first cousin of his, was haunted by his apparition wherever he was after sunset. The young man was afraid to speak to him, which the spirit seemed to want very much. At last, the apparition set upon him and beat him (because he did not speak), which compelled him to speak to him and to say to him: 'In the name of God! Howel, my cousin, what dost thou want with me?' To which he received this answer: 'God's blessing upon thee for speaking to me. There is a hatchet', in such a place (which he named), 'take it from thence and with all the strength of thine arm throw it into the lake' (Syfaddan lake, I suppose), 'and I will trouble thee no more.'[4] He did so, and was no more troubled with the troublesome apparition.

6. The Revd Mr T.L. of Llan-ddew gave me the following account of the Revd Mr Penry Bailey, curate of Llangamarch (I suppose) in the county of Brecon:

He was thought, by all who heard him and conversed with him, to be a godly man, both preaching in public and conversing in private with religious power and life. Mr Bailey was, when a boy, apt to study (and inclined to study) the magic art. He agreed, with two young persons, to go to Cefn Brith wood in Llangamarch parish to conjure. There, having made a circle, he called one of the spirits of hell who, it seems, came upon call (as they say they always will do). When it came and appeared, the terror was so great that the stoutest of the three fainted and lay dead for some time. Mr Bailey saw nothing, but he who fainted (whom they carried away with some difficulty) declared that he saw an exceeding dreadful appearance. They had to go with a candle into the place, which was put out — then, the terror came upon them.

Mr B. (by some means or other) knew, when he was from home, if any man was at his house enquiring for him, and whether it was a man or a woman that did inquire for him. For, upon a time, conversing with a friend at a distance from home, he said that a man and not a woman was at his house and had been a while there looking for him. He told the friend he knew it, and that it was a man who wanted to see him. The man, hearing that, said: 'I do not like you; I am afraid you are guilty of that which you are charged with, even conjuring or dealing in the black art. I will go home with you, to see whether it be as you say.' They went, and found it was as Mr B. said. The man still wondering, Mr B. (to make him easier) told him: 'I will show you my rules to know whether any person man or woman is at my house', and showed him some kind of writing in which the man could see nothing like conjuring or magic spells.

I once saw Mr B., and had pretty much conversation with him. To me, indeed, he seemed to be a godly man both in his speech and behaviour (something more than commonly so). How he could be guilty of anything that looked like dealing in the magic art, I cannot conceive. He was very young when I saw him, but he did not live very long. If it was not an evil thing to make a circle and cause an evil spirit to appear, one could have wished an Atheist, a Deist, or Sadducee to be in the circle, to be convinced of his infidelity (it being better for him to be convinced by any means that to live and die in the capital heresy of denying the being of spirits and the resurrection).

7. In the year 1769, David Thomas of Pantmelyn in Llangattock Crickhowell parish, Breconshire (a good man, a gifted brother, and a valuable preacher of the Gospel among our people), informed me that, being converted among the Methodists, and at one time thinking himself very courageous, he expressed himself to this purpose: that he was not afraid of one hundred devils (which, after the manner of Peter, was going too far in the way of self – which commonly meets with some check).

So it came to pass upon him. For travelling over Illtyd mountain in the county by night, all of a sudden he heard on his right hand a sound as strong and loud as five or six coaches could make at once. This caused so great a terror that it made him leap from the ground (and for a long time after any sudden sound would startle him). Upon hearing the strange mighty sound he said: 'In the name of God, what is here?' Upon which the sound ceased, and he heard it no more. He saw not the form of anything, but saw darkness on his right hand, where the sound was. He gained this good from it: to express himself afterward with less self and more modesty, as becomes a good man (and as Peter did after his fall). All Satan's work upon the saints of God are at least, one way or another, turned for good.

Would it be wrong for me to wish an Atheist, a Deist, a Sadducee, a ridiculer of apparitions, to be in good and honest David Thomas's place, to be cured of his infidelity, and to be a sober believer of an interesting reality, and not to go on in unreasonable, unprofitable, wild, and foolish incredulity? Here was a proof of the being of evil spirits to three of his senses: his ears, his eyes, and feeling, by a lasting impressing. If an infidel can suppose his sight to be deceived with the sight of darkness (though it appeared in the proper place where the infernal sound was heard) yet his ears could not be deceived. Such a sound in the ears of an infidel (a ridiculer of apparitions) might do him much good, and be a means of saving his soul from going to see the devils of hell – to be cured of his infidelity, forever.

8. Griffith Edward, a shoemaker born in Cardiganshire, was converted among the Methodists and came to the village of Tretower in Breconshire to live. He was disturbed in the night-time by a noise, like the rattling of iron chains. And once, if not twice, the enemy followed him (coming home by night from hearing the Methodists) in the shape of a turkey cock, piffing after him, and making such a sound with his wings which the turkey cock makes when he makes the piffing noise with his mouth (but something more disagreeable, which everyone that considers it may easily imagine was very terrifying both to see and hear).[5] Yet G.E. had courage to speak to him, and to reprove him for his ill will.

G.E. appeared to me to be a man of extraordinary piety, and to be fully alive toward God and heavenly things, and highly lifted up above the things of the present life. The means of his conversion was odd and extraordinary. For, endeavouring in hypocrisy to recommend himself to Mr Howel Harris, Mr H. (who was quick-sighted and honest to deal with men without respect of faces) said to him: 'Man there is nothing in you but hypocrisy, etc.' This was the means of G.E.'s conviction and conversion, as he himself told me. These secrets of God were with him, so that he foresaw and foretold several things as they came to pass. He is dead many years ago.

9. About the middle of the century, a young man of the parish of Llanfigan, Breconshire (who courted Ursula Powel, a young woman) was drowned when on the point of marriage. After, she mourned excessively and continued to do so immeasurably. At last, when she was in bed, she saw him come and he seemed to be on the bedside. She felt his face, as she thought as cold as a stone. He desired her to mourn for him no more, that he was where it was the will of God he should be (without telling her where he was) and departed, and she ceased the mourning. Here we see an instance that spirits (both good and bad) give but short accounts of the other world to the inhabitants of the earth. The reason, doubtless, must be because the human corruption of fallen mankind would be sure to abuse a larger knowledge of the things of the world to come. When men are gone to eternity, the goodly to Heaven, and the ungodly into hell, then they shall know – for then they are fit to have a large and full knowledge of the eternal world. It is a sign of the veracity and honesty of the young woman that she did not add to what the spirit told her – that he was in happiness (which some would have been strongly inclined to do from great love and respect). This account, also, I had from Mr T.F.

10. In the year 1767, Walter Watkins of the Neuadd in the parish of Llanddetty (a man of considerable substance in the world, a man of virtue, sense and learning) gave me the following notable relation of an apparition, as follows:

Some years past, being out at night towards Taf Fechan chapel, within sight and not far from his house, he could see a whitish kind of light near the said chapel.[6] It increased till it was as big as a church tower, and decreased again till it became as small as a star. Then, it would increase to the former largeness (doing so several times), so that he wondered at it (and no wonder he did) but felt no fear. He went to the house to fetch his father and mother to see it, and they all saw it in the same manner – to their great wonder (for, indeed, it was a supernatural, wonderful apparition to human eyes). Sometimes after, a neighbour was ploughing a field near the chapel. The plough stopped against a large flat stone, which the ploughers rose up. And, behold, there was a stone chest. In it was the jawbone of a man (a large one, for it encompassed the chin of the plougher, and it had the cleverest set of teeth that any man could have) and an earthen jug which was empty (supposed to hold the murdered man's blood, put into the earth to hide the murder). Who it was could not now be known, but shall be known in eternity. However, upon this discovery it was remembered by some that a man named Philip Watkins (living at the said Neuadd) was suddenly lost and never heard of. His wife married another man, taking it for granted that he was dead indeed, (or pretending to think it was so).

Some time after, asking a wandering sort of man, who used to be between the two houses, what news from Neuadd, he jocularly said that Philip Watkins was come home, and was well. This affected her so much that she fell sick and died. It was in vain for the man to say afterward that it was not true . . . that he only jested. If she was sorry for having married another man, it showed a tender conscience; otherwise, it looked like extreme guilt. There is a mystery in it, which must be left undecided this side of eternity, where all things which have been done on earth shall be known, according to our Saviour's saying: 'For there is nothing covered, that shall not be revealed; neither hid, that shall not be known', in the day when the secrets of men shall be revealed (Luke 12:2).

After this, the light was no more seen near the chapel (though often seen before). The spirits of men appear like light because they are knowing beings, properly resembled by light.

CAERNARVONSHIRE

11. About the year 1758, at the house of a certain farmer in the parish of Llanllechid, there was a great disturbance from an evil spirit, casting stones into and about the house, beating, and wounding the people.[7] The stones were of diverse sizes, up to twenty-seven pounds weight. Some clergymen from Bangor (on Bangor side) came there to read prayers and they did their best with a good design, but they were also beaten and obliged to go away. Reading prayers was too weak a means to drive an enraged evil spirit away; there was a necessity of some persons of a strong faith who had the spirit and gift of prayer in some great measure.[8] Most of the stones were river stones, taken out of the river which runs hard by. The disturbance was so great that the family removed thence. The person who related the story to the Revd Mr R.F. told him that he was struck with a stone of about five pounds weight, he thought.

CARDIGANSHIRE

12. I have little to say from this county, having neglected to make enquiry which, if I had made, I had certainly received many accounts of this sort, which upon earnest enquiry are sure to be had in every part of Wales.

That which I have to relate is concerning Sir David Llwyd, who lived near Ysbyty Ystwyth in that county, who was a curate (likely of that church) and a physician.[9] But, being known to deal in the magic art, he was turned out of his curacy and obliged to live by practising physick. His being called Sir David was after the manner of the other curates in Wales a long time after the Reformation, but ceased now. This was a relic of popery, which should have ceased just at the beginning of the Reformation – the pride of the popes of Rome causing them to make their curates equal to knights and baronets, and demanding the same honour to them. And here let us make a contrast between Christ the head of the Church and his pretended vicar and substitutes. Christ, the head of the Church indeed, made no diocesan bishops, archbishops, and cardinals, nor a vicar and substitute to supply his place. But the papists have made these for him without his leave, and against his will. Then, no wonder the popes have been such plagues in the Christian Church, to turn it into a harlot for themselves; for this, and no other, is the scarlet whore spoken of in Revelation 11, who became drunk with the blood of the saints, even the cruel persecuting Church of Rome (or Satan's Synagogue), opposite to the Church of God.

Of this Sir David I have heard several things. But I chiefly depend upon what was related to me by the Revd Mr Thomas Lewis, the curate of Llan-ddew and Talachddu.[10] Mr Lewis is a man of undoubted piety and veracity, an excellent preacher of the Gospel, and not sufficiently esteemed by his people (which not unlikely will bring a judgment upon them in time to come).

There was in those parts a tailor, a profane man and a great drunkard who, having been in a fair in those parts and coming home drunk, met (as he thought) a certain man on horseback. The man asked him: was he a tailor? He said he was. The man on horseback asked him: would he make clothes for him? He said he would. The tailor received a piece of cloth with a charge to be sure to be at home at such a day and such an hour to take his measure. The tailor said he would. Though he was drunk, the tailor observed that the man's feet who spoke with him were not like a man's but like a horse's feet. Some other circumstances made him concerned, and the more he considered it his fear increased: that not a man but something belonging to the devil had appeared to him. Being in great fear about the matter, he went to Sir David to ask his opinion about it, from whom be received the following advice: to delay the measuring him as much as possible; not to stand before but behind him; and bid him be sure to be at home the time appointed. (Sir David would come to him that time.)

The supposed man came and the tailor (in great fear) went about to measure him, fearing he was something not good. According to the advice given him, he delayed measuring him, pretending that he wanted this and that thing and was as dilatory as he could (in pain of mind and great fear). At last, the supposed man said to him: 'Thou art very long about it, and why standest thou behind my back? Why dost not come before me?' The tailor (now in greater fear) thought every minute a long time, expecting Sir David to come according to his promise. Accordingly, he came, and having looked on the strange man who was come to be measured said to him: 'What is your business here? Go away!' And, he went away. This the tailor told to all who enquired about it, and it passed about through the country.

13. Another time, Sir David, being gone on a visit towards the town Rhayader Gwy in Radnorshire, and being gone from one house there to another, forgot his magic book in the first house. He sent his boy or apprentice to fetch it, charging

him not to open the book in the way. But old Eve's son, his curiosity moved the more by the prohibition, opened the book and the evil spirit immediately called for work. The boy, though surprised and in some perplexity, said: 'Tafl gerrig o'r afon' ('Throw stones out of the river'). The evil spirit did so. After a while, having thrown up many stones of the river Wye or Elgy (which ran that way), he again, after the manner of confined spirits, asked for something to do. The boy had his senses about him to bid the spirit throw the stones back into the river, and it did so. Sir David, seeing the boy long in coming, doubted how it was. He came back and chided the boy for opening the book, and commanded the familiar spirit back into his book.

Another time, Sir David, being gone to Llanidloes town in Montgomeryshire (twelve miles from home) – as he was going home very late in the evening – saw a boy there of his neighbourhood. He offered the boy to ride behind him if he was for going home (which the boy accepted), and they came home in about two hours' time. The boy had lost one of his garters in the journey. But seeing something hanging in the ash-tree near the church, he climbed up to see what it was; it was the garter which he had lost – which shows that they rode high in the air.

It was thought that Sir David learnt the magic art privately, in Oxford, in the profane time of Charles II when many vices greatly prevailed. It was this man's great wickedness to make use of a familiar spirit, one of the enemies of God and man – a thing forbidden in holy writ (Leviticus 19:31). Seeking counsel of a woman who had a familiar spirit was one of the causes of Saul's destruction (1 Chronicles 10:11).

The bishop did well (whoever he was) in turning Sir David out of the sacred office, though he was no ill-tempered man. For how unfit was such a man to read the sacred Scripture, especially those chapters where seeking to familiar spirits is forbidden and condemned. How unfit to read the good prayers of the Church and to administer the holy ordinances of God! With what propriety and conscience could he ask the sponsors in baptism to undertake for the child to renounce the world, the flesh and the devil, who himself was in covenant with hell and familiar with one of the spirits of darkness? And how far was he from renouncing the devil and all his works (as he was engaged to do), who had told the bishop that he was moved by the Holy Ghost to seek ordination to the holy office to act against the kingdom of darkness?

Mr Lewis, who gave me the relation, knew her who had been his maidservant and the house where he lived.

CARMARTHENSHIRE

14. I am now come into that part of Wales where we shall meet with the most numerous and most notable account of apparitions. In the middle part of the bishopric of St David's there is the greatest account of the *cyhyraeth* and the

corpse-candles to be met with in any part of Wales. I am now to give some account of the *cyhyraeth* (a doleful foreboding noise heard before death) and enquire into the cause of this and of the appearance of the corpse-candles.

The judicious Joshua Coslet, who lived in that side of the river Towy (which runs through the middle of Carmarthenshire where the *cyhyraeth* is oftenest heard), gave me the following remarkable account of it. It is most apt to be heard before foul weather. The voice resembles the groaning of sick persons who are to die, heard at first at a distance, then comes nearer, and the last near at hand, so that it is a threefold warning of death (the king of terrors). It begins strong and louder than a sick man can make, the second cry is lower but not less doleful (but rather more so), and the third yet lower and soft (like the groaning of a sick man, almost spent and dying). A person well-remembering the voice and coming to the sick man's bed who is to die shall hear his groans exactly alike, which is also amazing evidence of the spirits' foreknowledge. Sometimes when it cries very loud, it bears a resemblance of one crying who is troubled with a stitch. If it meets any hindrance in the way, it seems to groan louder.

It is, or hath been very common, in the three commots of Ynys-Cenin. (A commot is a portion of ground less than a *cantref* or a hundred.[11]) Three commots make up this hundred of Ynys-Cenin, which extends from the sea as far as Llandeilo Fawr, containing twelve parishes (Llandeilo Fawr, Betws, Llanedy, Llannon, Cydweli, Llangennech, Pen-Bre, Llanarthney, Llangyndeyrn, etc.). These lie on the south-east side of the river Towy. There, some time past, it cried and groaned before the death of every man and woman (as my informant thought) who lived that side of the county. It also sounded before the death of persons who were born in these parishes and died elsewhere. Sometimes the voice is heard long before death; three-quarters of a year is the longest time beforehand. But it must be a common thing indeed, as it came to be a common thing for people to say, by way of reproach, to a person making a disagreeable noise and sometimes to children crying and groaning unreasonably: 'Oh'r cyhyraeth!'

15. D.P. of Llanybyther parish (a sober, sensible man and careful to tell the truth) informed me in the year 1767 that, in the beginning of one night, his wife and maidservant being together in the house (which was by the wayside) heard the doleful tone of the *cyhyraeth*. When it came over against the window, it pronounced these strange words of no signification that we know of: '*woolach, woolach*'. (Some time after a burying passed that way.) I confess a word of this sound, especially the latter part of the last syllable, sounds in Welsh like the twenty-third letter of the Greek alphabet (or, at least, as they pronounced it formerly in the schools). It was pronounced by a spirit of the night near at hand with a disagreeable hellish sounding voice that was very terrible and impressive upon the mind and memory.

16. Walter Watkins of Neuadd in the parish of Llanddetty, Breconshire was at school at Carmarthen. He and some other scholars, who lodged in the same house with him, were playing ball by the house late in the evening, and heard the dismal mournful voice of the *cyhyraeth* hard by them. However, they saw nothing (which was very frightening to hear). For though these sort of men are incredulous enough, yet they were soon persuaded that the voice was of neither man nor beast but of some spirit, which made them leave their play and run into the house. Not long after, a man who lived hard by died; (for this kind of voice is always heard before some death).

17. The woman of the house where the scholars lodged related to them many such accounts, which they heard with contempt and ridicule, believing nothing of what she said. One morning (sportingly) they asked her what she had seen or heard of a spirit that night. She readily answered that she heard a spirit come to the door, as it were walking in slippers and passing by her while she sat by the fire. It seemed to walk into a room where a sick man was. After some time, she heard him coming back and as if it fell down, or making a noise at the end of the room, over against the fire, as if one was fallen down dead in a faint and raised up. Very soon after, the sick man rose up (thinking to be able to walk), came into the room where the woman heard the fall, and fell down dead in that very part of the room where the spirit made the same kind of stir (which his fall made), and was made by those that raised him up. This made the scholars, who believed nothing of what she said before, to believe everything which she said afterward. For, that which she related came to pass, and she could have no other way to foretell these things but by some representations made to her from the world of spirits.

   Thus, these young men were cured of their evil inclination to Sadducism, and obliged (by a kind of prophecy accomplished and matter of fact) to believe the being of spirits against their natural inclination to it. The said Walter Watkins also told me (who was a man of family, substance, learning, and veracity) that he was sorry to hear that the Coedycymmer and Merthyr Dissenting professors ridicule the account of apparitions, and seek to make many honest men liars who speak of apparitions and the agencies of spirits from the most sensible experience. Is it any wonder indeed that apostates from many, and even from some of the most capital doctrines of Christianity (some of them to the Arminian, some to the Arian, and some to the Socinian heresies) should be also Sadducees? Yea! Some of them have not stopped this side of Deism and blasphemies against the word of God too shocking to relate.

18. A clergyman's son in this county (now a clergyman himself in England) was in his younger days somewhat vicious. He had been at a debauch one night, and came home late when the doors were locked and the people in bed. Fearing to disturb them, and fearing also their chiding and expostulations about his staying so late, he went to the servant who slept in an outroom (as is often the manner in

that country). He could not awake the servant. But while he stood over him he saw a small light come out of the servant's nostrils, which soon became a corpse-candle. He followed it out until it came to a footbridge over a rivulet of water. It came into the gentleman's head to raise up the end of the footbridge from off the bank whereon it lay, to see what it would do. When the corpse-candle came, it seemed to offer to go over, but did not go (as if loath to go because the bridge was displaced). When he saw that, he put the bridge in its place and stayed to see what the candle would do. It came on the bridge when it was replaced, but when the candle came near him it struck him as it were with a handkerchief. But the effect was strong; for he became dead upon the place, not knowing of himself a long time before he revived (such is the power of the spirit of the other world, and it is ill jesting with them).

A Sadducee and a proud ridiculer of apparitions in this gentleman's place, now, would have a pure reasoning for this pastime. 'Tis true, these men have not seen the corpse-candles of Wales, but they should believe the numerous and ever continuing witnesses of it and not foolishly discredit abundant matters of fact asserted by many honest, wise men. We have heard of others who, from an excess of natural courage or being in drink, have endeavoured to stop the corpse-candles, and have been struck down upon the place. But, now, none offer it, being deterred by a few former examples related, remembered, and justly believed.

19. Joshua Coslet (a man of sense and knowledge) told me of several corpse-candles he had seen, but of one in particular which he saw in a lane called Heol Bwlch y Gwynt (Wind Gap Lane) in Llandeilo Fawr parish. There, he suddenly met a corpse-candle of small light when near him, but increasing as it went farther from him. He could easily perceive that there was some dark shadow passing along with the candle, but was afraid to look earnestly upon it. Not long after, a burying passed that way. He told me, further, that it is the common opinion (doubtless from some experience of it) that if a man should wantonly strike it, he should be struck down by it, but if one touches it unawares, he shall pass on unhurt. He also said that some dark shadow of a man carried the candle along, holding it between three fingers over against his face. This is what some have seen who had the courage to look earnestly. Some others have seen the likeness of a candle carried in a skull. There is nothing unreasonable or unlikely in either of these representations.

20. Agreeable to what I have now related is the following. One William John of the parish of Llanboidy (a smith) was one night going home somewhat drunk and bold (it seems too bold). Seeing one of the corpse-candles, he went out of his way to meet with it. When he came near, he saw it was a burying. The corpse upon the bier was the perfect resemblance of a woman in the neighbourhood whom he knew. She was holding the candle between her fingers and dreadfully grinned on him. Presently, he was struck down from his horse (where be remained a while), and was ill a long time afterward before he recovered. This

was before the real burying of the woman. His fault (and therefore his danger) was his coming presumptuously against the candle. Here is also a sensible proof of the apparition and being of spirits.

21. The foreknowledge of these corpse-candle spirits concerning deaths and burials is wonderful, particularly as the following instance will show. One Rees Thomas (a carpenter), passing through a place called Rhiw Edwst near Capel Iwan by night, heard a stir coming towards him, walking and speaking.[12] When they were come to him, he felt as if some person did put his hand upon his shoulder and say in Welsh to him: 'Rhys bach, pa fodd yr ŷch chwi?' ('Dear Rees, how are you?'), which surprised him much, for he saw nothing. A month after, passing that way, he met a burying in that very place, and a woman who was in the company put her hand upon him, and spoke exactly the same words to him that the invisible spirit had spoken to him before, at which he could no less than wonder. This I had from the mouth of Mr T.I. of Trefach, a godly minister of the gospel.

22. About the year 1753, two women (Methodists) from Ystradgynlais parish were going to Tŷ Gwyn in the parish of Llangadog, Carmarthenshire, where lived one John Williams (who was thought to be a godly young man). They heard the voice of one singing psalms coming to meet them. They knew the voice to be the voice of John Williams. When the voice came near, it slackened and grew weaker (when it came within about twenty yards' distance); when just over them, the passing voice ceased, yet was soon renewed; and when about twenty yards distant, the voice was as strong as before. They heard some of the words, which were from Psalm 105. They did not hear all the words, but the beginning and end of the stanzas, which they heard with much surprise. The next Lord's Day at the Dissenting meeting at Cwmllynfell (to their great wonder) they heard that very psalm given out by John Williams, and sung. When they heard this, they said one to another (the people observing them to whisper one to another): 'that is the voice and the words we heard sung on the way.' The fifth Lord's Day after, John Williams was buried.[13] Here is another notable instance both of the being and foreknowledge of spirits.

23. A woman in Carmarthen town protested to Mr Charles Winter of the parish of Bedwellty (who was then at the Academy and since became a preacher of God's word) that she heard like the sound of a company, as it were a burying, coming up from a river. Presently, she heard as it were the sound of a cart coming another way to meet the company. The cart seemed to stop while the company went by, and then went on. Soon after, a dead corpse was brought from the river (from one of the vessels in the river, I suppose), and a cart met the burying till the company passed by – exactly as the woman heard. Mr Winter was no man to tell an untruth, and the woman had no self-interest to serve by telling an untruth. The wonder is how these spirits can so particularly foreshow things to come. Either their knowledge of future things near at hand must be very great,

or they must have a great influence to accomplish things as foreshown. Be it either way, the thing is wonderful: the very minute and particular knowledge of these spirits in the matter of death and burials.

24. I am now to give another remarkable instance, which I had from a good man, who also had it from creditable persons. (The place is not remembered.) A certain man in a field, burning turfs, saw the fairies come through the field where he lay blowing the fire in one of the pits. They went by like a burial, imitating the singing of psalms as they went and, doubtless, the very tune sung at the approaching funeral. One of them leaped over his legs. He rose up to see where they would go, and followed them into a field that led into a wood. Soon after, a real burying came through that field, and he lay down by the pit of turfs to see what they would do. One of the company actually leaped over his legs in passing by, just as one of the fairies had done before. They also sung psalms at the burial, as the fairies foreshowed.

25. R.D. (a good, wise, religious woman) gave me this remarkable account of one Reynold ——. He was a young man who heard it affirmed (as usually it is in that country) that if any man watched in any church porch for a night he would see those that would be buried that year come in at the church porch to be buried. One that did so, at last saw himself come in (as was said) and died that year. Having drank much to put himself in heart, Reynold ventured to go to the porch of the meeting-house at Henllan Amgoed, there being a burying yard by that meeting-house. Having sat there some time, there came a thick mist that darkened the place and filled him with terror. He felt himself heavy-laden (as if there was some weight upon him), and he left the place. When he came home, behold his hair on that side of his head which was next the apparition (though he saw nothing but dark mist) was turned white, and continued for all his days. She, who related the story to me, saw him. I asked what sort of hair he had, and she said it was lank hair and turning a little at the end. She thinks he was a sober-minded man (if not truly religious) and seemed penitent for his presumption. What he did indeed was no perfect necromancy, for he did not seek anything of the dead as Saul did. But it was a thing that bordered on it. This could not but be known in all the country roundabout, and it is a strong confutation of Sadducism. For here is the testimony of a sober man, and of the change of his hair against this unreasonable kind of incredulity, though it is but one of a thousand that might easily be found against it.

Let none think ill of Henllan meeting upon this account, for there is no place so sacred below heaven but Satan can come near it and into it. For he came into paradise, a more sacred place and a type of heaven. The Henllan congregation is one of the largest in Wales (much about 400 communicants), and contains abundance of good people, having had also excellent ministers to serve them: Messieurs Henry Palmer, Thomas Morgan, John Powel, and Richard Morgan (one of the best ministers, now, in Wales).

26. Before the light of the Gospel prevailed, there were in Carmarthenshire and elsewhere often heard before burials what by some were called *cŵn annwn* (hounds of hell), by others *cŵn bendith eu mamau* (hounds of the fairies), and by some *cŵn wybr* (sky-hounds). The nearer they were to a man the less their voice was (like that of small beagles), and the farther, the louder (sometimes like the voice of a great hound sounding among them), like that of a bloodhound: a deep, hollow voice.

About the year 1730, one Thomas Phillips (I think his name was) of Trelech parish heard these spiritual dogs, and the great dog sounding among them. They went in a way in which no corpse used to go, at which he wondered (as he knew they used to go only in the way in which the corpse was to go). Not long after, a woman who was come from another parish (Llanwinio, I think), dying at Trelech, was carried that way to her own parish in the very way in which these spiritual dogs seemed to hunt. What is very unlikely (and hardly credible) is that some people have reported concerning these death-hunting beagles: that they were finely spotted with white and black; that some have handled them (as thought) and shut them up in barns and stables (but when they went to look for them, they would be sure to find them gone away). This, I confess, looked very unlikely. On the other hand, I am loath to think but that some such experience sometime or other hath given occasion for this report.

27. An acquaintance of mine (a man perfectly firm to tell the truth), being out at night, heard a hunting in the air. It was as if they overtook something which they hunted after and, being overtaken, made a miserable cry among them, and seemed to escape. But, overtaken again, they made the same dismal cry and again escaped, and followed after till out of hearing.

28. I am now to relate one of the most terrible apparitions that ever I heard of. It was related to me in 1767 by R.D. (a woman appearing to me to be a true, living, experimental Christian beyond many) in relation to herself, as follows:

Being to go to Laugharne town on some business in the evening (it being late), her mother dissuaded her from going, telling her it was late and she should be benighted and terrified by an apparition which was both seen and heard by very many (and by her father, among others) at a place called Pant y madog. This was a pit by the side of the lane leading to Laugharne that was filled with water, and not quite dry in the summer. But she, then, not fearing anything, went to Laugharne and came back before night. Though it was considerably darkened, she passed by the place, yet not without thinking of the apparition. But being come but a little beyond this pit into a field uphill, where was a little rill of water (which as she was about to pass), and having stretched one foot over it, and looking before her, she could see before her (alas for the sight) something big – like a great dog. It was one of the dogs of hell coming hastily on to meet her. Being come within four or five yards of her (and it was well he came no nearer) it stopped, sat upon its backside, and set up such a scream – so horrible, and so loud and strong – that the earth moved under her. (She thought the rill was rent by it.) She, then, fainted and fell down dead upon the place, and did not awake and go to the next house (which was but about a field's length from this place) till about midnight, having one foot wet in the rill of water which she was about to pass when she saw and heard the apparition. She was very weak that night, and for a long time after a very loud noise would disturb and sicken her. She owned it was just punishment on her for her presumption and disobeying her good mother's advice. There was a strong and an effectual witness of the being of spirits both visible and audible, and both to some purpose.

Oh, that an Atheist, a Deist, a Sadducee, or the like sort of unbelievers, had been in her place. But it may be these sort of men are too wicked to obtain conviction in this way; hell and eternity must convince them.

Either a man was murdered and cast into this pit, or some money was cast into it. It should be searched to the bottom. Surely, it should.

29. About the year 1764, a man born in Carmarthen named George Griffith was engaged in the Carmarthen militia. Being gone to the west of England, at one time in bed, he received a terrible blow from an unseen agent. Soon after, the spirit of a tall man (the biggest he ever saw) appeared to him. He told him he was a German (a mariner) and had stolen some iron, some money, and some clothes out of the ship he was in, and had hid them in the earth. He persuaded George Griffith, very much, to go there and take them away, telling him where they were and promising he would trouble him no more (for he often appeared to him whenever he could find him in a secret place). At last (to have quiet from this extraordinary trouble), George Griffith was persuaded to go (it may be, chiefly for the money), enlisted himself with some regulars, and went to the wars in Germany. The spirit told him he should not lose his life in the war, but should come back safe (as indeed he came). He went to the place he was directed and found the iron and twelve shillings in moneys, but the clothes were spoiled and good for nothing. The iron he sold and the money he kept for his own use. When the apparition parted from him, he bid him not fear, but either shut his eyes and stand, or fall down with his face toward the earth. He chose the latter, and the spirit parted from him with such a noise as if the world about him was going to pieces. He returned home, and is like one desirous to mend his life.

Here is a man that is not, and durst not be, a Sadducee, a denier, and ridiculer of spirits and apparitions (as most are who have no experience of such things). But why this disembodied German spirit pitched upon this Welshman to act for him shall only be known by the all-revealing light of the eternal world (admirable to be known by all in heaven above and hell below): 'For there is nothing covered that shall not be revealed; neither hid, that shall not be known' (Luke 12:2).

30. I am now to give an account of another kind of apparition, which came to pass in a time of persecution upon the Dissenters in Charles II's time. There

lived at a place called the Pant in Carmarthenshire (which, I think, is between Carmarthen and Laugharne towns) one Mr David Thomas, a holy man who worshipped the Lord with great devotion and humility. He was also a gifted brother, and sometimes preached.

On a certain night, for the sake of privacy he went into a room (which was out of the house, but nearly adjoining to it) in order to read and pray. As he was at prayer, and very highly taken up into a heavenly frame, the room was suddenly enlightened to the degree that the light of the candle was swallowed up by a greater light, and became invisible. With, or in, that light a company of spirits (like children in bright clothing, and very beautiful) appeared and sung. But he remembered only one word of it: 'Pa hyd? Pa hyd? Dychwelwch feibion Adda' ('How long? How long? Return ye sons of Adam'), something like Psalm 90, verse 3. After a time, he lost sight of them, and the light of the candle again came to appear when the greater light of the glorious company was gone. He was immersed in the heavenly disposition, and he fell down to thank and praise the Lord. While at this, the room enlightened again, and again the light of the candle became invisible and the glorious company sung. He was so ravished and amazed at what he saw and heard that he could remember only the following words: 'Pa hyd? Pa hyd, yr erlidiwch Gristionogion duwiol?' ('How long? How long, will ye persecute the godly Christians?'). After a while, they departed and the candlelight appeared. Any Christian who enjoyed much of God's presence will easily believe that David Thomas was now lifted up very high in the spiritual life by this extraordinary visitation from heaven.

Here appears no gingle in the singing, so that it appears like the anthem way of singing or rather after the manner of the ancient Hebrews (in which there was little or no gingle, but tunes adjusted to the parts and measure of the words sung).[14] After this, he appeared to be greatly mortified to the things of time. He did not speak much, yet seemed to be a full vessel. He seemed to care little but for the things of the spiritual world and seemed like one who had a constant calmness and serenity in his mind. Christians who have had the extraordinary presence of God, in a less measure than Mr Thomas did, do know from their own experience that it leaves a serious humble sweet calmness after it, which continues to part of the next day.

But the sons of infidelity will question the truth, and cannot believe that the angels of Heaven did thus appear to any man. Some of the boldest and crudest of them may mock and ridicule the account. But why so? Did not the angels of God appear so many in times of old to Abraham, Lot, Jacob, Gideon, Manoah, David, Zechariah, and Cornelius, etc.? I grant there is less necessity (and, therefore, they more seldom appear) now, when revelation is complete. But doth not the Apostle say to the Christians of the New Testament: 'Ye are come to Mount Sion . . . to the spirits of just men made perfect', and to thousands of angels, etc. (Hebrews 12:22, 23)? That is, ye are come, through the grace of the Gospel dispensation, into union and communion with the members and company of the Church above. And, is it unreasonable to think that some of them may, upon some occasions, appear to some of their friends below? They are said to serve the heirs of salvation and to protect the saints (Hebrews 1:54; Psalms 36:7). And, is it unreasonable to think that they should sometimes appear upon great occasions to their friends whom they serve? There are reasons for their appearing sometimes to evidence the kindness of God administered through them, and to help the belief of it; to help the faith of eternity and the world to come; to prevent Atheism, Deism, and Sadducism; and to help to prepare for eternity. On the other hand, there are reasons against their appearing often, for the appearance of them is very discomposing and cannot be born without some inconvenience to the body, if not to the mind, in one respect or other. They also convey the souls of the saints to heaven after death (Luke 16:22) – then they will surely appear to the soul. And, is it unreasonable and unlikely that they should sometimes appear to the whole man before death? The primitive Church believed that an angel attended every saint; they said: 'It is his angel' (Acts 12:15). They are worse than the Pharisees (and that is bad enough) who deny the being of angels (Acts 23:7–10).

But to soften the displeasure of the sons of infidelity (for unbelief is very niggard in favours to God's people), I do not plead that they were angels (strictly so-called) who appeared to the holy man David Thomas.[15] For we never read that the angels did (for they should not) appear like children, for nothing childish belongs to them. Neither is it reasonable to think that they were the most eminent of the spirits of just men made perfect, who have more perfectly outgrown all childishness in the spiritual life. More likely, they were some of the inferior saints in glory and perhaps indeed godly children who received grace in their infancy, died, and were received into glory. These might properly appear like children in glory and not as grown men, as the more perfect saints and angels do and should appear.

31. Now that I am upon this kind of subject, I call to mind a similar case, which I heard several times from the mouths of several religious persons. It concerns Rees David (a man of more than common piety), who lived in this county of Carmarthen (towards the lower end of it, inclining towards Pembrokeshire).

In the time of his death, and a little before his death, several persons who were in the room heard (just as the time of his dissolution approached) the singing of angels drawing nearer and nearer. After his death, they heard the pleasant, incomparable singing gradually depart until it was out of hearing. Here was no deception, for several religious people (men of certain probity and sincerity) heard and attested it. The news of it spread far, and was by no means discredited by those who knew and heard of this holy man. I heard it from some of the ministers of the Gospel who were not, could not be, imposed upon.

Here the sons of infidelity again will be in the questioning, if not in the opposing and cavilling side against this account.[16] How shall we answer them properly? Surely, by saying that if the angels do rejoice at the conversion of sinners (as our Saviour, who perfectly knows heaven, saith they do) and if they do rejoice in the removal of sinners from the state of sin into the state of grace rejoice also, so far as to break out into singing (else they would not rejoice enough), do they not rejoice at their removal from this world of sin and misery into the state of glory, peace and felicity, which is a greater cause of joy and singing (Luke 15:10)? Here is an instance of it in this good man's account, nor was it the only instance of this kind of extraordinary mercy. For we have heard of other instances of this sort, though not of many. Is it not proper that there should be some instances in the world of the angels rejoicing in carrying the saints to the same happiness with themselves? It is surely proper and, therefore, hath come sometimes to pass.

Nor do I think it improper to relate a circumstance which came to pass in the day of his burial. These I choose to apprehend as a sign of his happiness, and so indeed as understood by those who saw it and by him, (a truly good man and a preacher of the Gospel) who related it to me and (I think) was there present and saw it. It was this: before the body was brought forth, a white dove came and alighted upon the bier in the sight and among all the company who stood about it, causing them to take notice with some wonder. The thing was so much the more remarkable, as doves are not numerous in that country.

Here proud unbelief (for unbelief is proud) will scorn and despise, and say that this is trifling – that it was a chance thing – and signified nothing. But soft and gentle . . . do the ravens and bird of the corpse appear and make noise before the death of many? This cannot come to pass without the agency of some spirits, because the birds of themselves know nothing of death and burial. And might not a dove appear in a significant manner, and as a good sign of this man's happiness (at whose death the angels sung, which was a greater miracle than the appearance of the dove) in a bold friendly manner upon the bier which was to carry the good man's body to the grave (and it was a delightful grateful sight to the company)? Doth not the Lord say: 'I will make a covenant for them with the beasts of the field, and the fowls of heaven' (Hosea 2:18)? And, is that for nothing, or is nothing to appear from this in any instance and at any time? He must be a strong unreasonable unbeliever that can think that nothing can.

32. Very many years ago, in coming towards home from Wrexham (Mr Perrot, the tutor at Carmarthen and the minister of the place, being dead), I was retained there to preach for some time and lodged at a house of Mrs Corrie, a widow. One night, being in an upper chamber, and none but myself in the room, Dr Cave's *Lives of the Fathers* – in which I had been reading, and lay on the table by my side – was suddenly thrown down. I was somewhat surprised at it, knowing it was some spirit that did it (there was no wind and none but myself in the room), and that it was no good spirit that threw down that book (which was an account of some of the best men in the world). I rose up and laid it on the table again and, in a little time, it was thrown down again. I rose up a second time and, after that, it was not thrown down. I indeed saw nothing, but saw and

heard this work of some bad spirit. The book made a noise when it fell down upon the floor, as being of a considerable bulk.

When I came back to Monmouthshire and lodged in a friend's house, I was put to sleep in a darkish room, which was partly underground and known to be an unfriendly place. I was not put there out of any ill will, but they thought (perhaps) I was too good a man for the enemy to trouble me (not considering that when the sons of God came to appear before him, Satan also came among them (Job 1:6)). After I had slept some time and awaked, the enemy violently came upon me. I heard him say in my ear: 'Here the devil comes in his strength.' (And that was true.) He made a noise by my face, such as is made when a man opens his mouth wide and draws his breath, as if he would swallow something. He also made a sound over me like that of dry leather and, by my left ear, a sound something like the squeaking of a pig. The clothes moved upon me and my flesh trembled, and the terror was so great that I sweated under the great diabolical influence. This, however, awakened me to pray unto the Lord of all, which otherwise I would not have done at that time. After some time, the cock crowed, and I had rest. To be revenged upon him, some time after I put the cock to sleep and to crow in that room, knowing the devil would not hurt the crow nor hinder him from crowing to shorten his night haunts and actings. For the devil had no moral advantage over the cock – who breaks no law (as we who are reasonable creatures too often do by doing Satan's work), which the unreasonable creatures do not, cannot, do. This chamber was never right after the death of a woman (in the former times of ignorance) who died in that room, to whom some sorceries were used in order to her recovery.

DENBIGHSHIRE

33. The Revd Mr Thomas Baddy (who lived in Denbigh town and was a Dissenting minister in that place), being gone one night into his study for quiet sake (and there reading or writing), thought there was one behind him laughing and grinning at him, which made him stop a little. It came again, if not a third time, and there Mr Baddy wrote on a piece of paper that devil-wounding scripture: 'For this purpose the Son of God was manifested, that he might destroy the works of the devil' (1 John 3:8). Mr Baddy held it backward, towards him, and the laughing ceased forever. For it was a melancholy word to a scoffing devil, and enough to damp him. And it would have damped him yet more if he had shown him: 'The devils also believe, and tremble' (James 2:19). But the devil had enough for one time. God's people should oftener wound him with the sword of the spirit than they do. But many are unskilful in the armour and word of righteousness, to their loss and discredit.

Mr Baddy was a sound substantial minister of the Gospel, and of an excellent character – a gentleman of family and substance (his elder brother one time being High Sheriff of the county) and a very comely man. The town of Denbigh did not understand his worth. He translated that excellent book (worth its weight in gold and more) Wadsworth's *Self-Examination* into Welsh (and very cleanly printed). It is not easy for any sober-minded person, that hath a competent measure of knowledge in spiritual things, to read it and not know whether he is a good man or not. I knew one man, Jeremiah James of Aberystruth, who had more life and tenderness in his soul than very many professors, who was greatly concerned to know whether he was a true Christian or no, but not being able to understand it from the preaching he was under (which, indeed, was not very spiritual and experimental). But, by reading of this clear, plain book he 'came to it' (as he expressed it), that he was, in some measure, a Christian.

Mr Baddy was the grandfather of the late Revd Mr David Jordine, who was the tutor of the orthodox Academy at Abergavenny, who told me of the before-mentioned passage concerning his grandfather.

34. I am now to relate one of the most extraordinary apparitions that ever was communicated to me, either by word of mouth or by letter. I received it from the hand of a pious young gentleman of Denbighshire (then at school), who was an eyewitness of it, as follows:

March 24, 1772

Revd Sir,

Concerning the apparition I saw, I shall relate it as well as I can in all its particulars. But as for the day and year, I cannot recollect. As far as I remember, it was in the year 1757 (about the seventh year of my age). In a summer's day, about noon, I was with three others, one of which was a sister of mine (about three years older than me), and the two others were sisters (one of which was eleven and the other eight years older). They are all alive this day (for ought I know), and they remembered it as well, if not better than myself. We were playing in a field called Cae-caled (in the parish of Bodfari in the county of Denbigh) near the stile which is next to Llanelwedd House.

There we perceived a company of dancers in the middle of the field, about seventy yards from us. We could not tell their numbers because of the swiftness of their motions, which seemed to be after the manner of morris dancers. (There was something uncommonly wild in their motions) (16). But, after looking some time, we came to guess that their number might be about fifteen or sixteen. They were clothed in red all over (like soldiers), with red handkerchiefs sprigged and spotted with yellow about their heads (all alike in everything, as we perceived), with the knot behind. They seemed to be a little bigger than we, but of a dwarfish appearance. Upon this, we reasoned together what they might be, whence they came, and what they were about. Presently, we saw one of them coming away from the company in a running pace. Upon this, we feared and ran to the stile. Barbara Jones went over the stile first, next her sister, next to that my sister and last of all myself. While I was creeping up the stile (my sister staying to help me), I looked back and saw him just by me, upon which I cried out. My sister also cried out and took hold of me under her arm to draw me over. When my feet had just come over, I fell crying and, looking back, we saw him reaching after me, leaning on the stile. But he did not come over. Away we ran towards the house, called the people out, and went trembling towards the place (which might be about 150 yards of the house). Though we came so soon to see, yet we could see nothing of them. He who came near us had a grim countenance – a wild and somewhat fierce look. He came towards us in a slow-running pace, but with long steps for a little one. His complexion was copper-coloured or reddish-brown, which might be significative of his disposition and condition (for they were not good but, therefore, bad spirits): the red of their cruelty, the black of their sin and misery . . . and he looked rather old than young.

> The dress, the form, the colour, and the size
> Of these, dear Sir, did me surprise;
> The open view of them we had all four,
> Their sudden flight and seeing them no more,
> Do still confirm the wonder more and more.

Thus far Mr E.W.'s letter.

FLINTSHIRE

35. I have not heard of anything of this nature from this county. This is certainly not because nothing of this nature came to pass in it (for accounts of this nature are to be had in all parts of Wales). Rather, it is because I had no opportunity of conversing with the inhabitants of this county, to obtain such accounts.

GLAMORGANSHIRE

36. Some years ago now, a certain coaster was going from Wales to Bristol. The weather being very fair and calm, and the vessel wanting wind to go, the captain (wanting patience) began to say: 'Blow wind, blow!', or as if the wind could hear him and was at his command. But, seeing no alteration, this son of Belial began to say: 'Blow devil, blow!', repeating it . . . 'Blow devil, blow!' Upon this, they could see a black cloud, eastward from them (they being on the coast of Glamorganshire), coming towards them. And the sky became darkened, and the sea became very tempestuous, and the vessel greatly endangered. So, the profane captain changed his note and said to the company: 'If ever you prayed, pray now, or we shall be in the bottom of the sea.' And he said but little. However, it was not long before the tempest ceased.

There being a religious man, who was amazed at the impiety, when the hurly-burly was over, and they in a capacity to hear, reproved the captain for his wicked speaking. The captain bore it patiently, as being now convinced that he had been too bold and presumptuous in commanding the wind and the devil (and as if the wind was at the devil's command). But observe, the captain at first wanted the devil's help, but the devil being too rough a helper and more like a destroyer (like many of his sort), then wanted the help of God to keep him from the devil.

This accident, being related about, took place with many, and put people farther off from the like profaneness (for it was indeed a thing deserving a sober notice and remembrance).

37. Many years ago there came an Englishman into Swansea, who was a Deist, who corrupted several people and disgusted others (who were aggrieved at his blasphemies against the Scripture and scriptural men). But the judgement of God reached him, and set him into the hands of the destroyer – for he shot himself to death. The people were not willing to put him into the earth and therefore cast his cursed body into the sea, to carry it away. But, as if the sea would not have him, it cast him back upon the sand. The people threw him into the sea again; the sea again rejected him, and then they buried him in the sand. Indeed, his unclean body defiled both the water and the earth about it, as being full of sin and rendered the curse of God. And as his burial was ignominious, so his resurrection will be to damnation – according to the Scripture (John 5:29).

38. I am now to give a melancholy account of another sort of burial. When the body of Elleanor Rowland, a gentleman's harlot in the parish of Gelli-gaer, Glamorganshire (and other ways, very ungodly), was brought to the church to be buried, there was such a storm and darkness in and about the church, the like whereof was never seen or heard of at such a time. The people were amazed (for they all believed it was an evil sign) and the parson could not see to read the burial office. He told the people to bury her as they could, and went away. By this means, he was happily delivered from being unhappily obliged to call this great sinner (now under signs of God's wrath) his dear sister in the burial office, and to say that God had taken her soul to himself, and that she was committed to the earth in sure and certain hope of the resurrection to life eternal through our Lord Jesus Christ, (when the Scripture saith that the resurrection of the wicked will be to damnation).

39. Mr W.T., curate of C—e, was a Deist, for I saw a letter of his to a friend of mine in which he recommended the book of Dr Morgan (the Deist) above the Bible (and, thus, W.T. was an odd man to preach the word of God). Being at Aber Pengam chapel, on a time, and after performing divine service (God knows in what manner), having stayed late at the gentleman's house hard by, he was going home. When he came near Ynis Erwith, where people were often dis-composed by an unnatural fear, the beast under him stopped and would go no

farther. He presently apprehended that something came behind him, and upon the beast. Surely, it was the devil. Then the beast set running (he must needs go whom the devil drives). Mr T. felt himself heavily pressed, and almost out of breath, and could do nothing but endeavour all he could to keep on horseback till the beast came home in a sweat, having had hard labour in carrying W.T. and the devil a long way (and of the two, the devil himself the heaviest). The curate was now convinced, by a very sensible experience, of what before he would not believe. He related it to several who, in this case as well as in many other things, were better believers than himself, and glad W.T. was convinced of his mistake.

Who are they in all the country who are not better believers than a Deist? Yea, in hell itself the devils are better believers than Deists. The Apostle James commends the faith of devils in a capital respect, and the damned in hell have the same commendable faith (James 2:19). They believe more, and better, than Deists, Socinians, and other heretics do to their everlasting shame and confusion. This man's speech hath much failed him, and things grow worse and worse with him, and never likely to mend.

40. Four men were coming from Llantrisant town, Glamorganshire, being come from the lane through a gate, which opens into the Rhiw, a long way downward towards Pontypridd. Presently, they could see a fifth person on horseback with them. They began to suspect him because the gate made no noise at his passing through it, as it did at other times. He had also a very dark disagreeable aspect. He was, indeed, pretty dark, but they could plainly see him going (sometimes by their sides and sometimes among them) a considerable part of the way. Yet none of them ventured to speak to him, fearing some hurt from him; only they spoke one to another, pretty low: 'Do you know what is among us? Do you see who was among us?' But three of the four only saw him; there was one of the company who saw him not. He was a proof that it was a spirit: for if it had been a man, every one of them would have seen him. So here were four witnesses of the being of spirits and apparitions.

This account I had from the mouth of Mr W.M. of the Hafod, a person of undoubted veracity, who was one of this company. He added that it vexed him to hear some persons saying that there is no such thing as apparitions, after he himself had experience (together with others) to the contrary. But it is what some inconsiderate people learn of one another – especially from the gentry, who do not travel so much alone and by night as others do. What further helped their suspicion (that it was an evil spirit that went along with them), was that they did not hear the sound of the horse's feet upon which he seemed to ride, and that they could not see his face.

41. Another person was commanded by a gentleman-like apparition (near a gentleman's house in the county of Glamorgan) to take a box of money from somewhere in the house and cast it into the river – which he did. In the same

county, another person was obliged (in order to have quiet from an apparition) to cast a trunk of copper money into the water.

Now, one cannot hear of the useful mercies of God being thus destroyed, and made useless, without some grief and anxiety to know the reasons why the spirits of those who have lived in the world do desire this thing, and God suffering it also to come to pass. For it doth not, cannot, come to pass without the will of God suffering it to come to pass. And what reasons can there be, but that partly the spirits of the dead do it out of envy that others do enjoy what they are deprived of? Partly, it may be because they foresee that what they have gathered amiss, and used amiss, will be yet used amiss (it may be more amiss), which will reflect upon themselves by way of punishment for providing means to make others more wicked and more miserable than otherwise they would have been. Dives' brethren would not have been in such danger of hell if less of the good things of life had been provided for them and enjoyed by them (Luke 16:28). God suffers this to come to pass because, by their ill way of getting, or ill way of using them – yea, of not using them at all for God – they have brought down like the curse of God upon them. This is agreeable to that notable scripture: 'If ye will not hear, and if ye will not lay it to heart, to give glory unto my name, saith the Lord of hosts; I will even send a curse upon you, I will curse your blessings: yea, I have cursed them already, because ye do not lay it to heart' (Malachi 2:2).

We have a notable instance of this in the golden calf, which Moses burnt, and threw the ashes into the water (Exodus 32). Here was the worth of some 10,000 pounds of gold destroyed, which might have enriched many and have been used to good purposes. But, being made an object of idolatry, it became an accursed thing – too bad for any use but to make the drink of jealousy for the idolaters, and to make their god pass through their filthy entrails for a reproach upon them. How often did the Lord destroy the precious fruits of the earth, in the land of Canaan possessed by his own people (and elsewhere), for the sins of the inhabitants? Some men's money must perish with them: 'Thy money perish with thee, because thou hast thought that the gift of God may be purchased with money' (Acts 8:20). If he who useth not his talent is to be bound in hell (where is weeping, wailing, and gnashing of teeth), what will come of them who use their talents ill? Let men be warned from all this to use their mercies well, to serve God and their generation according to his will.

42. In the year 1758, John, the son of David John Abel of Neath Abbey, Glamorganshire, was often troubled by the apparition of Thomas Watkin Lleision, who was his grandfather's or grandmother's brother. He appeared to J. with his white, long staff (just as he appeared upon the earth in his old age). At last, J. took courage to ask him what he wanted with him, to which the apparition answered (exactly in the voice of his dead uncle): 'Thou must come to meet me' (at such a time and such a place), 'and fear no hurt.' J. promised to go and, according to his promise, went. To be more in heart, J. drank two or three cans of ale; but when he saw T.W.L. coming towards him, he feared greatly – as

believing it could be no other but the evil spirit – so that he became very weak and faint. The spirit bid him, again, not fear, and bid him search the wall of the house or the barn (I remember not which), that he should find there twelve guineas. The apparition bid him take them, and he would trouble him no more. J. did so, as the spirit commanded him to do. When the spirit departed from him, he bid J. shut his eyes. The spirit did go, and departed from him with a great noise, which ended like the sound of thunder.

The young man now cannot look steadfastly in any man's face. Of this thing we have often heard, that such as see the spirits of the dead cannot afterward look steadfastly in men's faces, but we cannot understand the meaning of it in this world. This piece of knowledge is reserved for the other life, where the knowledge of it will be of some use for the extensive glory of God, and of some instruction to the inhabitants of eternity in heaven and hell. For there is nothing in being (either good or evil in earth or hell) but something will be produced from it (either direct or indirect), to glory God in this world or the next.

43. About the year 1756, Evan Gibbon (who was servant to Mr John Thomas of Tŷ'r Ffynon in Llanedeyrn parish, Glamorganshire) was troubled by a spirit in the night.

One night, going home, E.G. called at a house in the way. They told him, there, that he should see the spirit which appeared and terrified people in a certain part of the way he was to go (there, he himself had sometimes also felt some terror in the night), and sent two of the servants with him to keep him from fear. When they were gone part of the way with him, he saw her (the spirit) afar off, as it were waiting to speak with him. He then resolved to speak with her, and persuaded them to return. When he came to the farther end of the field, she sat on a stile as it were to stop his way. Then, in the name of God, he asked her what she wanted with him.[17] She, quarrelling with him, left him when he was gone out of sight, and hung the weeding instrument upon an ash-tree, and went away. She desired him to take the weeding instrument away, and she would trouble him no more. He asked her where she was, and she said: 'sometimes in the clouds and sometimes on the earth, seventy years' (some say she said eighty years) since her death. He was sorry afterward that he did not ask her whether she was happy or miserable. If he did, perhaps he should have a little or no answer to that; (eternity is much as secret in the present life).

He went on to see for the weeding instrument on the ash-tree. And, behold, the tree (being young) had grown about it, so that he could not take it away with his hands. Having told this, he went with a hatchet (or a bill) to hew it out, attended by several people. The weeding instrument was rusted and diminished into little – as small as his finger. At parting, she bid him lie down on his face. He did so, and saw a shining light departing. His description of her personal appearance was: that she was a young woman with a clean face; without a cap on her head; with her hair plaited or tied up (he could not tell which); and had a petticoat, such as he heard were worn by women in former times.[18] Here is another great evidence of the being of spirits and apparitions to keep the belief of it.

44. The following relation I had from an eminent, godly man and a preacher of the Gospel living in Llangynwyd Fawr parish, Glamorganshire, in relation to his wife.

Coming from market in the summer, about 6 o'clock, she saw a resemblance of a man before her with a rod in his hand. She lost sight for a while, yet saw him again and knew who he was. When she came home, she fainted (although a stout woman). She saw him afterward, several times, when none else saw him, and whenever she saw him, fainted. Her good husband advised her: when she saw him again to speak to him and ask him what he wanted with her. Some time after, she saw him and fainted in her husband's presence, and he asked the spirit: in the name of God, what he wanted with her. They (in the place) could hear him ask the question, but did not hear his answer (though so near), nor did see the apparition. When she rose out of the fit, she went into a barn hard by to fetch some hidden thing out of it. Her husband saw her come back and passing by the house, and she wept and cast it into the river not far from the house. But she would never tell what it was, nor who it was, that appeared to her. Her husband supposed it was her own father: T.T. of Llidiart. He once made a profession of religion but, breaking his religious vows and becoming a drunkard, he was excommunicated by the Revd Mr Lewis Jones and the congregation in that neighbourhood. It is a warning against entering hypocritically into the Church of God and continuing so in it, for it is the way to double damnation for the sinning against greater light, greater mercies, and obligations to piety than others.

45. I am now to give an account of the most wonderful actings of a disembodied spirit that ever I have heard of in this century. This came to pass in Tridoll valley (not far from the town of Aberafan), in a pious family in the house of Mr William Thomas.[19] The man was esteemed more than commonly pious by those acquainted with him, as also his wife and maidservant (who was a very courageous young woman, as the future account will show). The account I have in a letter from the Revd Mr William Evans of Llangiwg, who was there and had it from them verbatim, as follows:

About the year 1760, the maid durst not go with the candle about the room by night for the light of the candle would diminish, grow narrow (as if in a damp), and at last would go out (and the fire out of the wick), so that she was obliged to go to the room without the candle. When she came downstairs, the apparition would strike her on the side of her head, as it were with a cushion. While she was at private prayers, he would let her alone, excepting once or twice that she was obliged to give over (though a very courageous young woman). One time, she brought a marment of water into the house, and the water rose up out of the vessel about her and about the house.[20]

Another time, an abundance of pilchards came to the sea, so that the people could scarce devour them. The mistress and maid were desirous to have some of them; the maid asked of her master to go and fetch some of them. He, being a very just man, told her not to go, that the pilchards were sent for the use of poor people, and that they themselves wanted nothing. But she ventured to go, and brought some to the house. But, after giving a turn about the house and going to look after them, found them all gone and thrown upon the dunghill. Upon which her master blamed her, saying: 'Did not I tell thee not to go?'

One time, they had a pot of meat upon the fire and both the meat and broth were taken away (they knew not where), and the pot left empty, to their no small disappointment. Sometimes, the chapel Bible would be thrown, whisking by their temples and striking against something (and yet the Bible not much damaged). So it would do with the gads of the steeller.[21] Once the evil spirit struck one of them into the screen, where a person then sat, and the mark of it still to be seen in the hardboard. Such a blow in the man's forehead or temples would have killed him on the spot (but it did not touch the man). Once the china dishes were thrown off the shelf, and not one broke. And in divers particulars the evil spirit was evidently limited in its mischievous doings.

It troubled the maid very much in winter, taking away the clothes from her bed, and in summer, gathering more clothes to put upon her. Sometimes, when it began to take off the clothes, she would take hold and get upon them and go to prayer; when she prayed it would let the clothes alone for that time, which encouraged her the more to prayer. It was a great business with this light-hating spirit to throw an old lantern about the house, without breaking it. It would throw the candlestick also, and yet the candle would not go out of the socket nor break.

Once, she was going upon business before day, and being come into the highway a thick darkness – which was terrible to enter into – filled the way. Upon which, she thought once to go over the hedge to avoid it. But, presently, she thought it was not good to yield to the evil spirit and, therefore, went to prayer (I commend her for it) by the hedge-side. After she rose up the darkness went off, and she went her way. One night the evil spirit divided the books among them, when they were in bed: to the man of the house it brought the Bible; to the woman of the house, Allen's *Sure Guide*, Arthur Dent, and such books as she delighted in; and upon the maid's bed, the English books which she understood not. When it began to stir in the beginning of the night, the man of the house would call the family to prayer.

About two years' space, it continued, in all, to trouble them. In which space of time, it would sometimes be quiet for a fortnight or three weeks, giving no trouble. Once, it endeavoured to hinder them from going to meeting by hiding the bunch of keys and carrying them out of their place on a Lord's day (and for all their searching, could not find them). They were loath to appear in their old clothes at meeting. But the good man of the house bid them not yield to the devil, but to borrow some clothes of one another (something which one had, which another had not). But, at last, there was something wanted which they could not be without, and must have, or break the lock. They concluded to go, first, to prayer (and so did), and afterward found the keys (where they used to be, and where they had searched enough for them before).

Another time, the maid went to milking to the barn. And while she was milking the cow, the barn door was suddenly shut. She rose up to see what had shut it, but could see nothing, and came back to milk. And, then, the spirit turned the door backward and forward to make an idle, ringing noise. She, then, knew what it was and, before she had done milking, shut the door. But, when she attempted to open it afterward, she could not open by any means. She was going to open another door, but presently thought he might hold that fast shut. And that it was not good to yield to the devil, this heroine went to prayer against the enemy, as the best way of prevailing over him (which she did), and afterward the door opened as usual.

At one time, it endeavoured to make variance between the mistress and the maid, by strewing charcoal ashes upon the milk. When the mistress found the milk so, she charged the maid with some neglect, and watched the next milk herself. Yet, this was made more foul. At one time, W. Thomas and his wife went to watch to a neighbour's house, where was a dead relation. There was a young man, a first cousin to William Thomas, who would by no means believe that there was a spirit at W.T.'s house, and said they were only making tricks with one another. And very strong he was (a hero of an unbeliever, like many of his brethren in infidelity), and said he would lie in the house alone, and desired the keys of the house. He had them, and went to see if there was any spirit in it (but he had no disturbance). And if he was strong before (so strong, that the testimony of three sober religious persons had no weight with him), he was now strong with a witness, and very uppish (as high as the house top), and bantered them upon it. Some time after, he came and stayed over night. And hearing that the maid was disturbed in bed by the spirit, he said (in the hearing of the family): 'If anything comes to disturb thee, call upon me' (he lying either in that or the next room). Sometimes in the night, the spirit came to attempt to take away the clothes from the maid, and she cried out. He awaked, and suddenly rose out of bed to catch somebody who was playing tricks with the maid (as he thought), but saw now that there was nothing to be seen with her – but was made to know that there was an invisible agent in the place, which now severely handled him. (For feeling is believing.) He went to his bed in a worse condition than he came out of it, excepting that he was cured of his stubborn Sadducism. He never afterward bantered them, being made to believe that there was something more than human in the place.

One time – Mr W.E. (the author of this letter), being there, at prayer by his bedside – it struck the bed so violently (though it was but a trencher) that it made a report like that of a gun, so that both the bed and the room did shake.[22]

And, it did do twice – which greatly surprised him. Here was a pure room for a Sadducee to sleep in for two or three nights. One time, it made so great a noise that the man of the house, on a sudden, thought the house was going away, and was greatly terrified. It never after this made so loud a noise. Once, when they were at meeting, it threw a pad against the door, at the foot of the stairs, which made so great a noise as surprised and terrified those who were near the door especially.

One time, the Revd Mr Richard Tibbot (a Dissenting minister from Montgomeryshire), being come to preach that way (and he is an evangelical, holy minister of Christ), came into this house. Being in bed together with another person, and expecting the stir, he continued awake and talking a long time. At last, Mr Tibbot slept; his companion, keeping awake, heard the spirit come, and awaked Mr Tibbot. It began to pluck the clothes. They held them and prayed, and it let them alone a while. But, they being thoroughly awaked (by this time, kept awake), expecting it would come again to pull the clothes, therefore turned the clothes about them as well as they could. Accordingly, it came to pull them (which they held with all their might), so that they thought the clothes were broken between them (which, really, they were not). Having not prevailed this way, it struck the bed with the *cawnen* (a vessel to hold corn), so strongly that it removed the bed out of its place, and with so loud a stroke that W.T. heard it.[23] He brought light with him (they also calling for it), and they had quiet the rest of the night. They had, I think, been keeping the day before in a day of fasting and praying, which, it might be, enraged the spirit.

I imagine, in myself, how dreadful his companion's word was to Mr Tibbot (just newly awaking in the dead of night): 'Here it is coming!', when they expected to feel his power. Here was a pure place for a couple of infidel Sadducees (as to be in Mr Tibbot and his companion's place for the time): the proud bantering Mr S.B. and his companion in infidel mirth, Mr A.T., who have need of this conviction, which Mr T. and friend had not. (Though, even to them, it was a confirmation of what they rightly believed before.) It deserves to be observed, how this evil spirit was limited in its ill doings. For when the good man of the house (and such he certainly was) was shaving, it would not touch him while the razor was on his face. But when he would take it off, it would strike him on the side of the head.

The manner of its going away, and ceasing to trouble, was this: the man of the house, being in bed with his wife, Catherine Thomas, thought he heard a voice calling upon him. He, then, awaked his wife, and rose up a little in bed, and said to the spirit: 'In the name of the Lord Jesus, what seeketh thou in my house? Hath thou anything to say to me?' The spirit answered it had, and desired him to remove some things (telling what they were) out of the place where they had been mislaid. The good man, thinking it to be a devil, one of the fallen angels, made answer: 'Satan, I'll do nothing that thou biddest me any further then my Bible gives me leave; I command thee, in the name of God, to depart from my house.' Both of them perfectly knew the voice to be that of a dead relation (at least, that it perfectly resembled it). This gave them both a great concern, lest it should be the spirit of that relation of whom they hoped better things. However, from that time forth it gave no disturbance. For my part, I believe it was the disembodied spirit of that relation – which fought an alleviating circumstance to its bad state by the removal of those mislaid things (and wish they had removed them, as it always gives ease to them who appear on such accounts, and cease to give trouble to those to whom they appear) – there being no reason to be given why one of the fallen angels (properly called devils) should personate a disembodied spirit, but reason against it. It was the voice of a female relation more nearly related to Mr, rather than Mrs, Thomas, which they heard (of whom they hoped better things). Oh, that both men and women were more concerned, and laboured to the utmost to avoid a miserable, and to secure a happy eternity after life and death.

46. By the same good man (living in Llangynwyd Fawr parish), I was informed that the innkeeper by the church (a profane swearer), about the year 1767, while he lay in bed in an upper room, saw a numerous company with speckled clothes of white and red colour, one among them taller than the rest. Some of them sought to take him by the hand, which he refused (and it was well he did), and some (as he thought) threatened him the other side the bed. When he rose next morning, there was a strange, red substance on the chamber floor. He was so much terrified that he came to R.W. trembling, desiring his prayers and the prayers of the society of Methodists in that parish. He also desired the good man, R.W., to sleep with him that night. R.W. complied, and while they were in bed he told R.W. how 'he takes hold of my toe', to which R.W. replied: 'I don't care what is there, I will make him go away', and put his foot to the innkeeper's foot, and his toe was freed. The innkeeper was, afterwards, much mended in his language and some good came from the infernal apparition.

By their appearing with speckled clothes and dancing, with one taller than the rest among them, I'm inclined to think they were the fairy sort, of the kingdom of darkness, for so they used to appear, as a good man of my acquaintance, who lived in a place where they often appeared, declared to some of his acquaintance.[24] This taller spirit may be a principal one and the manager among them. Our Saviour, who perfectly knew hell, says it is a kingdom (Matthew 12:26), and a kingdom cannot be without order, rule, and subjection according to the holy, wise, just and sovereign power of the rector of all things.

For as God's works of mercy, so also his works of justice and punishment are orderly on earth and in hell (from the surface to the bottom of it), otherwise the stronger and crueller devils and damned would oppress the weaker among them. For whatever restraints may be without and about them, there is nothing to hinder them – neither mercy or justice to restrain them – from this. Hell cannot be beyond, or below, the government of God – and his government in hell must be wise, holy, just, and mighty . . . as it is on earth. And the God of all excellencies will have everlasting glory from his government of hell (something, even, from his goodness – indeed, only the negative sort of hell). For, but for God's wise and just government in it, hell be worse than it is. It is, indeed, a state of perfect misery; but it would be still worse for a greater oppression and cruelty in it (which is prevented by the justice of God, which measures the punishment of the wicked, which he hath taken into his own hands, and leaves it not to be managed according to the wills of the devils and the damned). For everyone is to receive in hell according to what he hath done in the flesh (and none, even in hell, is at liberty to alter it, to add to it, or diminish from it). And as God's government in hell certainly prevents a greater misery, here is something of God's goodness reaching downward to hell (agreeing with his word, which saith that his mercy is over all his works (Psalms 145:9)) – which kind of mercy – it may be, will be, at least should be acknowledged in hell, to the glory of his goodness. It should at least lessen their complaint of their miserable state, seeing and certainly be worse than it is, but for God's excellent government preventing it.

47. About the beginning of the eighteenth century, Lewis William Walter (a man of uncommon elevation of mind in the scientific ways, and of great skill in medicine) and John Mathew Howel (a person whom I knew and spoke with), drinking together in Merthyr Tydfil village, Glamorganshire, agreed both of them to go to conjure.

   The place they chose to go to was by a wall-side, which divided between the mountain and some fields some considerable distance from the village. Having drank very much to put them in heart against the approaching terror, being come to the place, Lewis (being the greater proficient in the black art) called one of the infernal spirits by name. Lewis ordered him to appear in the shape of a gosling, because it was a less terrible apparition. Accordingly, it came and demanded why they sent for him. But they, having drank too much, and their speech failing to give him a speedy answer, it rose up like a flash of fire – which took out Lewis William Walter's eyes. Thus, John Mathew Howel was obliged to carry back Lewis after having lost his most useful members and went into the village with great sorrow to himself and friends and the amazement of all his neighbours. The thing is also known far and near, and remembered to this day in those parts. A thing indeed to be remembered, and no good from it but the confirmation of the being if spirits and the eternal world against the atheistical and Sadduceistical heresy.

MERIONETHSHIRE

48. In the year 1694, there was a strange fire which kindled in the night about Harlech town in this county, chiefly in the night-time, and continued for several months, but was chiefly active in two months. It was a weak, blue flame which burned little else but corn and ricks of hay and the thatch of houses. Every night there was a hue and cry that such a house, hay, or corn was burning, and the

neighbours ran together to extinguish it. As it was not a very strong fire, they ran into it to extinguish it (though they must not stay long in it). Some, most of the learned, called it a meteor which came from the sea on the Caernarfon side. But if a meteor from the Caernarfon side, why not rather in Caernarfon than Merionethshire? Why in Merioneth and in no other place in Wales (or in the world) but Merionethshire? And, why at that time and neither before or after? The people gave another account of it in former days: that it was an effect of witchcraft (which is the more likely), as it cannot be accounted from nature.

Monmouthshire

Aberystruth parish

49. About the latter end of the seventeenth century and the beginning of the eighteenth century, there lived in the valley of Ebbw Fawr one Walter John Harry, belonging to the people called Quakers. He was a harmless, honest man (by occupation a farrier) who went to live at Tŷ'n-y-fyd in that valley. There, one Morgan Lewis (a weaver) had lived before him, and after his death had appeared to some and troubled the house. One night, Walter (being in bed with his wife and awake) saw a light come up stairs. Expecting to see the spectre coming on (with a candle in his hand, a white woollen cap upon his head, and the dress he wore in his lifetime), Walter resolved to speak to him, and did when the spectre came near the bed. Walter said: 'Morgan Lewis! Why dost thou walk this earth?' To which the apparition gravely answered, like one in some distress, that it was because of some bottoms of wool that he had hid in the wall of the house, which he desired Walter to take away – then, he would trouble them no more.[25] Walter then said: 'I charge thee Morgan Lewis in the name of God, that thou trouble my house no more', at which Morgan vanished away and appeared no more.

Morgan Lewis was no profane man nor openly vicious. It is like the poor man had indeed, in an hour of temptation, unjustly concealed these things of small value and was now troubled for it. He chose that these bottoms of wool should be of use to others rather than be of no use (though he neither charged them to make use of them nor forbid their doing it, but left it to their choice). Likely, they made use of them. For why should they do otherwise?

50. Long time after the death or removal of Walter John Harry, Thomas Miles Harry came to live in that house. Once, coming home by night from Abergavenny, Thomas was much oppressed with fears (as is usually the case before the appearance of evil spirits) in the way, when near home. His horse took fright, it seeing something that he did not, and ran violently with him towards the house. Nor did Thomas's fear cease when he was by the house. He was afraid to look about (expecting to see somewhat) and hastened to unsaddle the horse. But happening to cast his eye towards the other end of the yard, he saw the appearance

of a woman so prodigiously tall as to be about half as high as the tall beech trees at the other side of the yard. Glad he was of a house to enter in and rest.

51. Another time, the same person (coming home by night from a journey), when near Tŷ Llwyn, saw the resemblance of fire on the west side of the river, on his right hand. The next look, he saw it on the mountain near the rock Tarren y Trwyn, on his left hand. All of a sudden, he could see the fire, just by, on one side of him, and like a mastiff dog on the other side, at which he was exceedingly terrified. He called at Tŷ Llwyn, desiring one of them to come with him home.[26] The man of the house (knowing by Thomas's call and voice that he had seen an apparition) sent two of his servants with him home. My thoughts of Thomas Miles Harry are that he was a man of an affable disposition, innocent and harmless, and a respecter of what is good in his later days. His children also, his son and two daughters, were godly and religious. He was the grandfather of that eminent and famous preacher of the Gospel, Mr Thomas Lewis of Llanharan in Glamorganshire.

52. Thomas Miles Harry's son, Lewis Thomas (coming towards home from the Bedwellty side of the river Ebbw Fawr, over Pont Evan Llywarch bridge into the field beyond it), saw the dreadful resemblance of a man going on all fours, crossing the path before him, at no great distance from him. Upon which, Lewis's hair moved upon his head, his heart panted and beat violently, his flesh trembled, he felt not his clothes about him, and felt himself heavy and weak (although a strong, lively man). He remembered it all his days, and was ready to declare it, having been much affected with it.

53. At one time, two gypsies came to Lewis Thomas's house when he was not at home. Seeing his wife by herself, they began to be bold and very importunate for this and that which they wanted. But his wife (having an aversion for those kind of people) commanded them to be gone, which they refused to do until she took down a stick and threatening to beat them (being a strong, courageous woman). At this, the old gypsy went away muttering and threatening revenge. Some nights after, they heard like a boul rolling above stairs from the upper end of the chamber to the middle of the room, stopping a while, and then rolling down to the foot of the stairs.[27] Upon which, Lewis said to his wife (Jennet Francis): 'I believe the old gypsy is come to give thee a visit.' Next morning, when Jennet rose, she saw on the floor the print of a bare foot without a toe, dipped in soot, and gone from the foot of the stair toward the door.

Next Monday, when they went to churn, the cream began soon to froth – as if to turn to butter. But it did not turn to butter, though they churned much. They, therefore, poured it into a vessel, whereafter it had stayed some time; there was a thick slimy cream above, and underneath it was water a little like coloured with milk. They boiled the cream, having a notion it would torment the witch; whereafter, they were no more disturbed that way.

This indeed was no apparition, but the malicious trick of an old witch in compact with the devil. The fashionable incredulity is to deny the being of witches. I do not know whether they deny that ever there were such persons in the world, or that none at present are so. If they deny that ever there were such things as witches, the Scripture of truth and innumerable facts are against them. Therefore, to deny is an unreasonable, lying infidelity – which is a shame to those that have it.

Lewis Thomas Miles was a professor of some note in the valley of Ebbw Fawr (and much respected), being an honest, peaceable, judicious man, a good neighbour, husband, father, and an excellent companion (though not absolutely free from every kind of weakness, from which no man is free). He entertained a meeting at his house where the ministers of Penmaen, etc., preached. His wife, also, was of that communion (to whom he gave no trouble about baptism, nor to any who came to his house, being of a very catholic spirit – though he was in communion with the Baptists (and of that persuasion), as appears by what follows. For he was heard to say, that he liked to hear the Baptist preachers, because they preached the evangelick doctrine truly, till they went to preach about baptism when their subject did not lead to it, and when there was no occasion for it, to hear one of them dappling about it (so he expressed it), without bringing out anything clear about it, when he might have spoken somewhat else of greater benefit – that was displeasing to him. When he became old and infirm, he desired leave of his brethren the Baptist church at Tillery to commune, occasionally, with the Independents of Penmaen, who took the Lord's supper at his house. And they charitably gave him leave so to do. I mention this to their honour, and that none may say that all the Baptists are rigid, though too many of them give too much occasion to say so. For here is not only one particular person, but a whole Baptist church to prove the contrary. And it is right and just to speak of the good that belongs to all persons and things in heaven and earth. One cannot speak amiss of anything without being guilty of sin of some nature and degree or other, and worst of all to judge of good things and of great moment worse than they are; it is worse than to judge of evil things worse than they are, though even that is also a sin.

It is ever to be observed that the godly are the most moderate in all parties in religion, especially those who are most humble and mortified in creaturely sin (some allowance to be made for particular tempers and dispositions, and provocations to displeasure – for oppression makes a wise man mad (Ecclesiastes 7:7)). But the hypocrites of all parties are usually rigid and censorious, as the Pharisees, who were hypocrites, had the sour leaven of uncharitableness: 'Beware ye of the leaven of the Pharisees, which is hypocrisy' (Luke 12:1): because hypocrites are not sufficiently enlightened to see their sin and misery, and are therefore unhumbled, proud, and uncharitable.

54. About eighty years ago, there lived one John Jenkin (a poor man) near Abertillery, on the other side of the river. He hanged himself upon the hay-loft

in the daytime. When his sister (who lived with him) saw this, she cried out. Upon which Jeremiah James (who lived in Abertillery House), looking towards the house, saw the resemblance of a man coming from the hay-loft and violently turning upwards and downwards – topsy-turvy – towards the river. This was a dreadful sight to a serious godly man (and very impressing), for it could be no other but an evil spirit going with his prey (the self-murderer) to hell. Oh, that men would beware of Satan (the leader to hell) and not follow him – who delights in nothing but the sin and misery of mankind – to eternal destruction. They that go most softly in the way of sin make too much speed to go to hell. Many go swiftly in the way of destruction, but self-murderers make the greatest speed and take the shortest way to hell. Others follow after Satan, but these go to meet him. They need not make such haste, for one hour in hell will give them more than enough of it. Oh, that this was more considered.

55. John ab John of Cwm-celyn in the Valley of the Church, many years ago, was going very early in the morning (before day on May the 12th) towards Caerleon fair. In going uphill on Milfraen mountain, John heard (as he thought) a shouting behind – as it were on Brynmawr (which is a part of the Black Mountain in Breconshire). Presently after, he heard the shouting at Bwlch y Llwyn on his left hand, nearer to him, upon which he became oppressed with fear and heavy in walking, and began to suspect it was no human but a diabolical voice designed to frighten him (having wondered before, what people could be shouting on the mountain that time of night). Being come up to the higher part of the mountain, where his way was to go, he could hear the shouting at the Gilfach fields on his right hand before him, which confirmed his fear. But being past the Gilfach fields in the way of the cold springs, he could hear the noise, as it were of a coach coming after him. His terror increased on hearing the voice of a woman with the coach crying: 'Wow up!' Now, as he knew that no coach ever did or could go that way, and hearing the coach-like sound coming nearer and nearer (and that it must be an evil spirit following after him) he was greatly terrified, as anyone in his case would have been (though he was a strong man, the strongest in all the parish). Fearing if he kept the path that he should see some devilish, hellish appearance, he turned out of the way and fell on his face in the heath, not daring to look about until the hellish coach went by.

When it was gone out of hearing, his fear went by, and so much the more as the mountain birds began to whisper – singing one here and one there – as the daybreak increased. And seeing some sheep before him, his fear went quite off.

One may observe, here, that the evil spirit terrified and troubled this man – both behind and on every hand of him, but did not (because he durst not) stand before him to obstruct his way. And, truly, a Christian may, some time or other, have evils pursuing after him, and attending him on every hand; but while he goes on in the way of his duty, they will not be suffered to obstruct his way, or but so as he may either pass over them, go through them, or pass by them on the right or left hand – according to the blessed declaration of the Apostle: 'There hath no temptation taken you but such as is common to man: but God is faithful, who will not suffer you to be tempted above that ye are able; but will with the temptation also make a way of escape, that ye may be able to bear it' (1 Corinthians 10:13).

Some readers will have a curiosity to know what manner of man this person was, who had this remarkable trial in the course of his life. He never was a profane, immoral man, but an honest, peaceable, knowing man, and very comely person. And, in his latter days, after his conversion, he became wholly mortified to this world, very heavenly minded, and died happy. More of him may be seen in my *Geographical, Historical, and Religious Account of the Parish of Aberystruth*, published in the year 1779.[28]

56. W.L.M. told me that, going upon an errand by night from the house of Jane Edmund of Abertillery, he heard (as if) some people were speaking one to another at some distance from him. When he hearkened more attentively, he presently heard like the falling of a tree, which seemed to break other trees as it fell. After that, he heard a weak voice (like that of a person in pain and misery) hard by him, which frightened him much and caused him to turn back without going on to his journey's end. They were the fairies that spoke in his hearing. They doubtless spoke about his death and imitated the moan which he made when some time after he fell from off a tree (which proved his death). For the fairies, though not the worst of devils, yet are devils enough to delight in the miseries of men. This account, previous to his death, he gave me himself many years ago. He was a man much alienated from the life of God, though surrounded with the means of knowledge and grace. But there was no cause to question the truth of his relation, but reason to believe it.

57. If any think I am too credulous in these relations, and speak of things of which I myself have had no experience, I must let them know they are mistaken. When a very young boy, going with my aunt Elizabeth Roger (somewhat early in the morning but after sunrise) from Hafod-y-dafol towards my father's house at Penllwyn, I saw, at the end of the upper field of Cae'r Cefn (by the wayside which we were passing) the likeness of a sheepfold. The door was towards the south and over the door, instead of a lintel, the resemblance of a dried branch of a tree (I think of a hazel-tree). Within the fold there was a company of many people: some sitting down, and some going in and coming out, bowing their heads as they passed under the branch. It seemed to me as if they had been lately dancing, and that there was a musician among them. Among the rest, over against the door, I well remember the resemblance of a fair woman with a high-crown hat and a red jacket, who made a better appearance than the rest, and whom (I think) they seemed to honour. I still have a pretty clear idea of her white face and well-formed countenance. The men wore white cravats. I always think they were the perfect resemblance of persons who lived in the world before my

time. (There is a resemblance of their form and countenances still remaining in my mind.) I wondered at my aunt (going before me) that she did not look towards them (and we going so near them).[29]

As for me, I was loath to speak until I had passed them some way. I then told my aunt what I had seen, at which she wondered and said I dreamed. However, she came to believe me and told my mother of it when we came home. It was some time before I could be persuaded that there was no fold in that place. There is indeed the ruins of some small edifice in that place (most likely a fold), but so old that the stones are swallowed up and almost wholly crusted over with earth and grass. But it is a pleasant dry part of the mountain.

The fairies seem not to delight in open, plain grounds of any kind (far from stone and wood) nor in watery grounds, but in dry grounds not far from trees and hedges and the shade of grown trees – the hazel and the oak (the female oak especially, being more branched and shading) – where the ground is dry, even, and clear from brakes and bushes about them. Of all the places in the parish of Aberystruth they most frequently appeared at Hafod-y-dafol and Cefn Bach, which are dry, light, and pleasant places. Does not this correspond something with our Saviour's saying (who perfectly understands even hell itself) of the unclean spirits: that they walked in dry places when ejected out of the souls of men?: 'When the unclean spirit is gone out of a man, he walketh through dry places, seeking rest, and findeth none' (Matthew 12:43).

They often also came into men's houses (into some particular houses more than others), especially in tempestuous bad weather. For, though I cannot think that the weather can essentially effect disembodied spirits (or that they can feel heat or cold, wind, or rain), yet bad weather makes the place of their rendezvous less pleasant or more dismal and disagreeable. The poor, ignorant people (for fear of fairies) made them welcome by providing clean water in the house. They also took care that no knife was near the fire or other iron instruments (such as they knew were offensive to the fairies) were left in the corner near the fire. For want of which care, many people were hurt by them, and for cutting down the female oaks (some even unto death). Although now (and since the preaching of the Gospel, and men are come to have more faith in God), the female oak and all sorts of trees are cut down without any hurt. Some were afraid in those times of ignorance, superstition and want of faith in God to enter their gardens by night. There were few that had faith to oppose those spirits of darkness.

Nay, some were so ignorant as to think the fairies (at least for some time, and before they had more knowledge and experience of them) to be some happy spirits, because they had music and dancing among them. They are called by the odd name of *bendith y mamau* (their mother's blessing) in Monmouthshire. In other parts of Wales they are called *y tylwyth yn y coed* (the fair family or folks in the wood) because they were seldom or never seen far from the wood, especially from the female oak (likely for the sake of the paganism of the ancient Britons, which they greatly practised especially under the female oak). For that reason, then, it was and still is called *brenhinbren* (giant oak-tree).

58. My father (a pious man, and firm as a mountain in honesty and veracity) saw in a clear night the resemblance of an innumerable company of sheep, continuing a good while, to go out of an old fold built with stones (and open, as being of no use within the memory of man). And, at that time, he saw Catherine Richard, one of the next neighbours, passing through them on horseback from Abergavenny House. He wondered at first why she took no notice of them, till he considered that she did not see them – as indeed she did not. This was a trick to deceive his visive faculty. What end it could answer to themselves, we know not. To him, it answered to confirm him in the belief of being of those kind of spirits of the other world, and unreasonably denied by many.

59. Edmund Daniel of the Arail (an honest man, a constant speaker of truth, and of much observation) told me that he often saw the fairies after sunset crossing the Cefn Bach from the Valley of the Church towards Hafod-y-dafol. Before any falling out in the parish, they passed on – leaping and striking in the air – making a path in the air, much of this form:[30]

Of the truth of this observation, I saw a notable verification. For the last time he spoke to me about it, he told me beforehand that some mischievous contention would come to pass in the parish, and that it was not far off. He told me, also, where he thought it would be. The thing, indeed, unhappily came to pass – but not where he thought it would be, but in another place and among another people. This shows that he did not speak cunningly to gain applause of his foreknowledge of things to come. He was indeed above that meanness, and never apprehended to be a lying, guileful man by any who knew him. He was a discerning man and made conscience of telling the truth.

60. It was told me that Mr Howel Prosser, curate of Aberystruth, seeing a funeral going down the church lane, late in the evening, towards the church, imagined it was the body of a man from the upper end of the parish (towards Breconshire).[31] Having heard before that the man was sick (and thinking, now, he was dead and going to be buried), Howel Prosser put on his band in order to go to perform the burial office and hastened to go to meet the burial. When he came to it, he saw a people he did not know (and of which he took no notice), as they came from the borders of Breconshire. But, putting his hand to the bier to help to carry the corpse, in a moment . . . all vanished. And, to his very great surprise and astonishment, there was nothing in his hand but the skull of a dead horse. Mr Prosser was my schoolmaster and a right honest man of the best of morals. In former times, several have seen the likeness of a human skull carrying the corpse-candles, which may be some confirmation of the truth of this extraordinary thing.

61. But the following is a more certain instance. Isaac William Thomas (who lived not far from thence), being at one time at Hafod-y-dafol, saw (as it appeared to him) a funeral coming down the mountain – as it were to go towards Aberbeeg or Llanhilleth church. He stood in a field by a wall, which was between him and the highway leading to Aberbeeg. When the funeral (which came close to the side of the wall) was come just over against him, he reached his hand and took off the black veil that was over the bier and carried it home with him. It was made of some exceeding fine stuff, so that when folded it was a very little substance and very light. He told this to several. I knew the man myself, and in my youthful days conferred with him several times. I wish I had spoken with him after this had happened and had asked many particular questions about it – to have a more particular knowledge of this extraordinary supernatural affair, which related to some disembodied spirits of eternity. But the opportunity for this, in this world (as many others of this nature) is lost forever. But the light of eternity will show myriads of things which we cannot know here (nor are fit to know), and which we shall there certainly and infallibly know (without error) as they are and no otherwise.

It may be, some may wonder, how he escaped from hurt after doing this. For it was often found, by sad experience, that the fairies were easily offended and, like the spirits of hell, very implacable in their resentments (hurting many in those days of ignorance and want of faith in God). But they were willing he should do it, else they would not have come so near to him. For what reason they came so near, cannot be known in this present life.

The fairies appeared often in the form of funerals and of dancing companies, but when they danced they chiefly, if not always, appeared like children and not as grown men. They appeared in many other ways too tedious to number.

62. A gentleman possessed of every kind of virtue and goodness some time ago gave me the following relation. Many years ago (being, then, very young), walking out at Hafod-y-dafol in the dusk of the evening with his father's brother, they both saw a company going up the way towards the church. Among them, they saw the resemblance of a young child (which might be about ten or eleven years of age), and also of a big man whom this company of fairies seem to attend upon towards the church way. While they looked on them, the child seemed to part asunder and vanish into nothing, and (a little after) the big man, in the same manner. Not long after, the child of the man who saw the apparition sickened, and died in a little time. He himself fell sick – the very day that his daughter was buried – and died soon after. He was a man largely made (as represented in the apparition) – the richest man in the parish. In disposition, he was a plain, honest man, free from pride, guile, envy, and malice – a harmless, peaceable, and useful neighbour. Only he was too little concerned about religion and to seek and find out the way of salvation which, alas, is the fault and folly of almost all the world. When I think of several virtues of mind, which I saw in him, I am sorry for him that he was defective in that which is the greatest concern in the present life.

63. Reynold William, a sober, pious man of my acquaintance (for I was born and lived a long time in Aberystruth parish) declared that when he was a young man, working in a field, and had lain down to rest with his face downward, he heard a great talking coming towards him. He knew what they were and did not rise up, hoping they would pass by him. But when they came to him they stood and, after their usual manner, began to dispute about hurting him and where it should be done. He lay still until he heard one of them saying (the majority consenting to it): 'Thrust him in his leg!' Then, he started up and saw nothing. Had he lain down still, he would have been hurt and cured with difficulty. But, his starting up prevented it. Many were hurt by going inadvertently where the fairies were, when they had little or no occasion to go that way. At other times, the fairies suffered persons to pass through them unhurt.

64. W.E. of Hafod-y-dafol, going a journey upon the Beacon mountain (much above fourscore years ago) before sunrise, saw by his wayside the perfect likeness of a coal-race, where really there was none. There, many people were very busy: some cutting the coal; some carrying it to fill sacks; and some rising the loads upon the horses' backs, etc. This was an agency of the fairies upon his visive faculty. This wonderful extranatural thing made a considerable impression upon his mind, and he declared it several times (once in my hearing). He was of undoubted veracity, a great man in the world, and above telling untruth. (The power of spirits, both good and bad, is very great, having not the weight of bodies to encumber and hinder their agility.)

65. There were two brothers in one house in Cwm-celyn. One night, one of them lay in the chamber below and his brother above stairs. Sometime in the night, he who lay above stairs became very thirsty and rose up to come down for drink. When his brother heard him coming downstairs, he said to him: 'Be cautious, for the house is full of them.' The other (being a man of courage) answered: 'I don't care who is here, I will have drink.' The brother from the chamber saw the dancing fairies opening to give him way, both to go and return.

66. But the fairies often attempted, and sometimes prevailed, to change the children while the parents slept, leaving in their stead such as were of no growth, good appearance, or sense.[32] Dazzy, the wife of Abel Walter of Ebbw Fawr, nursed a child for another. One night, when her husband was absent, she awaked in bed and found the child gone from her and raised up upon the boards above the bed. But the spirit (or spirits) could not go with it any farther. Jennet Francis (in the same valley of Ebbw Fawr) told me that something – for she saw nothing – endeavoured, very sensibly, to take away her infant son Thomas from her arms in bed. As she worded it: 'God and me were too hard for him' (**15**). (Her son is now alive and a famous preacher of the Gospel.) But these evil spirits of eternity unhappily prevailed to change a son of Edmund John William, of the Church Valley (to the great trouble of his parents), leaving an idiot in his stead. He lived

longer than such children used to live, until he was (I think) ten or twelve years of age. I saw him myself: there was something diabolical in his aspect, but more of this in his motion and voice – for his motions were mad and he made very disagreeable screaming sounds which frightened some strangers who passed by. I remember not to have heard of any other hurt he did. His complexion was a dark, tawny colour. I heard of no changeling in Aberystruth parish besides.[33]

67. They sometimes took men in the night and carried them insensibly into other places – sometimes very far, of which take the following instance. Henry Edmund of Hafod-y-dafol had been with Charles Hugh of Coed y paun. Charles Hugh came with him as far as Llanhilleth, and persuaded him to stay with him there that night. Henry Edmund would not agree to, but chose to go home. Upon which, Charles told him he had better stay with him and not go farther. Henry went, but was taken up on the way and carried so far as the town of Llandovery in Carmarthenshire, which he well knew. He called at a public house, where he had been before. The people earnestly persuaded him to stay with them, to which he would not comply. Going out into the street, he was taken up again and carried back to Llanhilleth next morning. There he met with Charles Hugh, who saluted him with saying: 'Did not I tell you, you had better stay with me?'

68. Another instance is this: Mr Edmund Miles of Tŷ Llwyn in Ebbw Fawr, and some young men of the neighbourhood, went a-hunting to Llangattock Crickhowell in Breconshire (Mr Miles having, besides two or three estates in Ebbw Fawr valley, an estate in those parts). Among others, a brother of mine went with him (Mr Miles being my father's landlord). After hunting a great part of the day, they had sat down to rest and were concluding to return home, when up started a hare just by them. The hounds ran after it, and they after the hounds. After the hare had given them a long chase, the hounds followed it to the cellar window of Richard the tailor (who kept the public house in the village of Llangattock), and challenged the hare at the cellar window.

The village at that time was very infamous for witches in all the country round, and this man (among the rest) was believed to be one, and one who resorted to the company of the fairies. This begat a suspicion in the company that he was the hare which had played them that trick to make it too late for them to return home, so that they might stay to spend money at his house that night.[34] It being now too late to return home, and being weary, they did stay there. But they were very free in their suspicions and reflections upon him. Mr Miles, who was a sober, wise gentleman (although of few words), was not without his suspicion with the rest, though he persuaded them to speak less. And when my brother (sometime in the night) wanted to go out to make water, Mr Miles and others with him dissuaded him from going out but to do it in the house. He, disdaining to do, ventured to go out . . . but did not return. After waiting a while the company became uneasy and very stormy and abusive in language to the man of the house – threatening to burn the house if my brother did not return. So troublesome they were that the man and his wife left the room and went to bed. The company were still waiting and expecting his return, and slept little.

Next morning (not very early), my brother came to them. They were exceeding glad to see him, though he appeared like one who had been drawn through thorns and briars, with his hair disordered, and looking bad (who was naturally a stout man, and of a good healthy complexion). They were very curious to know where he had been and what had happened to him. He told them he had been travelling all night in unknown, rough ways. He did not know where he was until early that day, when he saw himself at Twyn Gwynllyw (near the entrance into Newport town).[35] There, he helped a man from Risca to raise a load of coal that had fallen from his horse. Suddenly after, he became insensible and was brought back into the place from whence he had been taken. In a few hours, therefore, he must have been carried by these infernal spirits through the air more than twenty miles (for so long the way is from Newport to Llangattock village). Let none say that this was impossible, or unlikely, since the devil is said in Scripture to carry the son of God through the air to the pinnacle of the temple. There, the devil tempted him to destroy himself – our Saviour suffering it, that he might be an experimental sympathizer and deliverer of those who are tempted, as many are with this kind of destructive temptation (Matthew 4:5–6).

The above relation I had not very long ago from the mouth of the Revd Mr Thomas Lewis, who then was one of the company. This notable turn came to pass about the year 1733. It was long kept from my knowledge (or under knowledge of my father and mother). It seems Mr Lewis had desired the company to keep it secret, so that it was not told me till many years after his death. After this, my brother became sober and penitent (especially after the death of my father and mother), who before was a stranger to the life of godliness and lived badly. He had some natural virtues, and had a respect for people whom he thought to be truly religious and sincere.

69. The last apparition of the fairies in the parish of Aberystruth was in the fields of the widow of Mr Edmund Miles (about thirty-four years ago), not long before Mrs Miles's death. Two men (one of whom is now an eminent man in the religious life) were moving hay in one of her fields on the Bedwellty side of the river Ebbw Fawr, in the morning before sunrise. At which time they could see the chief servant of the house coming through the field on the other side of the river towards them, and like a marriage company of people in white aprons to meet him (with some bravery). They met and passed by the chief servant, but of whom he seemed (to the two men) to take no notice. There was good reason for it – for he saw them not, as he told them when they asked him: Had he seen the marriage company? At the same time, they could hardly think that any marriage should come that way and that time of day. The appearance of the fairies, now, was partly a presage of Mrs Miles's death and partly (it may be) of the marriage

of her daughter with that servant a good while after (for they appeared, with some bravery, resembling a marriage company). This could not be kept so secret, but Mrs Miles came to know of it. It gave her much trouble of mind, for she understood it as a presage of her death – as indeed it was.

Bassaleg parish

70. I was told, August 30, 1760, that there was then living a woman called Anne William Francis. She, some time past – going by night into a little grove of wood near the house – heard pleasant music and saw a company of the fairies dancing here. She, seeing the place pleasant, went with a pail of water there to gratify them. The next time she went there, she had a shilling in the place, and so had in several nights after until she had twenty-one shillings. But, then, her mother, finding the money, questioned her where she had them (fearing she had stolen them). The girl would by no means tell until her mother went very severe upon her, if not to beat her. Anne then was obliged to tell how it was, but had no more money after that. I could not learn in what reign the money was coined, but was told it was no late coin. We have heard of other places where some persons had money from the fairies, and an instance of it in this parish (sometimes silver sixpences, but most commonly copper money pence and halfpence). As they cannot make money, it must be money lost and hid by men.[36]

71. Much above thirty years ago, William Daniel and William John Rees, both coopers and of the Baptist persuasion, were together with Thomas Lewis, a young man, apprentice to William Daniel. All three were of the parish of Aberystruth and now working at the cooper's trade in Bassaleg village.
    There, a lad (the son of a reputed witch) came to them every day and would not let the tools alone. Being weary of him, they put a trick upon him (for W.D. was a man of great levity for a professor of religion), desiring him to carry a stone to the smith, telling the boy that they had borrowed it of the smith to weigh their bread (which was not true). The stone, being heavy, the boy refused to carry it. But – they pressing him – he obeyed. But in the way, meeting with his brother (older than he), the boy was asked what it was he carried. He told him. His brother answered: 'O fool! It is no such thing, they only make a fool of thee.' They went, however, to the smith to enquire, who said it was no such thing. While they parlayed about it, the parson of the parish came there and they all saw it was a trick of levity. The boy told his mother of it. And even that day or the next, as the coopers and the apprentice were at work, W.D. (who, perhaps, was foremost in the trick) was struck with a stone. He, thinking it was the apprentice, said to him: 'Thou has struck me.' The apprentice said: 'No!', and went farther from him. Soon W. was struck again, and he said: 'Thou has struck me, again.' The apprentice answered: 'No! Sure.'
    Presently, they all could see a little stone fall among them. By and by, the stones came thicker and thicker so that they were obliged to go out of the room,

where they could see the stones coming through the air one after another (pretty softly), till they came near the vessels. Then the stones moved more swiftly, and struck the vessels violently with a great noise (and bruising some of them) without striking the men – till William John Rees went to read the Bible. Then he was struck with a stone, and a stone struck part of the Bible off without tearing off any word or even a letter of that. Mr Lewis, who was one of them, and related this to me, said that that mark must have remained yet upon the Bible (if the Bible remains). W.D., seeing all this, said: 'In the name of God, what is here? Here is some evil sure.' The stones were of divers sorts: some were bricks with old lime about them, some Cornish, and some flints, etc. They thought, at first, that the parson used magic spells against them till they called to mind that the boy's mother was a reputed witch, and they changed their minds.

While they were talking about it, a hare appeared near them. They began to pursue it, and it went into brakes and briars hard by, yet by searching could not find it. They encouraged the bitch to go into the brakes to drive her out. She did, but came back terrified and would go in no more (which increased their suspicion). T.L. said: 'I will make her go out', and took a large, heavy rod and began to beat the brakes . . . and out she came. They hooted after her, but they had no dog to hunt her. Two or three days after, the old witch came by them and they greatly abused her in words and did cast stones after her and her son.

Here was, I doubt not, an apparition of the witch, as witches often in former times transformed into a hare-like appearance (as the witch of Endor had to raise one, and had power to employ an evil spirit (1 Samuel 28:7)) to play tricks upon these men – seen and felt by them in the daytime, and three sensible men to attest it.[37] Mr T.L., who was one of them (now an eminent man in the religious life and one of the ablest preachers in all Wales among the Dissenters), gave me the preceding relation. Here is another strong proof of the being of spirits against the opposite infidelity.

72. A relation of mine, W.M. of Machen, told me many years ago (he himself now being dead many years ago) that a young woman who was maidservant at Graig y Saeson, going by night upon business, was met by the spirit of a man. The spirit told her that for many years he had waited for an opportunity to speak with her; 'And now', said he, 'I have had it.' He told her that a handbill was hidden in the cairn (a heap of stones) not far from Bassaleg village, and charged her to take it away from hence (or cause it to be taken away), or otherwise that she should have no rest. When he had told her this, he bid her turn her back upon him. He went away like a great flash of fire, with a great noise. This was so terrifying and affecting that the poor young woman was sick after this infernal visit a whole year, lived afterward but three years, and could not look steadfastly in any man's face (a common thing to those who have seen and conversed with the spirits of hell, though it may be not without some exception but the reason of it unknown in the present life). The bill was taken out of the heap of stones

much worn yet very clear and bright, as if it had been of some certain use. W.M., who gave me this account, saw the bill.

Here is a notable, though but a single, proof of apparitions and being of spirits, sensibly felt and notably proved. A Sadducee and ridiculer of spirits and apparitions in this young woman's place would have thought so, and believed (though for want of experience, he unreasonably scoffs at the real experiences of others). We also see in this, and other instances of like nature, that graceless men are sometimes troublesome both in life and after this life.

Bedwas parish

73. I was glad to have this account from a strictly honest and judicious man, perfectly free from enthusiasm and superstition (especially as he had been, in time past, disputing with me against apparitions). He did not indeed deny the being of spirits, but thought (though he thought unreasonably) that men were deceived, and also told untruths about apparitions.

Going home from my house late at night, he saw, going before him, the likeness of a big man. Having come to it, it was a dark thing without regular members. He, therefore, forbore saying good night to him, whom before he thought to be a man. He, also, at that instance, remembered what he heard his father say: that once, travelling by night upon a lonesome mountain, and seeing an ill-looking man (as he thought) coming to meet him, his father said: 'Nos dawch' ('Good night' (to you)). He had no answer, but was seized with terror, upon which he said to himself: 'I am mistaken, no good night belongs to thee.'

Another time, while lying in bed in the chamber by himself, a strong pluck was given to the hair of his head so that his head was sore for three to four days after. This, he owned, could be done by nothing but a spirit.

I was glad that a person of his great excellences of mind and office was cured of this branch of infidelity (it being very improper that a preacher of the Gospel, and a soldier against the kingdom of darkness should deny the agency and appearance of the spirits of darkness upon the earth). Mr Lewelin is a preacher of the Gospel in Suffolk, in a Dissenting way.

74. Henry Williams Hugh was a schoolmaster with whom I was acquainted, as having been in the same school with him.

Going one night towards home, and being come to a field in the way he saw, by the stile and a holly-tree by it at the farther end of the field, the resemblance of a man but of somewhat odd figure. At the sight, the hound that was with him was exceedingly frightened and squalled, and Mr Hugh himself was terrified. When he came near, to his yet greater terror, the black man became two men; then he knew he saw a devil, and was studying what to say to him and thought of James chapter 4, verse 7: 'Resist the devil, and he will flee from you.' But his tongue cleaved to the roof of his mouth, and he could by no means say anything (and thought also that his tongue filled his mouth). When he came just to the place of the apparition, it changed into a pillar of fire – terrible to look upon.

When H.W.H. came to the house, the hound squalled again and ran its head into a wooden pot, out of which they could by no means take his head, so that Mr Hugh was obliged to break the pot with a hatchet. His wife, seeing all this – and his telling her when he came to the house not to stir the fire lest he should faint (as they commonly did who saw evil spirits) – was frightened so much that she knew not what she did. However, she told him (and she told the truth too) that he had brought the enemy with him into the house. Anyone that reads the account may easily imagine what disturbance of mind here was from the hound's squalling in the pot, beating it about the house in endeavouring to get his head free, and squalling so much the more when one of them drew the pot forward and the other pulling the hound backward.

Some may wonder how the dog who thrust its head into the pot could not draw it out. The answer is: its ears closed with its head in going in, but were doubled in drawing back and made the passage more strait. Anyone may imagine what a clutter was there between the melancholy incessant noise, and the dispute between the man and his wife about it – enough to make an ill-natured devil laugh who (having lost all happiness himself) envies all their happiness, even the least measure of it, and delights in all the miseries of men and every measure of it. Such is the devil whom men choose to serve and will not be persuaded to leave his service, but live and die in it to their eternal destruction. I even suspect that this devil had measured both the dog's head and the mouth of the vessel, and frightened him to put in his head that the devil might have to this hellish sport, though he was little the better for it (but that he delights in mischief). The history of this passage the schoolmaster related to several persons.

Bedwellty parish

75. Very many years ago, there was a watch-night at the house of Meredith Thomas after the death of his child (about four years old). The watch-nights, then, were being very profanely kept in some parts of Wales. The relations of the dead were so silly as to suffer it (though it looked like an insult upon their mourning and misery) and had not the sense and courage to forbid it.[38] Few besides the Dissenters did, but suffered it as a custom and because the pretence was to divert the relations of the dead and to lessen their sorrows. The watch-nights improperly and impiously turned the house of mourning into a house of mirth, contrary to the Scripture declaration: 'It is better to go to the house of mourning than to go to the house of feasting: for that is the end of all men; and the living will lay it to his heart' (Ecclesiastes 7:2). Now, God be thanked, the light of the Gospel hath prevailed against this madness. There came into the house at this time some sober persons: Margaret Andrew and William Harry Rees (both of the Baptist persuasion). But there came also two profane men: Thomas Edward Morgan and Anthony Aaron (not much to the liking of the rest

of the company), who went to play cards and swearing very badly. But none else did play with them.

While they were playing and swearing, a lamentable groaning noise was heard at the window, which surprised all except the two men. William Harry Rees persuaded them to give over, and for some time they did desist, and the groaning noise ceased. When the noise ceased, they went to it again (for very wicked men are commonly very incorrigible) and then the lamentable and lamenting noise was renewed and was louder. But when they were again desired to desist, they said it was nothing but somebody that played tricks to frighten them. Upon which, William Harry Rees told them it was no man but that the evil spirit had been a while by the house and might come in and appear if they did not desist, and desired them to give over. These hardy men would not venture out to see who played tricks. One of the company (bolder than the rest), for they all now began to fear, said: 'I will take the dogs with me and scour about the house, and see if there it any person about it.' Accordingly, he took the prime staff and began to hollow, to call the hound and the dogs to go out. But the dogs would by no means go out (having likely heard the groaning sound and feared), but sought to hide themselves under the stools and about the people's feet. And though they pouted and beat them, yet they would not go to the door. Upon which William Harry Rees sharply told the two men to give over, all the rest joining with him – for now they were fully persuaded that there was an invisible agent near them. The two men themselves at last gave over, being convinced there was somewhat extraordinary in it. The thing was reported about, and had effect to prevent this wicked practice in that neighbourhood and about unto this day – and may it be forever.

This was related to me by Elizabeth Isaac, an eye- and ear-witness of this extraordinary fact, a woman of care, and conscientious to tell the truth.

We have heard of other places where people played cards until the devil came among them, which hath much lessened the practice, which yet alas much abounds in many places in this very sinful, profane kingdom. Our parliament is busy in seeking the welfare of this kingdom. It is to be wished they would extend their virtue against this wicked, dangerous recreation. But, alas, it doth not enough appear that they are careful to prevent sin and profaneness, which is the only thing that can prevent the ruin of this kingdom, whose welfare they continually seek and study in another way. Though, after all this, the only way to prevent it, is to prevent all manner of sin and profaneness, as far as it can be done. They do indeed see the misery of the kingdom (for it is great), and they experience it, and justly lament it. But they do not sufficiently attend to the only cause of this great sinfulness in the kingdom. Should any great effect be considered, and the cause be overlooked, without which the effect would not be, could not be. It is a wonder to many, how so many wise and clear-sighted men in other things cannot see this. They are men of learning, readers of histories, and cannot see but sin hath been the ruin of empires, kingdoms, families, and particular persons. The Duke of Richmond (I think it was) did, once, in the House of Lords speak to this purpose (and we honour him for it): that sin and profaneness was the cause of all our evils, and that the king should be addressed upon this head. But, it seems, he was not much minded, though nothing could be more properly and necessarily spoken. He was not seconded by the bishops, who should be foremost in this work. What sort of men are these bishops?

76. Mr Charles Winter, who lived near Bedwellty church, many years ago, told me that (having been disputing about original sin in the house which is nearest the churchyard) when he went home through the churchyard, he heard like the voice of a child crying about the top of the steeple – which somewhat impressed him. Mr W. was a Baptist, but not agreeing with his brethren (whom he thought were too rigid in the Calvinistic doctrines), he went to be instructed in learning in the Carmarthen Academy. There he imbibed, or farther imbibed, the Arminian notions. But not plainly discovering himself (or being not understood), he became a minister among them. The differences continuing and increasing among them, he and some of the congregation separated into a church by themselves, where they still continue separate from the rest of the brethren, and are the only Arminian or Arminianish–Baptist congregation in all Wales. I doubt, therefore, that it was Mr Winter himself who disputed that night against original sin, which, if he did, here was a voice against him from the dead; for the crying of children – a sign and expression of some misery – is as certainly the effect and equally the proof of original sin (madly denied by Deists, Socinians, Arians, and Arminians) as the pain of conception and birth is and declared to be so (Genesis 3:16).

77. H.A. was a sheep-stealer, and stole sheep from William David Richard of Rumney. The said William David Richard, or some person employed by him, went to a dealer in the black art who did something to H.A. so that he could not see William David Richard's sheep. He could see all other, but none of William David Richard's sheep. This was a pretty punishment for a thief – if it did not come from an evil cause.

78. About the end of the seventeenth century, there lived in the valley of Sirhowy in this parish David Ziles, an honest, substantial freeholder. His house was often troubled in the night by witches, who were very mischievous (destroying the milk, etc.). The thing was known far and near. In process of time, Hopkin David (a Quaker, by trade a turner) came there to work. One night, when he was there, these witches made a disturbance and (as he apprehended) moved his tools. Upon which, he rose out of bed and came down, and saw them in the shape of extraordinary looking cats. Knowing what they were, he spoke to them and asked one of them: 'Who art thou, and what is thy name?' To which she answered: 'Elor Sir Gâr' ('Carmarthenshire Eleanor'). He asked another: 'Who art thou?', and was answered, 'Mawd Anghyfion'

('Unrighteous Mawd'); and the other answered the same question: 'Ishel Anonest' ('Unjust Jezebel'), to which he answered: 'Unjust is thy work in meddling with my tools', and he severely reproved and threatened them – for now they had betrayed themselves and were in danger of punishment. They did not trouble the house afterward. This good the honest Quaker did to an innocent honest family.

Had His Majesty King George II read the history of witchcraft, and known as much as we do in some parts of Wales, he would not have called upon his parliament to determine that there are no such things as witches (and his parliament would have hardly complimented him therein). If they thought that there never were such things as witches in the world, the Scripture is against them (both the Old and New Testaments). For there were witches in the days of Saul, and also in the days of Paul, else he would not have wrote: 'O foolish Galatians, who hath bewitched you, that you should nor obey the truth?' (Galatians 3:1). Yet His Majesty is in some measure to be excused, as there are much fewer of those sort of people in Wales since the preaching of the Gospel hath prevailed in it. As for me, I knew but one woman in all the parish of Aberystruth who was supposed to be a witch. Her son-in-law was nearly positive that she was such. I doubt so too, though her daughter was certainly a good woman – yea, good beyond many good people.

True, here was no proper apparition of spirits; here was an apparition of persons transformed by and acting under the influence of evil spirits in the house of David Ziles, in the valley of Sirhowy.

79. From under the hand of the Revd Mr Roger Rogers (born and bred in this parish) I have the following very remarkable relation. A remarkable and odd fight was seen in July 1760, acknowledged and confessed by several credible eye-witnesses of the same: that is, by Lewis Thomas Jenkin's two daughters (virtuous and good young women); his manservant and maidservant; Elizabeth David (a neighbour and tenant of the said Lewis Thomas); and Edmund Roger (a neighbour).

They were all making hay in a field called Y Weirglodd Fawr Dafolog. The first sight they saw was the resemblance of an innumerable company of sheep, or somewhat like them, over a hill called Cefnrhychdir, opposite to the place where the spectators stood, about a quarter of a mile distant from them. Soon after, they saw them go up to a place called Cefnrhychdir Uchaf, about half a mile distant from them, and then they went out of their sight . . . as if they vanished in the air. But, again, they had another sight of them about half an hour before sunset; they all saw them at the same time, but all of them did not see them in the same manner, but in different forms. Two of these persons saw them like sheep, some saw them like greyhounds, some like swine, and some like naked infants. They appeared in the shade of the mountain between them and the sun, though the people that saw them stood in the sunshine. The first sight was as if they rose up of the earth. This was a notable appearance of the fairies, seen by many credible witnesses. The sons of infidelity are very unreasonable not to believe not only many single but also double and treble witnesses of the appearance and being of spirits.

80. Mathew Howel, a young man in the parish of Bedwellty, was much given to play bowl and puis on the Lord's Day.[39] That not satisfying, he went with a neighbour (Edmund Thomas) to play upon a Lord's Day night. While M. stood at one end of the alley (and his companion at the other end), with the bowl in his hand ready to throw, a little dog that was with them squealed out for fear and sought to climb upon him. At the same time, hearing as it were the noise of young pigs dancing and thumping the ground, M. held the bowl in his hand and cried 'hist' ('silence'). At which, E., wondering, went to him and asked why he did not throw the bowl. Upon which, M. told him what he heard. But E., little minding that, took the bowl in his own hand (to throw), but heard the same noise, and could also see something like young pigs dancing. At whom, and among whom, he threw the bowl. But as soon as it went out of his hand, he was so terrified that he felt his hair moving upon his head, and they both ran home. When M.'s father heard this story, who before was angry with his son for breaking the sabbath, and seeing a miraculous sign against it, he offered to strike him with a staff, and M. narrowly escaped a severe blow. M. took warning, and gave over bowling on the Lord's Day.

Here, some may wonder how evil spirits can act at any time to prevent sin (as, in many instances, we find they have done). The answer must be that the spirits of the kingdom of darkness are not all equally bad (though none of them good, and cannot do any good from right principles to good ends, but indirectly on some selfish or other principles). Some of them are too malignant to do any kind of good, but only to be instruments of justice in the punishment of men; (like the flesh of the asp, the dipas, the drine, the rattlesnake, the macas, of whose flesh no medicine can be made – they are so poisonous).[40] But the flesh of vipers, and other serpents, is of use in medicines; so some of the serpents of hell, through the ruling power and virtue of God's providence, are indirectly of some use in the kingdom of God (as Satan's buffeting was to Paul, and to other Christians, to whom every thing and therefore Satan's temptations shall work for good (Romans 8:28)). Dives in hell wanted that his brethren should be hindered from coming to hell, and therefore from doing that which should bring them there (Luke 16:27–8). It might be the spirit of the dead relation in the kingdom of darkness, who might give this warning against sabbath-breaking (though none of the worst spirits of darkness, for it did not appear in the shape of dogs creatures wholly unclean, but of young pigs, but half unclean in the sense of God's law (Leviticus 11:7)). This story was related to me by M.H. himself, in the year 1772.

81. E.T., travelling by night, many years ago, over Bedwellty mountain towards the valley of Ebbw Fawr (where his house and estate is, within the parish of

Aberystruth), saw the fairies on every side of him. Some were dancing; he heard also the sound of hunting and of the hunting horn, so that he began to fear. He called to mind his having heard that if any person saw the fairies about him and drew out his knife, they would presently vanish.[41] He did so, and he saw them no more. This the old gentleman seriously related to me, not long ago. He is a sober man, and of such strict veracity that I heard him confess a truth against himself, when he was like to suffer loss for an imprudent step. I mention this to obtain credit to the above relation, to weaken the Sadduceistical infidelity – for infidelity sometimes (and this among the rest) is very obstinate to yield to both reason and experience.

82. John Jacob, a tailor in this parish (whom I knew) was a man of sense and judgement, far enough from being fanciful and superstitious. Many years ago now, travelling by night, even in the neighbourhood, he lost his way. The fairies, among whom he was now fallen, caused the ways (which he well knew before) to look strangely different from what they really were (which indeed they had power often to do). All of a sudden, to his great surprise, he saw himself for some time in a town and the resemblance of shops (as there are in towns), which all of a sudden vanished. He saw where he was and came to a neighbour's house, where he sat mute and heavy. Being asked the reason of it, he declared what he had seen, and he was more heavy. He did not live long afterward. We have little apprehension, in our embodied state, of the power of disembodied spirits, till the all-showing light of eternity opens upon us – which will amaze us with the new and great knowledge of things past and present.

Caerwent parish

83. About the year 1757, David Griffith (a carpenter in the parish of Caerwent) was going from his work. Being a little past the river rheen, he was suddenly and exceedingly terrified by a sound in the air – like the braying of an ass, but more disagreeable (something hellish and more tangible in the sound).[42] To add to his terror, he saw a dark roller, rolling by his side, and passing on to a hedge before him.[43] It made such a noise as if all the hedges about were tore to pieces – so amazed, and terrified and confounded he was. (Who, in his case, would not have been so?) He knew not how he went home. When he came to light, he fainted and became as a dead man, and was ill about a fortnight after that.

    Here was a witness of the being of an evil spirit, both in his eyes, fears, and feelings. Oh, that a Sadducee, an Atheist, or one of the ridiculers of apparitions had been in his place to be cured of his foolish infidelity. Here was also a witness of it to others, and to those who saw him fainting, and to those who saw and heard of his keeping his bed upon this account, and losing his health for a time upon this occasion.

Christchurch parish

84. Many years ago, the Revd Mr T. Evans, the curate of Caerleon, writing below stairs at night, heard (near the fire) like the sound of sweet, small bells. He called Mrs Evans from bed to hear it. She came, but heard nothing. He called the maid, and she also heard nothing. Mrs Evans desired him to go to another room to see if he could hear it. He did, but could hear nothing. That time, two years hence, their child died in that room, and that part of the room where he heard this sweet bell ringing. Here it is plain that this was the agency of some invisible beings or spirits who exactly knew the time of his child's death, so long before (to the farther conviction of Atheistical, Deistical men and Sadduceistical principles, which have no foundation but the corrupt, perverse fancies of men).

Llanfihangel Llantarnam parish

85. Mr Thomas Edwards, a right good man and a sound preacher of the Gospel, told me that, lodging one night at a house called Pentre-bach in the parish Llanfihangel Llantarnam, Monmouthshire, he was troubled in bed by an evil spirit. All night long, till the crowing of the cock, it made a squeaking noise in his ear, somewhat like the squeak of the pig (an unclean creature), for it was made by an unclean spirit and malignant who, as far as he durst, tormented a good man. But, behold, as soon as the cock crowed that troublesome noise ceased in a minute, and T.E. had quiet to sleep the rest of the night (which he could not possibly do before). Mr E. was made, by experience, to see and believe the virtue of the voice of the bird of day (which he little minded or believe before), and to thank God for it.

Here we may take occasion to observe the wickedness of cockfighting, whose pastime it is to destroy these useful birds. And may we not justly think that the devil hath a great hand in promoting this inhuman, cruel, reproachful recreation out of revenge to this bird of the day, who cuts him short in the night walks and exercises? The devil's malice is doubtless very extensive, extending not only to everything but to the least thing crossing his proud, evil nature.

Formerly, if not still, the family durst not stay up in the house after 10 o'clock, but must go to the bed out of the way, otherwise there was a stir about them which they could not but know was made by an evil spirit, and it grew worse and worse till they went out of the way. A great family lived there in former times, where likely there was (as in many other great houses) much wickedness. There is in a room in that house a stone wall with pretty many letters upon it, resembling Greek letters. But I have not heard of any that have read them.

86. Edward Frank, a young man of this parish, having been to mend his shoes, and going home by night, heard something walking towards him. Presently, he saw some big, tall, dark thing, without any regular shape, before him on the way. With much difficulty, he was enabled to say: 'In the name of God, what is here?

Turn out of my way, or I will strike thee.' It, then, disappeared. Pretty soon after, he was seized with the greatest terror, so that he felt not his clothes about him. Presently, on the way before him, and between him and the hedge, two dun-coloured things (like posts) appeared.[44] This put him to the utmost terror, so that he could hardly walk on. But seeing a cow not afar off, he went towards her, to lean upon her, because he could scarce stand; she stayed for him, smelt him, and suffered him to lean upon her. Going forward, and being scarce able to go, he called at a young woman's house (with whom he was acquainted). He was so weak that he could not tell her who he was when she asked him, and she would not open the door, because she did not know his voice. But, apprehending he was a person in distress, she did open the door and did let him in – and saw it was her well-known neighbour. He could not go home that night. This story was told me by Abraham Lewelin, a wise, religious man, who lodged in the same house with this young man.

Llanhilleth parish

87. Rees John Rosser, born at Hendy in this parish, was a virtuous man and led a very holy life to the day of his death. After he was come from the army of the parliament and the civil war was ended, (when a young man), going early before day to feed the oxen at a barn called Ysgubor y Llan, and having given hay to the oxen, he went to sleep upon the hay. While he rested there, he could hear fine music coming near the barn. Presently, a large company came in to the floor of the barn with striped clothes (and some of them appeared more gay than others), and there danced at their music. He lay down as quiet as he could, thinking they would not see him, but in vain. One of them, a woman (appearing better than the rest), brought him a striped cushion with four tassels (one at each corner of it) to put under his head. After some time, the cock crew at the house of Blaen-y-cwm hard by. Upon which they appeared as if they were either surprised or displeased – and the cushion was hastily taken from under his head – and went away. These spirits of darkness do not like the crowing of the cock, because it gives notice of the approach of the day (for they love darkness rather than light). They surely belong to the kingdom of darkness, who hate and avoid the light of the sun. If they are averse to the light of the natural sun, how much more to the light of Christ – the sun of the spiritual world? It hath been several times observed that these fairies cannot endure to hear the name of God – so far they are alienated from him – and become his enemies. This is the work of their creaturely sin in perfection of strength.

88. Llanhilleth mountain was formerly much talked of (and still remembered) concerning an apparition who led many people astray both by night and by day upon it. The apparition was the resemblance of a poor old woman with an oblong, four-cornered hat; ash-coloured clothes; her apron thrown backward upon her shoulder; with a pot or wooden kann, with two hoops about the middle

of it, in her hand (such as poor people went about with to fetch milk).[45] She was always going before them at some considerable distance, sometimes crying out: 'Wow up!' Whoever saw this apparition, whether by night or in a misty day (though well acquainted with the way) was sure to lose his way. For they did not see the way as it really was, but very different. So far (sometimes) the fascination was, that they thought they were going to their journey's end (when they were really going the country way). Sometimes, they heard her cry: 'Wow up!' (the very word which hunters use in this country when the hare is killed), when they did not see her. Sometimes the cry was heard by some when they went out at night to fetch coal or water, etc., hard by. Presently, they would hear it afar off (upon the opposite mountain, in Aberystruth parish) and sometimes passing by their ears.

The people have it by tradition that it is the spirit of one Juan White, who lived time out of mind in these parts and was thought to be a witch (because the mountain was not haunted with her apparition before, but after, her death). At first, when people lost their way and saw her, they thought it was a real woman who knew the way – and were glad to see her. They endeavoured to overtake her, and to enquire about the way. But they could never overtake her (nor would she ever look backward), so that they never saw her face.

89. She has been sometimes seen and heard upon other mountains, even as far up as the Black Mountain in Breconshire. For Robert Williams of Llangattock Crickhowell, a substantial man of undoubted veracity, who died some years ago, travelling over part of the Black Mountain by night, saw her. Having lost his way, he was glad to see her, to enquire about the way (thinking she was a real woman who knew the way, and was travelling that way) and, therefore, called upon her to stay for him. But having no answer, he thought she was deaf and hastened his pace. That not availing, he ran – thinking to overtake her (but could not, but rather lost ground by running). At this, he wondered – for he could not think it was a spirit be saw and heard. For, when in seeking to overtake her, he happened to stumble or put his foot in a plashy pit, and his vexation increased.[46] He heard her laugh at it, like an old woman. At last, he saw himself in a dangerous place and, being greatly wearied and in much trouble of mind, had other thoughts of the apparition. But happening to draw out his knife to some purpose, she vanished away – and he saw where he was, found his way home, and was glad to be delivered from the unmerciful delusion.

90. She led one man backwards and forwards in a misty day at Pen y ddoi-gae mountain.[47] For, after travelling much, he still came to a bush of rushes, this gave him so great a concern that he, afterward, made a song of complaint and reproach against her (in which he mentioned her four-cornered hat, etc.). But her chief haunt was on Llanhilleth mountain. I remember, when I was a young lad in Aberystruth parish, that, now and then, we heard of this and that person having lost his way in coming home from Pontypool market upon that mountain.

I once met a woman of the next parish who, together with her young daughter, had lost her way in the daytime and were very weary (especially the young lass, whom I put in the way).

Indeed, I myself lost the way two or three times in the daytime on this mountain, though I knew it very well and that it is no more than a mile and a half long and about half a mile broad. Once I lost the way and, being come from the mountain, I called at a house (where I had never been) and, finding an uncommon inclination to it, I offered to go to prayer (which they admitted), and I was greatly welcomed. I was, then, about twenty-three years of age and had begun to preach the everlasting Gospel. They seemed to admire that a person so young should be so warmly disposed – few young men of my age being religious in this country then. Much good came into this house, and still continues in it. I think the Lord answered my earnest prayer and, if so, the old hag got nothing by leading me astray at that time. Often it is that the malignity of evil spirits is turned for good to them that fear God (and wonderful is the mercy that makes all things to work for good). Another time, going over the mountain, a-horseback, on a misty day, and thinking she might be near me (for she was very busy on that mountain, observing who passed over it), I said (in faith): 'Do thy work thou old devil, I will not lose my way' (and did not at that time). I think I once saw her in the daytime, for I saw one exactly answering the description, crossing the way at no great distance from me. I am not quite sure it was not a real, old woman (though I must suspect it, because she never once looked towards me and crossed the mountain where there was no path).

Of late years, there is little talk about her – the light of the Gospel hath driven her to closer quarters (in the coal-pits and holes of the earth), until the day when she shall be gathered in the body to receive the everlasting curse: 'Depart from me, ye cursed, into everlasting fire, prepared for the devil and his angels' (Matthew 25:41).

91. Far back in the seventeenth century, Jenkin John David was coming home late in the night from the parish of Aberystruth and, in the way, passed by the great thorn-tree upon the mountain dividing between Llanhilleth and Trevethin parishes, not far from Blaen-nant-ddu fields. (He was thinking to go over the mountain to Blaen y Cynw, a way about half a mile long.) However, he travelled much. At last, the bridle unaccountably fell off the horse's head. He alighted to put it on and, looking where he was, saw that he was at the great thorn (having rode his way backward). He went a-horseback again, thinking, then, he could not miss his way. But, after travelling much, the bridle again was taken off the horse's head. The horse stood still and would go no farther, as if it apprehended that his rider missed his way. Having also tired, Jenkin alighted, looked, and saw he was again at the great thorn. When he saw that, he did not go a-horseback again nor attempted to cross the mountain, but went by the hedge-side to Ysgubor y Grug Llwyn barn, under the eves of which he and his horse stayed all the rest of the night (which was a long night in the month of November).

92. Thomas Andrew, living at a place called the Farm in this parish, coming home by night saw, by a wall-side in his way, the similitude of a dark man creeping on all fours – scraping the ground and looking aside (this way and that way, and aside backward), and also making some dreadful noises. By which (as well he might be) he was terribly frightened – for it was indeed, to every one that will particularly consider it, a dreadful appearance.

93. Another time, he was coming towards home (and some persons together with him) in the night-time. He heard, as he thought, the sound of hunting. He feared they were hunting the sheep, and hastened on to meet and hinder them. He heard them coming towards him (though he saw them not). When they came near him, their voices were but small, but increasing as they went from him. Down they went the steep way, towards the river Ebbw (dividing between this parish and Mynyddislwyn), whereby he knew that they were: what are called *cŵn wybr* (sky-hounds), but in the inward parts of Wales *cŵn annwn* (hounds of hell). I have heard say that these spiritual hunting dogs have been heard to pass by the eves of some houses before the death of some in the family. Thomas Andrew was an honest, religious man, who would not have told an untruth either for fear or for favour. He is dead many years ago.

94. Mary M., living by Crumlin bridge many years ago now, standing upon the bridge, heard a weak voice like that of one in distress going up the river saying: 'O Dduw beth a wnaf fi? O Dduw beth a wnaf fi?' ('O God what shall I do? O God what shall I do?'). At first, she thought it a human voice of one in distress. But while she considered the voice, suddenly a great terror seized her, so that she thought that her hair moved, and she could not move either forward or backward from the place. Seeing a young cousin of hers standing in the yard of the house near the bridge, with great difficulty she called upon her (who also had heard the voice, and came to her). When Mary came to the house, she fainted. The lamentable voice, which she heard, was most probably the voice of some disembodied spirit who had lived and died in sin and felt the wrath of God for it (which will make all impenitent sinners cry at last). Our Saviour, who perfectly knows hell, saith that it is a place of weeping and gnashing of teeth – in anger at themselves for having unnecessarily lost heaven and fallen into misery (Matthew 25:30).

Oh, that we could prevail with men to fear hell, and damnation, and the sin that leads to it. Voices from hell are sometimes heard, yet prevail not. This woman is still living who heard the lamentable voice and was terrified, is not yet converted to God (though she leads not a profane, vicious life). It is time for her to turn to God, lest she should be made to make the same moan herself under the wrath of God in the other world.

95. From a house called the Farm in the parish of Llanhilleth, Monmouthshire, the family used to see by night (as some of them told me myself) a light moving

about the holly-trees by a house (which is by the river Ebbw side) called Tŷ Llan y Dŵr, moving sometimes about them on all sides. More often, the motion was upwards above the trees, and then back again downwards. It appeared also in different sizes, sometimes increasing and appearing as a large star and larger (nearly large as the moon), and then decreasing and appearing like a small star. It also, sometimes, appeared and disappeared in the motions about the trees. The colour was rather whitish than reddish, and most apt to appear before a change of weather for the worse. This place, not then inhabited (though in a delightful part of the earth), is about a measured mile from the farm on high ground above it.

Some would call this a meteor (and such things indeed there are). But can any meteor move so orderly as this: round about the trees, and upwards and downward? What hath a meteor to do with the hollies more than other trees? And, if a meteor, why by that house more than another is too difficult to account for in the way of nature. And, if a spirit, why about the holly-trees? (We have heard before of an evil spirit appearing by this tree.) If it signifies anything, it must be partly because of the roughness of its leaves, which are pricking and painful to handle. Because of this, the tree is made the flail to thresh the corn to obtain bread for the support of life. The devil may like it, as it beats the corn (which represents the people of God). And as the beating with it represents the beating of God's people with afflictions (in which the enemy delights), for which reason the Lord calls his church: 'O my threshing, and the corn of my floor' (Isaiah 21:10).

Here, one of the consumptive believers will say: 'Fy! This is too fanciful and enthusiastical.' Soft and fair! I have not spoken positively, though I speak according to my inclination. And what have I more to say for than any man can say against? For who can say and make it good that the malice of devils against God's people is not particular to the utmost extent? He hates not only the persons of God's people but everything that represents them, and everything that belongs to them in any beneficial way. Besides, doth not the Creator delight more in the trees which he calls good trees, some of whom represent himself and his Son – such as the Tree of Life in Paradise and the apple tree (Revelation 2:7, 22:14; Canticles 2:3) – some of which represent his Church and people.

I, myself, saw a representation of a bush of thorns with the top downwards coming through the air against me as I was travelling upon a mountain between sunset and dark night, and passing by me on the left hand. I am sure it was no natural bush, but a supernatural apparition. To me, it was a prophetic sign of troublesome men (like thorns, to which troublesome men are compared (Ezekiel 2:6)). Yet, there were the resemblance of many round drops of air in the visional, thorny bush, which surely represented a mixture of mercy with these affections. There was a sensation of terror upon me when I saw this apparition, which signified what it was (which night was ominous of the affections that followed).

Machen parish

96. About the year 1748, J. W. James was going by night from Bedwas (with a young woman whom he pretended to court) towards Risca church-wakes on horseback. Before they came over against Certwyn Machen hill (the east side of it facing the parish of Risca), they could see the resemblance of a boy going before them part of the way. They suspected, by something in the appearance, that it was not a real boy – as, indeed, it was not – but a hellish dangerous boy, as it soon appeared. For while they looked upon it, they could see it suddenly putting its head between its legs and, transforming into a ball of light, tumbling a steep way towards the Certwyn, which is the top of the high Machen mountain (it being as easy for a spirit to go up as to come downhill).[48]

Presently after, to increase their fear, they could hear the jingling sound of iron and, together with that, they saw many great stone-horses with some darkness about them. It was as if they were drawing some load between them until they came to Pontymister bridge and somewhat beyond it, and then turned to a cross-lane leading towards a house where a man newly dead was. When they were gone a little way farther, they could see the earth cleaving and opening, and out of the pit came up a pillar or beam of fire, very shining and waving in the air. It made an impression upon the young woman's handkerchief of a yellow colour, yet as if somewhat singed by the fire, which could never be washed away but continued as long as the handkerchief (and seen by many, and among others by my brother's daughter, living in Machen).

It was a heavy night, which they could never forget. Here was both an eye- and ear-witness, and something to purpose to witness the being and appearance of spirits. And this the more to be credited, as it made a serious impression upon them – for the man afterwards soberly confessed he intended to debauch the young woman in this journey, but this prevented his evil intention. Was there not enough to convince a Sadducee, an Atheist, the stoutest of them all, had they seen this apparition?

97. About Michaelmas in the year 1773, H.J., a widow woman in Machen parish, was a midwife and (as to her disposition) ready to do any kindness in her power (and this was her commendation). On the other hand, she cared not for the word of God and did not hear it, and so had not God in the world nor a ground of hope of eternal life (though the parson buried her in sure and certain hope of the resurrection to life eternal). She was a drunkard, and was drowned in the ditch of the forge where the water was not so deep (but that she was drunk and unable to help herself). Some time after, she appeared to a young man, who could durst not go out at night but he saw her. Upon which, he complained to his master and asked his advice whether he should speak to her or not.

Accordingly, some night after, he did. In answer to which, she said: he must come with her into the great field, which is near at Machen church, and take up a key and a purse with fourteen pence in it in a certain place in the field. He obeyed, and followed her three miles and passed over Llanfihangel bridge and Machen cymmer (or wooden bridge), came to the field, and took up the iron key and fourteen pence. When she parted from him, she bid him hide his face and not to look about and charged him not to tell who she was (and he did not). But people, being curious to know who she was, have named the one and the other to him, to which he answered 'no', till naming Hannah Jones . . . when he said nothing. From this, people do conclude who she was. She also told him that this was the only thing that troubled her and made her appear to him. Perhaps it was the iron key that troubled her more than the copper money, for there is something very mysterious in hiding of iron things to trouble the spirits of the dead, which we cannot understand in the present life.

Magor parish

98. Many years ago now, Mr Matthews (a schoolmaster at Magor village in Monmouthshire), being gone to a great house was put to sleep in a large empty room with high windows by himself (where he was afterward told none could sleep). The family knew (and perhaps would exercise) his courage and faith, as sometimes hath been done in other great houses by others (especially with some Dissenting ministers who travelled about to preach). Before he slept, he could hear (as he thought) the stirring of the corn which was in that corner of the room. But he soon came nearer and heard the sound of one walking (as it were) in his stockings above the bed, rustling the bedclothes as he passed. After he had gone for three or four times about the bed (whereby he greatly terrified Mr M.), he fell upon Mr M. (which terrified him to the utmost), and he tumbled out of the bed and the bedclothes before him into the chamber floor, and was some time before he came to himself. Having come to himself, he went to bed again, but could not sleep all night. He was told, afterward, that a man had fallen down from the garret into the room and died. If it was his spirit (as likely it was), it was a very malignant one to torment his fellow creature (who had done nothing against him). Doubtless, wicked men become devils after death, and some of them are almost devils here in flesh and blood. (Our Saviour called Judas a devil upon earth, before he went to hell (John 6:70).)

Mynyddislwyn parish

99. A young woman of my acquaintance, who going from Lanhither towards Abergweidd in the parish of Mynyddislwyn by night, was filled with a great terror upon the way so that she felt not her clothes about her.[49] She presently saw a bowl of fire – as large as a pompion – skipping before her, out of which came forth flames about half a yard long (sometimes changing into blue – the brimstone-flame colour – and sometimes of a greenish colour).[50] After some time, it receded, and went by her side, and sometimes followed her – all which was very terrible, so that she felt not the ground under her feet nor the weight of

her own body. For some part of the way it disappeared, and then appeared again, continuing and increasing her terror till she came to the village, where it decreased to the size of a tennis ball, and then entered into a shop in the village. When she came into the house, she fainted.

Some time after (and ever since), this young woman hath met with uncommon troubles, occasioned by her obstinacy, disobedience to parents, and a fiery temper (though a person of great understanding, and also of some virtues). I did not remember to ask her whether the living, fire bowl (which had the life of hell in it) receded back by her left side and passed forward by her right, or the contrary way. I also wish I had asked Mr W. whether the spectre which turned about him, began to turn on the east side of him and went forward from the east to the north, from the north to the west, and from thence to the east, or was it the contrary way.[51] For I have observed that the very circumstances of some apparitions bore a resemblance of the circumstances of the evils to come. For, as evil spirits delight in the troubles of men, they must delight to show them as particular as they can.

100. Mr Henry Lewelin was sent by me to Samuel Davies of Ystrad Dyvodog parish in Glamorganshire, to fetch a load of books (Bibles, testaments and Watts's *Psalms, Hymns and Songs* for children) on the 3rd October 1766.

On coming home by night towards Mynyddislwyn, and having just passed by Clwyd yr Helygen alehouse into a dry, broad, and fair part of the lane, the mare which he rode stood still. She would go no farther, but drew backward. Presently, he could see a living thing, round like a bowl, rolling from the right hand to the left, crossing the lane, moving sometimes slowly, sometimes very swiftly (swifter than any creature on earth could, if not swifter than a bird flying, though it had neither wings nor feet). It altered, also, its size: appearing three times, lesser one time than another; it appeared least when near him, and seemed to roll towards the mare's belly. The mare, then, would go forward, but he stopped her to see more carefully what it was. He stayed, as he thought, about three minutes to look at it, but (fearing to see a worse sight) thought it time to speak to it, and said: 'What seekest thou, thou foul thing? In the name of the Lord Jesus, go away'. (Would a Socinian or an Arian say so?) Upon his speaking this, it vanished into nothing, as if it sunk into the ground near the mare's feet. It seemed to be of a reddish colour, with some mixture of an ash colour. (Near Clwyd yr Helygen, in time past, and near the place of the apparition, the Lord's Day was greatly profaned. It may be, also, the adversary was angry at the good books and the book-bringer, for it knew what burden the mare carried.)

101. Many years ago, John, the son of Watkin Elias Jones (a substantial man of this parish), after his father's death, ploughing in a field, when the oxen rested sent the lad which drove the oxen to fetch something which he wanted. Before the lad came back, he saw a cloud coming across the field towards him, which came to him and shadowed the sun from him. Out of the cloud came a voice to

him, which asked him of which of three diseases – the fever, the dropsy, or the consumption – he would choose to die (for one of them he must choose in order to his end). He chose to die of the consumption. He let the oxen go home with the lad, and finding himself inclined to sleep, laid down to sleep. When he awaked, he was indisposed and fell by degrees into the consumption whereof he died. (Yet, he lived more than a year after he had seen the apparition of the cloud and heard the supernatural voice out of it.)

Some say that he saw the similitude of a venerable old man in the cloud speaking to him. I believe it was so, and that it was the disembodied spirit of some good man (likely one of his ancestors) and not an angel – for angels do not appear like old men, nor is it proper they should because there is no decay in them as in men subject to mortality. It is not unreasonable to think that (sometimes at least) the spirits of the saints departed are ministering servants to the heirs of salvation, as well as the angels and under the name of angels (seeing they have a nearer relation and, therefore, an equal, if not a superior, propriety to do this). It is thought to be the spirit of a departed saint who spoke to John: 'And I fell at his feet to worship him. And he said unto me, See thou do it not: I am thy fellow servant, and of thy brethren that have the testimony of Jesus: worship God: for the testimony of Jesus is the spirit of prophecy' (Revelation 19:10). It would be odd that the angels should serve in the church militant upon earth who were never members of it, and that none of those who have been members (and have more experience of it) should never serve it.

He became very serious after this, though sometimes a little fretful. He would often read and shed tears in reading, and (before his death) gave good advices to the family to be weaned from the world: to think of the shortness of time; the certainty of death; to prepare for eternity, etc. He did not tell of the apparition till within six weeks of his death.

His great-grandfather was an excellent minister, the Revd Mr Watkin Jones at Penmaen, several of whose family have been, and are, religious, and fair and beautiful persons. The promise is but too little minded and pleaded that: God sheweth mercy to them that love him, to the third and fourth generation. And what a sinful neglect and hurtful folly it is to neglect this great and precious promise which, if pleaded in faith and earnestness, would be accomplished by him who hath said: 'Ask, and it shall be given you; seek, and ye shall find; knock, and it shall be opened unto you' (Matthew 7:7).

102. But there is an account of a different kind of spirit which, about fourscore years ago, came to the house of Job John Harry. He was living at the Trewyn in this parish, and stayed there from some time before Christmas until Easter Wednesday (which was the last day of his abiding there). In which space of time, it spoke and did many things which were very remarkable, as being done by an invisible spirit. The report of it spread very far, and was in every man's mouth for a long time, and is still remembered and spoken of at times. Being aware that some things might be added in the report, and other things altered from what

they really were, I choose not to relate all that I heard, but what I judge most likely to be true.

At first, it came knocking at the door (chiefly by night), which it continued to do for a month's time (by which they were often deceived to open it). At last, it spoke to one who opened the door, upon which they were much terrified, which, being known, brought many of the neighbours (ten or twelve in a night) to watch with the family. T.E. foolishly brought a gun with him to shoot the spirit (as he said), and sat in the corner. But as Job was coming home that night (having been abroad), the spirit met him in the lane near the house and told him that there was a man come to the house to shoot him. 'But', said he, 'thou shalt see how I will beat him.' As Job was come to the house, stones were thrown at the man who brought the gun (and he had sore blows), and in vain did some of the company seek to hide and defend him from the blows (for the stones did hit him and none other), so that he was obliged to go home that time of night. When the spirit spoke (which was not very often), it was mostly out of the oven by the hearth's side. He would sometimes, in the night, make some music with Harry Job's fiddle. One time, it struck the cupboard with stones, the marks of which were to be seen (if they are not there still).

Once he hit Job a gentle stroke upon his toe, when he was going to bed. Upon which Job said: 'Thou art curious in smiting.' To which the spirit answered: 'I can hit thee where I please.' They were, at last, grown fearless and bold to speak to the spirit. His speeches and actings were a recreation to them – seeing he was a familiar kind of spirit which did not hurt them, and informed them of some things which they did not know. An old man, more bold than wise, hearing the spirit just by him, and threatening to stick the spirit with his knife, had this proper answer from him: 'Thou fool! How canst thou stick what thou canst not see with thine eyes?' The spirit told them that he came there from Pwll y Gasseg (Mare's Pit) – a place, so called, in the adjacent mountain – and that he knew them all before he came there.

One notable passage was this: B., the wife of M.R. of L—l, desired one of the family to ask the spirit who had killed W.R., the Scotchman. As soon as Job came home, he did so. The spirit's answer was: 'Who bid thee ask that question?' Job replied: 'Blanch y Byd' ('Worldly Blanch'). (By which name B. was often mentioned afterward.) She was a creditable substantial woman, of no evil qualities, but that she was uncommonly industrious to gain the world – though still in an honest way – and she would also do some charities. (Some of her posterity are virtuous, creditable, substantial people.)

On Easter Wednesday, the spirit left the house, and took his farewell of the man of the house in these words: 'Dos yn iach Job' ('Farewell Job'). To which Job said: 'Where goest thou?' He was answered: 'Where God pleases.' The person whom he seemed chiefly to regard was Harry Job (if he regarded any, for the spirits of hell – the least wicked among them (for they differ much in degrees of wickedness) – cannot be thought to be right friends to men (who are enemies to God), or if they be so in any measure, it is from selfish views (as Dives in hell was concerned for his brethren upon earth (Luke 16:27, 28)). Doubtless, this was one of those sort of spirits which the Scripture in several places calls familiar spirits, and speaks much about them, warning the people of Israel from seeking after them (Leviticus 19:31). Which intimates, they would not have come to them if they did not seek after them, and therefore are more in fault in that respect than the spirits themselves; ordering the seekers after, and the workers with, familiar spirits to be stoned to death and to be destroyed from the land of the living (as not fit to be among men on earth but among the devils in hell – yea, very meet to be with the devils in hell, who desire their company on earth). This shows what a capital sin this was, which deserved an immature, violent death. It is mentioned as one of the monstrous sins of Manasseh, that he dealt with a familiar spirit (2 Chronicles 33:6). It is said, that the Lord slew Saul, king of Israel, because he asked counsel of one that had a familiar spirit (1 Chronicles 10:13, 14). They are called familiar spirits because they make some poor show familiarity, and do some kind of services. But their services are evil, and for evil ends.

This spirit at the Trewyn in Mynyddislwyn was of this sort. He never showed any signs of virtue and goodness in any respect. I choose not to think that it was one of the fallen angels (properly called devils), but a diabolized human spirit who had lived in sin and died in a state of enmity to God. I had once an opportunity to speak with David Job (whom I several times saw at the meeting at Penmaen, who seemed to me to be a sober man), and asked him about the agency of this spirit at his father's house. He owned the substance of what was reported, but hinted that the cause of the spirit's coming there was his brother Harry's making use of some magic spells (yet without a design of bringing the spirit there, but for some other, idle purpose). Harry Job was a scholar, and brought up his son to be a considerable scholar. He, for some time, kept school, and rose up to be a clergyman in the Church of England. I did not hear much commendation of him. He was a remarkable, beautiful young man, had a most lovely complexion, and his countenance very attracting to the sight. It is not easy to see the like of him.

Newport town

103. From D.J., of the town of Newport, I had the following remarkable account in July 25th, 1767:

Passing through the churchyard in the night, he came within about two yards distance from the ash-tree in the churchyard and heard a dismal groan (like that of a sick man), which somewhat discomposed him. When he was come over against the ash-tree, he heard it again, and then it was most terrifying. When he was passed two yards from it, he heard it the third time. He soon recollected himself and said: 'Whatever thou art, God is stronger than thee', and the terror left him. Some of the neighbours also heard the groan. It was a presage of death;

for there was then a sick man in the neighbourhood, who soon after died. Some years after, D.J. (who heard the groans) married this sick man's widow.

This looks, and for my part I have no difficulty to believe it, that the spirit (whether a fallen angel, but more likely a disembodied human spirit), who imitated the groans of the sick man to D.J., certainly knew that the sick man would die and that D.J. would marry his widow. I have said before (and now repeat it) that the spirits of eternity have a wonderful knowledge of future things (at least in relation to death). This D.J. is a good, religious man (the son, also, of a godly father and of a very good mother), and would not tell an untruth for any man's sake – a man for whom God did indeed a miracle to save his life from drowning many years ago.

104. Mrs Morgan of Newport, a godly gentlewoman, told me that (some years before) there were two or three persons drinking in a public house (two of them officers of excise). One of them, to show his courage and, it may be, because he did not believe the existence of spirits (there being of late, in the towns especially, much Atheism and infidelity taking place in the minds of men), said he would go to the charnel and fetch a skull from thence. He did so, and they judged it might be a woman's skull, though the grave nearly destroys the difference between male and female before the bones are turned into dust (and the difference then quite destroyed and known only to God). After they had seen it, he went with it back. But in coming from the church, a strong wind – like a whirlwind – blew about him, which brought with it a great terror, so that he declared he would not do such a thing again for much. His wife (a smart, sensible woman) told Mrs Morgan that, afterward, in the night, his cane (which hung upon the wall) did beat smartly against the wall, and she was sure that it was done by some spirit and no accidental thing.

Here was a witness of the being of spirits (directly and immediately) – in all likelihood, of the being of that spirit whose skull was wantonly disturbed.

105. I have heard of a man, who lived in my time (a man greatly estranged from all good), and was thought to use a dead man's skull to no good purpose, who, not long after, fell sick and lay in his bed above stairs. It was said that a man appeared to him with a skull in his hand, with which he gave him a violent blow upon his head, so that he cried out and his nose bled. They heard the blow below stairs, and were not a little troubled at it (as indeed well they might). He died some time after. Oh, that he had died penitently.

They who have gone through the troubles of life ought to rest in their graves until the resurrection and Last Judgement, when all shall receive from God according to what they have done in the flesh (from the judge of all (2 Corinthians 5:10)). The burning of the bones of the idolatrous priests of King Josiah is another thing, related in 2 Kings 23:16. They were the ministers of Satan, and the wrath of God justly reached into their graves, and burned the bones of these foul murderers. Extraordinary wickedness hath followed into the graves of some, and hath prevented many from going into the grave – as Jezebel, Jehoiakim, and the house of Jeroboam, etc. – which is the worst judgement upon the body that can be in this life.

Pant-teg parish

106. About the beginning of this century, Margaret Richard of this parish was gotten with child by one Samuel Richard (for which she was very sorry and ashamed). He promised to marry her and, on the day appointed, she went with two or three persons to Pant-teg church to meet him (who then lived somewhere in Glamorganshire). But he did not come, being sick (or pretending to be so). After long waiting, and seeing he did not come, she fell on her knees and prayed God he might neither have rest in this world nor in that which was to come.

Presently (after his death), he came to appear to her and to trouble her. He never did appear when the sun was on the sky, but always between sunset and sunrise. She sometimes saw him by her side, and she would sometimes say to him: 'What dost thou want?' or 'Be quiet! Let me alone'. Others saw him not, though she complained of his haunting her. But they often saw signs of his being with her, whence she came to be called Marged yr Yspryd (Spirit-Margaret). One notable sign was this (which was seen several times): for bringing the milk towards the house, and finding herself ready to faint, she would hastily throw the pail of milk upon the table and the milk would not spill upon the table, nor even move in the pail (which was indeed miraculous). And it came to be a practice with her to do this, which convinced all that saw it that it was the work of the spirit which haunted her.

Sometime or other, she came to the house of Mr Hercules Jenkins at Trostra. She stayed till it was late, in discourse with Mrs Jenkins about the apparition, who desired her to stay longer. Margaret answered: 'I must go now, or else shall be sure to meet with him in the way.' Mrs Jenkins, a sober, wise gentlewoman, advised her to speak to him, 'to tell him thou dost forgive him'. Margaret went away, and as she was going over a stile at the end of a footbridge where (like Balaam's ass, she had no way to go by him, either to the right or left) he stayed for her at the stile. Then she asked him what he wanted with her all along, to which he answered: 'I want nothing but do thou forgive me, and God will forgive thee. Forgive me, and I shall be at rest, and never trouble thee any more.' She did forgive him. He took hold of her hand, shook it in a friendly way and departed, and never appeared to her any more. Here is a lesson from the world of spirits against fornication, and a warning to people not to deal amiss with one another in this life. His hand did not feel like the hand of a man, but like moist moss. And before she forgave him, he seemed to have but half arms. But after she forgave him, he seemed to have full arms and bare up to his elbows. This story was told me by Justice Jenkins (the son of Mr Hercules Jenkins and of Mrs Joice Jenkins his wife) who had it from his honest, wise, virtuous mother. He related it to me March 1767, who farther told me that she had a daughter then living in the parish.

No man will question Mr Jenkins's veracity, who is either acquainted with him or hath heard of his character (a gentleman of too much goodness to falsify a story, and too wise to question the being of spirits). Here is another additional and remarkable proof of the being and apparition of spirits from the other world, which it would be unreasonable to question.

Risca parish

107. One W.J. (a religious man) was sent to fetch me to baptize his master's child. Upon the way, hearing him speak like a truly religious man, and enquiring how he came under religious impressions, he gave me the following extraordinary and wonderful account.

Being a great sabbath breaker at Risca village (where he used to go to break the sabbath), one Lord's Day, having played, and afterward gone to the alehouse and staying there till night, when he went towards home, he could hear something walking after him in the way. Turning to see what it was, he could see the likeness of a man walking, now, by his side. His face he saw not and he was afraid to look on it, as fearing it was not a man but an evil spirit. Therefore, he did not speak to it to wish him good night, and it was well he did not. This dreadful, dangerous apparition sometimes walked after him, sometimes by his side (always on his left side). At last, the man-like appearance came to appear like a great mastiff dog, whom he heard coming after him, and sometimes saw him on his left hand. At which, he was so terrified that he felt not his clothes about him, neither did feel his own weight – the terror was so great. And, which made it yet greater, after it had gone with him about half a mile, the dangerous companion – the hellish dog – blazed into a great fire (as large as a small field) with such a noise as the fire makes in burning gorse. When he came to the house, he went to bed without looking on the fire least he should faint (as they usually do who have seen evil spirits). He had a dismal night of it, thinking the evil spirit still near him. It was suggested to him that the devil might have gone away with him for his wickedness, and that if he amended not that the devil would have him. For some time he was serious and concerned to amend, yet after that he became vain and regardless (but not to break the sabbath as before, but was fully reformed by the preaching of the word).

He related this to some young people (his companions in vanity), who wanted to know the reason of his change. They gave him the hearing but mended little or nothing (so true is the saying from heaven: if they hear not the word, they will not hear though one from the dead came to warn them (Luke 16:30, 31)). Here is an instance of it in these young people, and in the young man himself (the relater of the extraordinary vision) – for that did not convert him.

This was one of the terrible apparitions I have heard of, and I have been thinking if an Atheist, a Deist, or Sadducee had the like trial which this man had, whether he could continue in the unreasonable monstrous unbelief of the being and apparition of spirits. One would think it is impossible.

St Mellons parish

108. In the parish of St Mellons (in Welsh: Llaneirwg), some time past, was heard the *cyhyraeth* coming the same way as the corpse was to come to church. Those that lived in the village near the church could not well sleep in their beds that night. Once, a certain boy (being sent to fetch a horse upon some occasion) heard it crying in the church – at first in one place, then, it removed into another place and cried there, and from thence into another place, where it rested. Some time after, a corpse was brought to the church to be buried, but some persons came and claimed the grave. They went to another place, and that was also claimed. They removed to a third place, and there had quiet (just as the boy declared). Now, it is plain that the boy told the truth of what he had seen, for he knew not what was to come to pass. On the other hand, this crying spirit exactly knew what would come to pass; the knowledge of spirits, good and bad, infinitely exceeds the knowledge of men upon earth. I never heard before of the *cyhyraeth* being in any part of Monmouthshire; it is chiefly to be heard in Carmarthenshire, etc.[52]

Trevethin parish

109. There was a woman born in this parish, who once was thought to be virtuous and well disposed, but afterward was alienated from God and gave to the lust of the flesh. After her death, she appeared to her brother (a truly religious man) in his sleep, and gave him a push on his breast to awaken him to more attention. He knowing in his sleep that she was dead, said to her: 'N. What dost thou here now?' Upon which, she groaned and said nothing. He then asked, where was she and how was it with her. Her answer was that she was in a sore, cold place, and that there was a sword over her head. When he said to her: 'Give God praise' (much such a word as Joshua said to the malefactor Achan: 'give glory to the God of Israel' (Joshua 7:19)), her answer was: 'No! I will not', and departed. Her brother thought he saw R.W.J. with her (with whom she had sinned against the Lord).

   They are in a cold place indeed who, after death, are sunk below the mercies of God, and the comfort of his mercies, where the warmth of his mercies never reaches. (When God's people, here on earth, are deserted, they are in the spiritual cold and sorely complain of it (Lamentations 3:16, etc.). Yet, it is not so cold as in hell.) And they shall not come into the sun again, for the sun of righteousness warmeth none in the bottomless pit. There is the eternal cold of discomfort and the tormenting fire of God's wrath. By the sword over her (woe and alas for it), nothing can be properly meant but the impending sentence of the final curse which shall be pronounced upon all the wicked in the great day of account: 'Then shall he say also unto them on the left hand, Depart from me ye cursed, into everlasting fire, prepared for the devil and his angels' (Matthew 25:41). Oh, that people were afraid of this endless sad condition.

110. Francis William Watkin and William White of this parish of Trevethin were friends and companions in life. But W.W. died, and after his death appeared to Francis after sunset whenever he could find him alone (and this continued for a year and a half to F.'s great trouble). One time, washing his feet at the well, F. saw W.W. and to avoid him (as he thought) he ran towards the house, but the spirit was before him; then he ran another way to avoid him, but he was still before him. When F. saw that, he fell down upon his knees and said: 'In the name of God, what wantest thou with me?' To which the spirit answered: 'Hadst thou done this long before, it had spared much trouble to me and thee.' Then W.W. desired him to take a razor or two (hid in the wall of a barn that is next to Pontypool), and bid him be sure to do it – and he would trouble him no more. At parting, the spirit bid F. to fall down upon his face to the earth and not look about, and bid him not fear if he heard a noise. The spirit did go, and presently there were so strong and loud a hollow as if all was going to pieces. But F. had no hurt, and he was no more troubled with the apparition.

That the spirits of men are troubled after death for hiding iron instruments and tools is fact proved by numerous instances, but there is a mystery in it that cannot be understood by men upon earth. The spirits who are troubled have never revealed it. I never heard of any who ventured to ask one of them about it and, if any did, I question whether any of them would have revealed the secret: for the spirits of eternity, both angels and men, good and bad, are very short in their accounts of the other life.

111. Many years did the spirit of Jenkin Parry appear, and to several after his death (having given away his large estate from his relation), for a warning to all around to beware of this kind of injustice, which gives so much trouble in the other world.

112. This puts me in mind of what was told me by an honest man, concerning Thomas Cadogan of Llanfihangel Llantarnam. He had a large estate (nearly reaching from the mountain to the river), and yet saw it not enough, but removed his landmarks (being ignorant of the Scripture which forbids it: Deuteronomy 19:14, or disobedient to it) farther off into the land of a widow woman (which was yet worse), in order to enlarge his own. This, after his death, was trouble to him and, therefore, he appeared to a woman of the neighbourhood, travelling by night, by a stile, which she was to pass over. She, in a surprise, not recollecting that he was dead, suddenly asked him: 'Mr Cadogan, what makes you to be here now?' To which he answered: 'I was obliged to come', and desired her to tell such a one to remove back the landmarks which had been long injurious to the widow woman. Presently, he vanished away. Upon which she recollected his death, and was much terrified. And well it was that it was kept out of her mind (like Nebuchadnezzar's dream) for a time. She declared the apparition and his request to the person he named, and it was done as he desired. He had no son but three daughters to inherit his estate. But, as if the judgement of God

followed the oppression, they were ill married and the estate is gone from the family.

Had Mr C. known and obeyed the word of the Lord (which forbids the oppression of widows and threatens for it (Exodus 21:21–3)), he would not have been troubled for injustice, and nothing like judgement had followed his posterity for it. But the world is still bad, oppressions are still continued and attempted, though there are warnings from heaven and hell against it, and judgements for it executed abundantly upon the earth, in all places and at all times.

113. Very many years ago, Hugh ——, a shoemaker of the parish and village of Merthyr Tydfil, Glamorganshire, was going home from Pontypool (whether by day or by night, I was not told – most probably in the misty dark day, for who would attempt to go by night from Pontypool to Merthyr Tydfil fifteen or sixteen miles by night). When he was come to the mountain from Pen rhiw traine, he could see a man walking before him, and sometimes by his side, at no great distance from him. He did not speak to him, to bid him good night (according to the usual manner), having some fear and oppression of spirit upon him (which hindered his speaking). He was willing and chose to think it was a man, until he looked upon his feet and saw they were not like human feet but like the feet of a horse. Then he believed it was not a man but an evil spirit that walked with him (in whose company it was dangerous to be), and justly feared. Surely, it was an un-clean spirit, for it had the feet of a horse (a beast of travel, indeed, but counted an unclean beast in the holy ceremonial law of God (Leviticus 11:3, 4)). Therefore, these unholy walkers to and fro through the earth (as Satan told the Lord he did (Job 1:7, 2:2)), do properly appear, as they should appear, with the feet not of clean but of unclean beasts. Either they will not appear with the feet of clean beasts out of the prejudice, or they durst not do it from fear of the lord of all things.

114. Long time ago, a man and a woman were going through the wood the west side of Pontypool by night, and talking together. They could see the resemblance of a woman, somewhat well dressed (with a high-crowned hat, such as the women wore in former times), coming towards them followed by a black dog. When she came to them, and passed by them, she made a most dreadful noise, crying: 'Ooh!' Presently, she rose up and did fly like mad over the trees, hedges, briars, and thorns till she was out of sight (at which they were amazed). Here was an apparition both seen and heard by two persons and they, proof of the being and apparition of spirits. Had only one person seen this apparition, it might have been a heavy trial which two persons together might bear without hurt. Most likely, she was a human spirit gone into the kingdom of darkness, and the black dog was a devil attending her. Oh, the misery of lost sinners!

115. Anne (the daughter of Herbert Jenkins and sister of the late Revd and eminent minister of Christ, Mr Herbert Jenkins of Maidstone in Kent), a lovely

young woman, eminently well disposed to what is good, gave me the following relation of an apparition, which she had seen in the daytime.

Going one evening to milk the cows by Rhiw-newynydd, and going through the wood under Rhiw-newynydd to seek them, she saw like a black man standing by a holly-tree. The bitch, which was with her, saw him also and ran towards him to bark at him, upon which he stretched out his black tongue. The bitch was frightened, and ran back to the young woman turning about her feet for fear. The young woman herself was much terrified, so that she could not use her tongue. She went on, found the cows, and brought them back to their own field from whence they had strayed.

Passing by the holly-tree, back again, she feared to look upon it lest she should see the same sight again. But, being past it, she saw him again – very big in the middle and narrow at both ends – going before, treading very heavily, so that the ground seemed to tremble under him. He went towards a spring in that field which is under Rhiw-newynydd, called Ffynnon yr Yspryd (Fountain of the Spirit), because of an apparition formerly seen by it. About which, he fetched a turn and went over the stile from that field into the Rhiw-newynydd (the common way so called), and there he whistled so exceeding strong that the cwm (the narrow valley) echoed it back. Then he departed, and she felt herself well. I make no doubt of the truth of this from so virtuous a young woman, who indeed feared God.

116. This young woman's grandfather, William Jenkins, for some time kept school at Trevethin church. Coming home late in the evening, he used to see the fairies under an oak within two or three fields from the church between that and Pont Newynydd. And one time, he went to see the ground about the oak, and there was a reddish circle upon the grass, such as have been often seen under the female oak, called in Welsh *brenhinbren* (giant oak-tree), wherein they danced.

He was more apt to see them on Friday evenings than at any other day of the week. Some say, in this country, that Friday is apt to differ often from the rest of the week with respect to the weather; that, when the rest of the days of the week are fair, Friday is apt to be rainy or cloudy and, when the weather is foul, that Friday is apt to be more fair. If there is anything in it, I believe it must be with large and frequent exceptions. Yet, there may possibly consist with some measure of reality in the matter. (But of this I am no judge, having neglected to make observation of the matter.) However, the prince of the kingdom of darkness is called the prince of the power of the air, and doubtless not for nothing so called (Ephesians 2:2).

The fairies dance in circles (which some writers, on the side of infidelity, unreasonably explain another way) in dry places; the Scripture saith that the walk of evil spirits is in dry places (Matthew 12:44) – chiefly under the oak-tree (the female oak, more especially). This is likely because of its more spreading branches and of a greater shade under it. It is perhaps, also, and very probably, because of the superstitious, idolatrous use made of it beyond other trees in the dark times of paganism – which is an apostasy from God and true religion in which the spirits of darkness delight. Formerly, in the days of ignorance (when men had no knowledge and faith in God), it was dangerous to cut down the female oak in a fair, dry place. Some were said to lose their lives for it, by a strange aching pain which admitted of no remedy (as one of my ancestors did). But now that men have more knowledge and faith, this effect follows not.[53]

117. P.W. lived at the Ship in Pontypool, and was born, also, in Trevethin parish. She was an honest, virtuous woman who, when young and going to school, at one time saw the fairies dancing in a pleasant dry place under a crab-tree. She saw them like children, much of her own size. Hearing pleasant music among them, she went to them, and was induced to dance with them. She brought them into an empty barn to dance. This she did at times, both going and coming from school, for three or four years. Though she danced so often with them, yet she could not hear the sound of their feet; (they were spirits, and had no feet to sound with). Therefore, she took off her shoes that the might not make a sound with her feet (which she imagined was displeasing unto them). Some in the house, observing her stockings, said: 'This girl walks in her stockings to school.' But she did not tell them of her adventure with the fairies. They had all blue and green aprons, all of a small stature, and looked oldish.

They might well look oldish, as having their existence long before (none on earth knows how long). Neither doth the appearance of youth and beauty become the children of darkness. To appear young and glorious is the property of the angels of heaven, and not of the spirits of hell who live in sin and misery – even of those who are least in the hellish state, and but just in it on the other side of the unpassable gulf between heaven and hell, mentioned by our Saviour (who perfectly knows heaven and hell, and all the devils in hell). For there are many sorts of them – some worse than others – as our Saviour declares: 'This kind can come forth by nothing but prayer and fasting' (Luke 16:26; Mark 9:29)).

All the spirits of hell cannot make as good appearance and divert themselves in the hellish state, as the fairies do (who are nothing else, after all the talking about them, but the disembodied spirits of men who lived and died without the enjoyment of the means of grace and salvation). When she gave over going to them to dance, they showed their displeasure. And because they could not prevail, they did hurt her by dislocating one of her walking members (which was afterward put in place). Here is one instance of their malignity, and shows to whom they belong.

But, it seems, this girl – who was so long with them, and heard the music so often – learned none of their tunes. Yet, there is in the county a tune called the 'Tune of the Fairies'.[54] Perhaps it is a tune learned from them (which they say was very difficult to do), or a name devised and given to the tune from mere fancy. The tune which goes by this name is (in my apprehension) a well-composed tune of curious parts: the bass and tenor well-answering to one another, and somewhat brisk and long. If it was learned from the fairies, it may justly be apprehended to have something very curious in the composition, and the sound expressive of something – if not in their condition, yet of something in their disposition – which a curious mind would have some delight to know. But, at present, it is one of the innumerable things of eternity not to be known in the course of time.

118. About the year 1760, John Llewelin, a Breconshire man born (and a tailor working with Benjamin Jenkins, living in the parish of Trevethin), was coming home by night from Cwm y gollen. Being come into a field called Mynach (Monks' field), where it was a deep, hollow, woody pit of ground, he heard as it were the sound of a big, strong bird flying out of it. But there was something too strong and terrifying in the sound. Presently after, he saw like a bowl running before him; after that, a dark blackish cur-dog going along with him; and, after that (which was a yet more terrifying), a great dog – as big as any bear-dog – walking by his side, with one eye towards him (which was very terrifying indeed).[55] Now, he drew down his hat over his eyes so that he could only see the way just before him, and that he might not see the dreadful-looking great dog. It also came to stand between him and the stile he was to go over, which obliged him to go over the hedge. Then he saw, first a calf and then a hart skipping before him. At last, he could not see this stile and, therefore, went over the hedge to Pen y Lasgarn lane.

Now, he could see the resemblance of a young man (a gentleman's huntsman) with whom he had been acquainted (and had been his companion in drinking and vanity) standing in the lane before him (as if he wanted to speak with him), and walked with him part of the way. At first, J.L. was glad to see him, till he recollected that the young man was dead two years before, and was, then, afraid . . . but he lost sight of him. Then, he saw like a bowl rolling before him towards the wood before him. When J.L. came in to W.J.'s field, the horses were so exceedingly frightened at the sight of the young man that they ran so as to tear the ground.

J.L. came to his master's door weeping and crying and, being let in, told his master and mistress what he had seen and desired his master to be in bed with him. But his mistress, being frightened by the relation, could not part with her husband (especially as, at that time, they heard some puffs of strong wind about the house, though elsewhere it was the calm). However, both the master and mistress were willing to sit up and watch with him. In the meantime, his master began to tell him that he feared J.L. had been doing some wickedness with that person who had appeared to him. J.L. absolutely denied he had done any great scandalous thing, except drinking and being very vain. His master also advised him to reform, for J.L. was light and vain and did not go to hear the word of God. He did reform a little, but afterwards relapsed and went to live in Monmouth town. His master (who told me this story) declared that he heard his workman relate this account in many places without ever varying in his story – an argument that he was careful to tell the truth.

Here is another strong proof of the being of spirits. For could any man's eyes be so often deluded, without cause, to see so many things which we had no reality? And, if his eyes could be supposed to be thus deluded, why not the eyes of some others? Or, can this man be supposed to divine this without any cause or any selfish end to serve by such a relation?

119. Mr Thomas Williams, who lived in Trevethin parish, was sometime agent in the ironworks. He and a Mr Hanbury, going over Eglwys Ila mountain in company with another man early in the morning, could see a white thing in the form of a pyramid. It was broad at the bottom and narrowing towards the top, passing on the side of the way before them, inclining to cross their way, and went on (as they thought) as swift as a horse. Upon which, his companion said to Thomas Williams Thomas: 'What is that?' Being a fearless man, W.T. called out to it: 'A hey!' Upon which, it stood and moved not a step farther. They passed by it and ventured not to speak to it, though it seemed to stay for them at the call. Then they feared, lest it should change its appearance in to some terrible form, or blaze into a great blaze of fire. Truly, there was some danger of it – from a too bold call upon at a spirit of darkness. (That most heavenly Mr Thomas Brooks said in one of his books, it is ill jesting with four things: one, was sin; two, with Satan; three, with the Scripture; and fourth, with the majesty of God.) They thought the visional pyramid to be about ten yards long upwards, and about ten yards abroad at the bottom. Its form was very notable, and seemed to represent its state and disposition: that it grew narrow upward, and into nothing heavenward (as a pyramid doth in the natural heavens or the air); but was broad downward – backwards from the heaven towards the earth and hell – as far as the earth gave it a place to do. What other reason had it to appear in this odd form?

I have often observed (in many instances too tedious to relate) that there are many circumstances in the apparitions of spirits, both good and bad, which denote their state and disposition. I will instance only in one out of Scripture, even in the apparition of the angel Gabriel to Zacharias (Luke 1:11–20). The words are an extraordinary account of the appearance of the angel Gabriel to Zacharias (a holy priest in the Jewish Church), together with the place of his standing, his posture, and speech to the priest. But, now, I am only to take notice of the place of his standing, and posture in the place:

1. Of the place where the angel stood. It was on the right side of the altar of incense (which represented Christ in his exalted state). And where could the angel as properly appear as in the temple? And where in the temple, as at the altar of incense? For there was no Ark in the second temple for him to stand by. For if there had, it would have been a more proper place than the altar, because the cherubims of glory were placed in the Ark, which represented the angels in connection with Christ and in his presence in heaven. But, then, had the Ark been in the most holy place in the second temple, and had the angel stood by it, Zacharias could not see him to converse with him. Therefore, no place was so proper for the angel to appear at the Altar in the sanctuary, where the priest offered the typical incense to God.

2. Nor at the altar could the angel properly appear, but only at the right side of it. For if he stood beyond it, he would then have had his back towards the holy place – representing heaven, the habitation of the angels (called therefore the angels of heaven). He would also have stood directly in Zacharias's face (the glory of whose countenance the priest could not have born), and also stand, as it were, between the priest and the holy place, and in a way of the incense (which he directed towards the holy place which represented heaven). Therefore, this would have been no proper place for him to appear in. The same impropriety would have been if he stood before the altar, and he would have stood in the priest's way to perform his office. Therefore, he did well not to stand before the altar.

3. Nor would it have been proper for him to stand on the left side of the altar, as if he had been out of Christ's favour. (For the left hand, is typical and meta-phorical in Scripture, and signifies being out of favour; for so we are to understand Matthew 25:41, where the wicked are said to be at Christ's left hand on the Day of Judgement.)

4. And beyond all, it was not proper for him to stand upon the altar (great as he was), as if he was superior to Christ, and Christ under and below him. Amos 9:1 saith that he 'saw the Lord standing by the altar'. I am glad the word is not: 'I saw an angel standing upon the altar', and that such expression is not in the text; for it would have been a stumbling block to me had such a word been in Scripture. But it is an everlasting delight to me to observe the wisdom and propriety of everything in God's word, and that it is a word every way worthy of the wisdom of its author (and no stumbling block in it but to ignorant and erroneous minds, who use not the right way to understand it). Therefore, the angel had no proper place to stand at the altar, but on the right side of it (and therefore he wisely appeared). In every other place about it, he would have been faulty in circumstance. Here is an instance of the perfection and rectitude of angels in their motions and agencies. They have never erred in thought, word, or action – and never will. How great the happiness of men that shall arrive to the same perfection (Hebrews 12:22–3).

120. Evil spirits often appear either willingly or unwillingly in significative circumstances. Some have been seen like men, but with the feet, not of sheep and cows, but of horses, and some not with fingers (which are useful members), but with claws, the destructive members of beasts and birds of prey. I know a good woman who, going from a place of worship by night, was followed by a black sheep a long way. For some time, she thought it a black ewe, but following her a long way and leaping every stile. After, she wondered at it and told a pious young woman who walked before her, who would not turn back to look on her. The first time she told her of it, the young lady said nothing to it. The second time she told her of it, the answer the good woman had (if I remember right)

was: 'Come thou on!' The third time, the good woman spoke strongly: 'Why Mary! Here is a sheep again.' Yet, the young lady would not turn back to look on it, as being either afraid to do it or was hindered by the evil spirit from looking (for they care not to appear to two persons at once).

Being not able to prevail with her good companion to look back – the black ewe still following and very near to them – she turned back to look upon the ewe. And, behold, the ewe had a dog's mouth, though it had the appearance of a sheep (it was a sheep with the dog's head) – the picture of too many hypocrites in the Church of God who, though they appear like sheep, yet are black with sin and have dog-like mouths of reviling and calumny.

I myself once met with a spirit in the way, which appeared in a significative circumstance of its condition. Going home one night from the meeting-house, and being near the bridge over a small river in the way, I could see the resemblance of a man coming hastily down the lane towards the bridge, as if in haste to come over it before I came to it. It seemed to be all life without any bodily weight, which indeed it had not; it came very near but did not pass by me, but went at the river making a noise in the water. I, then, perfectly knew what it was, and yet had no fear. Having passed the bridge, I heard the cracking of sticks in a hedge and then I felt a terror about me, which followed me till I was near the house. When it was near me, it had this resemblance of a man, except the head which was not a man's head, but little and deformed, and difficult to be described. I suppose it was the spirit of an ignorant man who had no head of knowledge (who lived in a little house near the bridge now demolished, and the stones removed to another place a long while before). It appeared very narrow also towards the head.

121. In the year 1740, I and my wife removed from the parish of Mynyddislwyn into an empty house called the 'Transh', not far from Pontypool in the parish of Trevethin. We heard that the house was troubled by an evil spirit before we came to it, but there was no place open for us to go but that. Here we had numerous and great experience of the being of an evil spirit in a house, in the space of twelve years (for so long I and my dear excellent spouse dwelt in that house). To speak of all its actings and signs of its being there would be too tedious by far. I shall speak, therefore, of it in the general, and only some particulars as it shall come in my way.

It did not indeed destroy anything (either within or about the house), nor did much appear (for we must by no means wrong the devil), but made divers kinds of noises. If we stayed up after ten o'clock, it would stir more and be more uneasy. Every night throughout the whole year, we might hear it after ten. Its manner was to strike a blow near, or upon, the stable (which was near the house); the next blow would be at the door; and a third, in the house (oftenest upon the pewter dishes). The good woman (my spouse) used to go to bed before me, and for some time I stayed up in order to read and write, but I could make no hand of it for the stirs. For after I heard the first stroke, I expected to hear the second and, after the second, to hear the third stroke – there being no great distance between them. I did sometimes speak to it, and reproved it, telling him: 'Dost think to make me afraid? I will not go from here till I please', etc.

It made other kind of stirs. I have heard it like the grunting of a hog, the jetting of the weasel (unclean creatures – for it was an unclean spirit that made the sounds) and, once, like a coughing of a horse above stairs.[56] After we were gone to bed, if we were to hear any bad news the next day, it would strike the table – as it were with a rod. Sometimes the stroke would be gentle and low, sometimes smart and strong, according as the news was very bad or not. This was a frequent exercise of it, whereby it was a frequent prophet of evil to us, and gave us the vexation beforehand. This plainly showed to us that it knew all that passed in the country about, and that, therefore, it must either go about to know what came to pass or was visited by spirits who went about. We are to remember that Satan told the Lord that he walked the earth to and fro (Job 1:7; 2:2). There are, therefore, far more news and knowledge of those things on earth in hell than earth itself – things better and more particularly known in hell than on earth by far – and much more knowledge also of things to come.

Often people heard the sound (by night and by day), like the sound of a horse coming towards the door, so that we often opened the door to see who was there, and saw there was none. It was perfectly the sound of a horse's feet (only a little more low and soft), and there was no other difference in the sound.

122. Another time, my spouse went to see her brother and his family. I was then at home and to be myself in a house that night, alone. I confess, I was somewhat afraid (for the truth must be spoken when it is necessary to do so, whether it be for or against one). I knew, indeed, it could not hurt a hair of my head, and I could hear its stir. But, if it should make a stir hard by me, just when I was going to sleep (as I feared it would do), that would be to me a most disagreeable, startling thing. However, for shame, I resolved to bear it out. Often, I had barred and locked the door.

An acquaintance and a neighbour (who was a tailor by trade and a very knowing, religious man) called at the door and came in. I asked him would he stay with me that night. I was resolved not to press him to it, but had rather he should stay, and he did, and came with me to sleep. While we were talking about this spirit in a house – and he was greatly admiring my spouse's courage and faith (for he heard of the before-related passage) – a heavy blow was given to the round table, just below us. I told him: 'There, a stir is!' He answered: 'I do hear it.' This made him to admire her more than before, and he spread it about the neighbourhood (having had an experience of what was reported before). This made her to be much admired in the neighbourhood, and others at a distance (less acquainted with her), hearing of this, and beholding the goodness of her personal appearance, look upon her in the market with attention and respect.

123. One time, when I was gone from home to preach (as I often did in those times), the good woman (my spouse) being by herself (for we had no ability to

keep a maid, and she would have none to keep from fear in the night as King Solomon had, who had less faith (Canticles 3:7, 8)), being gone late in the evening to a neighbour's house, returned in the beginning of the night. When she came to the stile, which entered into the yard before the house, there appeared a light in one of the windows of the house, and presently in three windows – one below, and the two others above stairs. This plainly told her it was a spirit light, there being no candlelight in the house, and the fire was little when she went out (it being in the summertime). When she saw it, she was on a sudden somewhat startled, but presently said: 'I do not care what is there, in the name of God I will go to my house', and went. When she opened the door, she confessed that she then felt a disagreeable influence passing over her, but went in and stirred the fire to make it flame and give light. That was all that passed then.

We had kept the stir in the house much a secret till now. My spouse (who was a wonderful woman) was not loquacious. Her way of speaking was rather in short sentences with authority, and constant care to speak aright in the fear of God. But happening to relate this passage, it flew about the neighbourhood – none questioning the truth of what she said and admiring her courage, as indeed well they might.

Montgomeryshire

124. About the year 1712, Edward Lloyd, in the parish of Llangurig, was very sick. Those about him thought there were some people talking about the house. Accordingly, they went out to see but could see nothing (for the talk of spirits was nearer to them in the house and in the room where they were). Soon after, they heard these words, spoken by something unseen: 'Y mae nenbren y tŷ yn cracio' ('The uppermost beam of the house (the rafter at the top) cracketh'); then, soon after: 'Fe dyr yn y man' ('It will presently break'); and, soon after, heard the same voice say: 'Dyna fe yn torri' ('There it is breaking') – just when he died (which much affected the company, as indeed well it might).

Pembrokeshire

125. If this be not enough to confirm the exquisiteness of their knowledge of burials, I have another notable proof of it from under the hand of Mr Morris Griffith (a man truly religious, and a lively preacher of the Gospel among the Baptists), which came to pass in Pembrokeshire, as follows:

'About eleven or twelve years ago, when I kept school at Pontvaen parish in Pembrokeshire, as I was coming from a place called (in Welsh) Tredavid, and was come to the top of a hill, I saw a great light down in the valley (which I wondered at, for I could not imagine what it meant). It came to my mind that it was a light before a burying, though I never could believe before that there was such a thing. The light, which I saw then, was a very red light, and it stood still for about a quarter of an hour in the way which went towards Llanychlwydog church. I made haste to the other side of the hill that I might see it farther, and from thence saw it go along to the churchyard, where also it stood still for a little time and entered into the church. I stood still, waiting to see it come out, and it was not long before it came out and went to a certain part of the churchyard where it stood a little time, and then vanished out of my sight.

Few days afterward, being in school with the children about noon, I heard a great noise overhead, as if the top of the house was coming down. I went out to see the garret, and there was nothing amiss. But in a few days afterward, Mr Higgon of Pontvaen's son died. And when the carpenter came to fetch the boards to make the coffin (which were in the garret), he made exactly such a stir in handling the boards in the garret as was made before by some spirit or spirits who foreknew the death that was soon to come to pass. And in carrying the body to the grave, the burying stood where the light stood for about a quarter of an hour, because there was some water across the way, and that the people could not go over it without wetting their feet, and were, therefore, obliged to stop there so long till those who had boots helped them over. The child was buried (as near as I could guess) in that very spot of ground in the churchyard where I saw the light stopped after it came out of the church and vanished away. This is what I can boldly testify, since I have seen and heard what I relate. A kind of thing which, before, I could not believe' (Morris Griffith, 1777).

Here, everyone may see, was a very particular and wonderful knowledge of what came to pass beforehand, though it is but what is apparent in most of these kind of apparitions. But whence they have it, is the question? We cannot see that they can have such knowledge from the influence of the stars, though they have an influence upon the lives and deaths of men (whatever many say to the contrary). Where else these spirits of darkness have this particular knowledge will remain a secret in the present life, but not in the life to come.

126. From this county I heard many things of apparitions, all of them too tedious to relate. From all of them, however, something profitable might be learnt in relation to this world and the next by an ingenious mind who hath the noble skill to turn every thing to mental profit. Some of them are these following:

About forty years ago, there lived in this county one John Jenkin (a schoolmaster and, also, a conjuror). Being known to be such, one of his scholars (who was alive some time ago), having a mind to it, told his master he had a curiosity to see the devil. His master told him he might, if he had courage for it, but told him (withal) that he did not choose to call an evil spirit till he had some employment for him.

Sometime after, a man came to him who had lost some money, and desiring to know who had stolen them. 'Now', said the master to the scholar, 'I have some business for him.' That night, the conjuror and his scholar went into a wood and drew a circle, and came home. Some night after (and it was a fair, clear moon-shining night), they went into the circle and the conjuror called an evil spirit by his name. Presently, they could see a light and some motion in the sky afar off. After that, a bowl of light shot like lightning toward the circle and turned round about it. (I suppose to see if there was any gap in it, that he might come in and destroy them both.) The conjuror asked him who had stolen such a man's money. But, by his answer, he understood that that spirit knew not who had done it; so the master told the scholar that that spirit knew not who had done it, and that he must call another. Having sent that spirit away, the conjuror did call another and, presently (in answer to the call), the resemblance of a bull came flying through the air – so swiftly and fiercely as if he would go through them – and turned round about the circle. He asked this spirit, also, who had stolen the money, and received much the same kind of answer as from the former. The conjuror told his scholar (now almost dead with fear): 'This also won't do; I must call another.' This bold-hearted – too bold-hearted – Welshman was not afraid of those dreadful appearances and dreadful voices of these terrible and dangerous spirits of hell.

And after the young scholar was a little revived and recovered from his terror, his master (for, alas for it, he knew the names of several of the fallen angels of hell, which he had better been ignorant of) called another of them by name. And, behold (in answer to it), a spirit came out of the wood, all in white – as white as a linen sheet – much shining in the moonlight and coming towards the circle. When the conjuror saw him, he told his scholar: 'We shall now hear something from this.' When he asked him the same question, the spirit answered: he knew the man who had done this, told him who he was and other circumstances concerning that matter which the conjuror asked him. The young man (who was still alive in 1764) declared that neither of these spirits could speak and answer the conjuror till they had worked themselves into the human shape. But the man has never been as well as another man since that time.

127. Not far from Glanbrân in Carmarthenshire lived a tailor who was also a conjuror. Coming at a time into the house of Mr Gwynne of Glanbrân, Mr Gwynne began to talk to him about his conjuring, rather in the way of blaming him. The tailor was a little, mean-looking man. Mr Gwynne told him: he wondered how such a man as he was had the courage to look upon the devil. The man affirming he had that courage, Mr Gwynne (either designedly or inadvertently) happened to ask: 'Canst thou show him to me?' To this the man replied: 'You are not able to look upon him.' To this Mr Gwynne replied: 'What! Thou able to look upon him, and not I?' The man answered: 'If you are able to look upon him I will show him, if you will.'

The gentleman consenting, he went out (it was in the daytime) and made a circle, after the usual manner, in a little grove of wood in a field not far from the house. He called one of the fallen angels (now become a devil) into it. He returned to fetch the gentleman to see him, who met him just at the door, and said to him: 'Come with me, and you shall see him.' Mr Gwynne followed the tailor to the stile, which entered into the field where the horrible sight was. The tailor said to him: 'Look yonder. There it is!' As soon as the gentleman saw it, there was something so horrible and terrible in the sight that he said to the tailor: 'Oh, take him quickly out of my sight.' And so, he did. I remember not to have heard anything amiss of this gentleman, but if he (after the manner of too many of the gentry) did not believe the existence and apparition of spirits, he had a rare and doubtless effectual conviction to his infidelity.

128. John James David, a tailor and said to be a man of great piety, was going by night through a fair plain called Blaenwaun in the parish of Cilrhedyn, Pembrokeshire. He saw a grove of wood with the leaves trembling in his way (as he thought), where no such thing really was. Having occasion to pass that way another time, he saw a couple of mastiff dogs fighting about the way. He thought once to turn back, but again recollecting he was in his way (and that God only tried his faith by this appearance) he was encouraged to go on, and the infernal dogs turned out of the way (for Satan cannot stand before strong faith (1 Peter 5:8–9)). Next time he came that way, the apparition was changed into two brands of fire striking against each other (a double sign of evil to come). Some time after, two wicked men quarrelled and one murdered another in that place (a wickedness seldom heard of in that part of the world). Here is another instance of the foreknowledge of spirits of things to come; they know many things to the third and fourth generation from the declared threat and the implicit promise of God contained in it (Exodus 34:6–7), and by forming a judgement about the tendency of contingents they can see far into futurities.

129. Mr D.W. of Pembrokeshire, a man of mean mental abilities, and religious, and far from fear and superstition, gave me the following account in relation to himself. He was travelling by himself through a field called the Cottesmore, where two stones are set up called the Devil's Nags (at some distance from each other) where evil spirits are said to haunt to trouble passengers. Once, passing by that way, he was thrown over the hedge and was never well afterward. Mr W. went with a strong, fighting mastiff dog with him, but suddenly could see another mastiff dog coming against him. He thought to set his own dog against him, but his own dog was exceedingly frightened and closed to Mr W.'s legs. Mr W., being yet without much fear, bowed down to take up a stone to throw at the other dog. Then, a flash of light opened upon him, and then he knew it was one of the infernal dogs of hell – one of those kinds of dogs against whom David prayed: 'Deliver my soul . . . from the power of the dog' (Psalms 22:20). Now, he was so terrified that he felt not his clothes about him, and he went the rest of the way in much dread and discomposure.

130. At another time, between sunset and dark night, he could see the likeness of a man but could not see his arms (and he was without a hat), at some distance

from him, going round about three or four times, and at the same distance from him. He spoke to it several times, and asked what it wanted, etc., but had no answer. As yet, he did not fear him, but said to himself: 'Perhaps it is somebody that wants the way', and so turned out of the way to give way to it. Then, a terror came upon him, which increased as be went on. (It is not good to give way to the devil (it makes him bolder), but to resist him courageously in the faith (1 Peter 5:8–9).) When he was got some distance from the place, and going up the hill, he looked back towards the place of the apparition and he saw there a ball of fire. When he came to the house the people saw him look bad and discomposed, and asked him if he had been frightened. He was ready to faint, though a stout man. They gave him some cordial, which kept him from fainting and recovered him from his trembling.

That as the appearance of angels is a sign of good so, I have observed, the extraordinary apparitions of evil spirits have often been signs of trouble to those that saw them. For so it came to pass upon this man with a witness.

131. In the year 1767, David Powel (the son of Rees Powel of Llanybyther parish, Carmarthenshire) gave me this relation:

His father (who was an honest man), being gone to see his brother who lived in Pembrokeshire (and was another sort of man), and having had a great difference with him, took his horse to go home by night (though he had eighteen miles to go). Being gone not far from his brother's house, he could see something odd by the wayside, at which his horse snorted and would by no means go forward.The horse was so affrighted that it made that odd sort of noise which horses sometimes will do when they are in great pain, in great rage, or greatly affrighted. When he suffered the horse to go back, it ran. He was sensible that the enemy was behind him, and the horse went madly on. He, then, prayed to God and thought the evil spirit went off, and the horse slackened pace. But, soon after, the evil spirit came again behind him, and then the horse again set running till he came to his brother's house, where he was obliged to tell them this as reason of his coming back.

This was an odd turn made by an evil spirit of the night, not easy to be accounted for. I would have thought it was the spirit of a dead relation who (Dives-like) wished well to his brethren, even out of hell (Luke 16:27–31).

132. I made an excursion into Kybidiog in Pembrokeshire, hearing of a grave-stone which had the Latin letters upon it. When I went to seek for it, it was taken from the grave and put on a hog sty belonging to Mr Perkins of Rhadland.[57] I crept into the hog sty, with a candle in my hand to blacken the letters with the flame of it to make them legible. Mr Perkins (a friendly, affable man), seeing my curiosity, said that, for that satisfaction of the curious, it should be taken off that I might read the stone writing in an easier posture. I opposed his removing it, but in vain. The words upon the stone seemed to me to be 'Valantine Raave',

meaning, that the ground under it was the grave of Valantinus Raavus (for the name being inscribed in the genitive case implied sepultus (the grave)). This was the name of the Roman, and shows that the Romans extended to west Wales (as doth also Tŷ'r Polin, that is, Terra Paulini (Paulinus; his land), in Carmarthenshire, showeth).[58]

But, to the design in hand; after viewing this gravestone and being the occasion of its removal, I went that night into Mr David Harris (his house), a godly gentleman in the neighbourhood among the Dissenters. That night, in bed, I was greatly troubled by an evil spirit, so that I could by no means sleep. Though I saw nothing, yet it moved the bedclothes and caused such a terror as caused me to sweat and my flesh to tremble all night until the cock crowed. I believe it was because I meddled with the dead man's gravestone and, likely, it was his spirit that troubled me. But they shall be known in eternity where everything (the least that concerneth us) shall be known; for something for instruction shall at last be obtained from everything that have passed in the world, both in heaven and hell, though this among many other things and things of far greater importance – yea, of the greatest importance and consequences – are little considered by the ignorant stupid world.

RADNORSHIRE

133. In the year 1737, in the house of Edward Roberts, in the parish of Llangynllo, came to pass a strange thing.

As the servant man was threshing, the thresher was taken out of his hand and thrown upon the hay-loft. He minded it not much, but being taken out of his hand three or four times gave him a concern, and he went to the house and told it. Edward Roberts not being at home, his wife and the maid made light of it and merrily said they would come with him to keep him from the spirit, and went there (the one to knit and the other to wind yarn). But, they were not long there before what they brought there were whipped out of their hands and tumbled about in their sight, and they went away more sober than they came there, and shut the barn door. It is not wisdom but folly to make sport of such things. For the agency and the apparition of spirits, whether good or bad (if men were wise enough to consider), is generally very significative and of serious consequences, as it was here. For, presently after, they could see the dishes on the shelf move backwards and some things also thrown about, and they could see them move to and fro. Most of the earthen vessels were broke, especially in the night (and they had great vexations), and the pewter dishes much damaged. Things were so thrown down in the night that, next morning, they could scarce tread but upon some wrecks upon the ground.

This, being noised abroad, brought the neighbours together to visit them in kindness. Some came from far to satisfy their curiosity (some from Knighton). One came from thence to read, confident he would silence the evil spirit, but had the book thrown out of his hand up stairs. There were stones cast among them, and sometimes upon them, but they were not much hurt by them, though they were often hit with them. Some iron was cast among them from the chimney, and they knew not whence it came. The stir continued there about a quarter of a year. At last, the house took fire about the door, which the woman of the house quenched with water. But the next day, or soon after, the house took fire, which they attempted in vain to quench. They saved most of the furniture, but the house was burnt to the ground, so that nothing but the walls and the two chimneys stood as a public spectacle to them that went to and came from Knighton market.

The apparent cause of the disturbance was this: Griffith Meredith and his wife (the father and mother of Edward Roberts's wife) were dead, and their son, who was the heir of the house, listed himself a soldier and went out of the country. Roberts and his wife, who were tenants in the house that was burnt, removed into their father's house (now dead). The house being decayed, they repaired it and claimed it as thinking it their own and that her brother would never return. But, in that year, the brother unexpectedly came home thinking to see his father. He wondered to see the house altered and, making enquiry, went to his sister and claimed the house. She refused, as having been at charge with it. At last, he desired only a share of it (which she also refused). At last, he desired but two guineas for it which, she still refusing, he went away for Ireland, threatening his sister that she should repent for this ill dealing (and she had cause to repent).

Now, here was very plainly the work of some spirit, enough to convince or at least confound an atheist of the being of spirits. But whether it was her brother's own spirit (after his death) or an evil spirit, which he employed to work this revenge upon an unnatural sister, cannot be determined. But, the last is more certain.

134. In Llynwent (a place so called in this county), there an old chapel had been built (and appears to be so by its fashion), but now turned to secular use. At a certain time, when the man of the house and his wife were gone somewhere else upon occasion (while the rest of the family were at supper), three of the servants heard the sound of horses coming towards the house. Thinking their master and mistress were coming, they said: 'There, they are coming', and went out to meet them – but they saw nothing, wondered at it, and the rest laughing at them. They sat at the fire and heard, as it were, the sound of people passing by them, and going upstairs, and talking among themselves, which – they telling – the others at the table laughed at them. Herein, their levity (too apt to be on such occasions) was wrong. For, behold, not long after, three of the family sickened and died.

Now, were they more in the right who heard a sign of what came to pass, or they who wantonly laughed at them? Some of them also heard the mill grinding (when none was in it), and like the sound of the falling of trees – both signifying the deaths that followed (for death, in Scripture, is resembled to the falling of trees: 'Where the tree falleth, there it shall be' (Ecclesiastes 11:3)).[59] The grinding of the mill might be (nay most likely was) a sign of the much grinding of corn and making of bread occasioned by the burials. The foreknowledge of spirits of the end of men's lives is wonderful.

THE CONCLUSION INFERRED FROM THESE ACCOUNTS

Are not all these numerous instances, together, sufficient to convince all the Sadducees and atheistical men of the age (or any age in the time to come) of the being of spirits, and of their appearance in the world? Surely, one would think they are, and that it is monstrously unreasonable to believe the contrary. The Scripture of truth saith, that by two or three witnesses every word shall stand (Matthew 18:16). And should not the being of spirits be believed – attested by more than threescore witnesses, which carry in them the plain, undeniable marks of the judgement and sincerity of the writer, and of the authenticity and truth of the relations? And what confirms it much more is that these relations are but few of many more that can be produced to prove this great interesting subject: the being of spirits and the resurrection (absolutely depending upon the being of spirits). For why should the body be raised if there is no spirit of life to dwell in it? And the resurrection is so great and interesting a subject of faith and religion that the denial of it deserved the sentence of excommunication (out of the Church of God), by the Apostle (2 Timothy 2:17, 18).

Will nothing serve the prevailing human corruption, but either the over-believing of things that have no reality; believing things, more than they are, otherwise than they are; or the not believing things that really are; or as far as they are; and being against the necessity of believing them in order to obtain felicity? Some are so reduced in the faculty and exercise of believing that they scarce believe their own existence as rational men. (Some deny their own spirits, and lay they are mere machines.) So strong hath unbelief prevailed in the world, that the faculty of believing – which God created in the understanding of the first man (the parent of mankind) – is so impaired in many of his fallen posterity as to be in some nearly annihilated into nothing, and in all mankind by nature so weak, that it cannot believe the things necessary to salvation without being repaired by the special grace of God (for which cause faith – which is the true exercise of belief – is called the gift of God to salvation (Ephesians 2:5, 8, etc.)).

The instances produced in this book prove sufficiently the being of spirits, of angels and men – good and bad. This, again, helps to believe the being of God, who is a spirit and the father of spirits of all flesh (Numbers 27:15–16), and should influence the lives of men in order to a due preparation for the future world and immortality.

Epilogue

The significance of Jones's collections of spirit narratives does not stand or fall on their ability to establish irrefutably the existence of a world of spirits. They represent a spellbinding and illuminating example of both paranormal and Welsh visual culture. Jones describes apparitions which are sometimes striking in their oddity. Equally remarkable is his ability to visualize, in a vivid and earthy manner, the sites these bizarre and often malevolent beings stalked. Jones evoked a rural landscape that would have been very familiar to readers in eighteenth-century Wales. As a result, the apparitions alarm not because they appear (as so often in nineteenth-century ghost-stories) in mysterious and remote places (of a frightening aspect). On the contrary, like awful crimes, they are the more appalling for having occurred within a customary and an otherwise reassuring domain – the pastoral seclusion of lanes, farms, fields, forests, rivers, and mountains with perfunctory names and mundane associations.

The clarity with which Jones described the various supernatural entities renders his collections an important source for studying the iconographical origin, the significance and the evolution of apparition types. Apparitions are a visual phenomena, 'seen' either in the mind's eye of a witness or as part of the external world. They are, in an honorary sense, artefacts, too – the product and representation (or projection) of the religious imagination, usually appearing as substantial as ordinary objects, places, or persons. Apparitions possess attributes of shape, colour, and significance – just like tangible visible images. (Accordingly, they are as much within the province of the historian of art and visual culture as within that of the theologian and psychic investigator.) The visual 'style' of apparitions is often fashioned by the unconscious influence of religious images (where available), as well as prevailing theological notions regarding the nature of supernatural entities. Consequently, Jones's accounts reveal as much about the witness's mental furniture and convictions as about the putative nature of the entities themselves. In these respects, his collections provide a welter of material for investigating the representation of the occult in art and literature in relation to the imaginings of spiritual entities by witnesses.[1]

Treating apparitions as (transient) artefacts does not imply that (like the atheists and materialists against whom Jones's book was, designedly, a tub-thumping polemic) one need deny their supernatural basis. Apparitions can be real and at the same time idiomatic of the witness's culture: preconceptions about what an apparition *ought* to look like act as an interpretative filter which conditions the way a witness perceives and describes a phenomenon (that is, they simply make sense of the strange and unknown by reference to the familiar and known).[2] Nor does a belief in apparitions in theory mean that one must subscribe to every account recorded by Jones. (Testimonies given by witnesses after an evening spent in an alehouse are, perhaps, the most suspect.) Indeed, one may be sceptical of every account without abandoning faith in the supernatural, for the veracity of these narratives (as of all accounts of paranormal phenomena) is predicated upon not only the existence of a spiritual realm but also the reliability of the witness's experience and the integrity of transmission — the accurate communication of that experience to others. As with all testimonies to paranormal sightings, the witnesses in Jones's accounts describe their experiences either verbally or literally. The recreation of the apparitional image in words, passed from person to person (in a game of Chinese whispers sometimes over several generations), reforms and deforms the initial experience, often considerably. Even though the vast proportion of Jones's accounts described encounters which supposedly took place within sixty years of the book's publication (that is, within his lifetime), they have inevitably suffered from this process of reconstitution to varying degrees.

More often it is Jones's confident assertions about their authenticity that give rise to our gravest doubts. He was sometimes embarrassingly credulous: too eager to believe, too desperate to persuade, and too quick to deduce too much from too little. Not once did Jones countenance the possibility that any of the supposedly supernatural phenomena could have been due to a natural cause. Jones's weakness was shared by his contemporary and fellow collector of supernatural relations, John Wesley (1703–91), who, 'after satisfying his under-standing that supernatural acts and appearances are consistent with the order of the universe, sanctioned by Scripture, and proved by testimony too general and too strong to be resisted . . . invalidated his own authority, by listening to the most absurd tales with implicit credulity, and recording them as authenticated facts'.[3]

The insistence, which underlies Jones's work, that apparitions were the evidential proof of the spiritual realm, is wholly absent in nineteenth- and early-twentieth-century collections of Welsh folklore. In an age in which belief in ghosts, witches, and fairies was largely outdated,[4] folklorists aimed not to challenge scepticism, but to provide a historical account of spirit narratives as only one of a number of other categories and examples of myth, tale, custom, and superstition.[5] While, in keeping with Jones's collections, works such as William Howells's *Cambrian Superstitions, Comprising Ghosts, Omens, Witchcraft, Traditions, Etc.* (1831), Wirt Sikes's *British Goblins* (1880) and Jonathan Ceredig Davies's *Folk-Lore of West and Mid-Wales* (1911) were concerned to establish the origin, reliability, and provenance of apparition accounts, they did not attempt to determine the authenticity of the sightings at source. Nor did they, like Jones, collect and comment out of a personal conviction and experience of his subject. Indeed, they assumed that the stories were no more than curious fictions, the origins of which were rooted in the ancient mythologies and philosophies of other countries and cultures. To the contrary, Jones held what Sikes called a 'poetico-religious theory', believing his accounts to be no 'cunningly devised fables' (to quote the Apostle Peter), but recent manifestations of the real agents of good and evil, whose origins were in the far more distant times of the Bible. Fairies and ghosts were 'part and parcel of the Christian faith';[6] possessed of a theological dimension; significative of spiritual conflict and moral imperatives; to be not only seen but also 'read' – and therefore requiring the interpretative gloss of the preacher to extract their exemplum (a dimension wholly absent from later collections of spirit narratives).

Jones was concerned about the essential nature and purpose of apparitions. Thus he writes of their genus rather more than their species, with little attention to those sub-classifications and categorizations of spirits and fairies which later writers conspicuously delighted in. Consequently, we find no reference in Jones's work to terms such as *pwca*, *coblynau* (mine fairies), *gwyllion* (mountain fairies), *ellyllon* (pigmy fairies), or types of goblin, like the *bwbach*, although, with the exception of goblins, Jones refers, in a general way, to apparitions of all these sorts and places.[7] Sikes suggests that since goblins were averse to piety, and Jones exhibited this attribute in abundance, this was the reason why he saw so few.[8] Sikes's collection describes many other types of apparition of which Jones makes no mention, such as doppelgangers, mermaids, and spectral villages under the sea. Their inclusion, in some cases, would not have assisted his argument. For instance, the doppelganger (or apparitional double of a living person) implied that death and the afterlife were not, after all, the necessary pre-supposition or precondition of apparitions. Again, mermaids (belief in which may have stretched the bounds of even Jones's credulity) would have presented a profound theological difficulty. The conjunction of a woman and a fish confused the fundamental distinction between mankind and animal-kind, which God had established at the Creation (Genesis 1:22–7). Furthermore, unlike demons (which frequently exhibited a confusion of types), mermaids were physical rather than spiritual creatures and, as such, unserviceable to Jones's end. In these ways, their absence from *A Relation of Apparitions of Spirits* may reflect an astute editorial policy on his part.

Regardless of the fundamentally different outlook and purpose of Jones's apparition accounts, the sequel became a major source for nineteenth- and twentieth-century collections of Welsh folklore. Ceredig Davies and Sikes incorporate a liberal number of references to and retellings of Jones's narratives.[9] Howells includes several relations with certain similarities to those cited by Jones (in terms of the names for places, witnesses and informants, details and narrative development), but makes no mention of either Jones or his books.[10] This suggests that Howells's accounts were either derived, unacknowledged, from *A Relation of Apparitions of Spirits* or else recorded independently from the same sources as Jones's accounts. Thus Jones's relations, in some instances, may either have become or else echo folk tales.[11]

At the cusp of the twentieth century, Evangelical claims to visualize spiritual phenomena re-emerged in Wales. The context was, as it had been for Jones's book, religious revival and an atmosphere charged with emotion and expectation. As Jones had done, ministers and the lower orders of society – coalminers and agricultural workers, in this case – experienced and appealed to the phenomena as evidence for the existence of the spiritual realm.[12] However, during the revival of 1904–5, the phenomena comprised visions, which witnesses interpreted as having derived from God for good, rather than from the devil for evil (as many ghosts and spirits in Jones's day were believed to have done). Visions of Christ were the most common by far – the perceptible expression of God's love and means of redemption, which doctrines the revival emphasized above all others. In contrast to their eighteenth-century counterparts, Nonconformists in 1904 could more readily visualize Christ, along with the devil and angels, for engravings and litho- graphs printed in illustrated Bibles and devotional material during the nineteenth century furnished their imaginations with the raw materials for their mental portraits. Jones's accounts make no mention of apparitions of Christ. The author's Calvinistic sensibility would not have countenanced the representation of God, or other heavenly creatures, for that matter – he was reluctant to interpret even the radiant white children seen by David Thomas of Carmarthen- shire as necessarily an apparition of angels: 'for nothing childish belongs to [angels] . . . More likely they were some of the inferior saints in glory' (30).[13]

Several notable apparitions in Jones's book bear a striking resemblance to some of those seen in 1904–5, including fireballs and strange lights. A pastor in Abertillery, Monmouthshire saw, in a vision, a ball of fire (like that which followed a woman travelling in Mynyddislwyn) descend upon the church.[14] A star (similar to that seen in Breconshire by Walter Watkins (10)) featured in an extraordinary vision witnessed by Mary Jones and numerous others at the epicentre of the revival, in February, 1904.[15] Mary Jones was a Methodist farm woman who had lived all her life at Dyffryn on the west Wales seaboard. She described herself as the female counterpart of Evan Roberts (1878–1951) (the revival's figurehead), a prophetess, and a recipient of visions that were, like apparitions, both figural and abstract. The latter included an encounter with unusual luminescence and a brilliant star. Before the first appearance of the star, she saw a vision of a different type, one which bore more than a passing resemblance to Edmund Jones's apparition of the cloud-bow, mentioned earlier (see p.12). It was of a luminous arch, like a misty rainbow, one end resting on the sea, the other on the mountain top, bathing in soft effulgence the roof of the little chapel where she preached. The star (which was of unusual brilliance and magnitude, and could travel at great speed) emitted dazzling sparks, like flashing rays from a diamond. It appeared in the near southern sky and would vanish with the appearance of 'the lights', which either preceded (in the manner of the corpse-candle) or followed her, illuminating the roads that led to the chapel.[16] Like several apparitions in Edmund Jones's accounts, Mary Jones's visions represented the confluence of the everyday world and biblical motifs, like the star that went before the Magi to Bethlehem and stood in the sky over the stable (Matthew 2:9–10). Mary's star signified heavenly approval of her mission, divine guidance, and evidence of God's particular regard for the land of Wales.[17] In these ways, visions and apparitions connected contemporary Wales with God's unfolding plan of redemption, biblical history, and events in the future.

Today, there is a widespread interest in the paranormal, occultism, and encounters and abductions by unearthly beings, unparalleled since the beginning of the twentieth century. This revival is, in part, a response to the excesses and limits of scientific materialism, as it was in Jones's century. At the beginning of the new millennium, *Apparitions of Spirits in Wales* has, therefore, a renewed relevance as not only an antiquarian curiosity but also a telling anticipation of our contemporary yearnings.

Notes

NOTES ON INTRODUCTION

[1] His facility for preaching, demonstrated in early manhood, never matured into even competent oratory. Rees described Jones as being not a popular preacher, having a feeble voice and slow delivery (Thomas Rees, *History of Protestant Nonconformity in Wales, from its Rise in 1633 to the Present Time*, 1861, 2nd edn. (London: John Snow, 1883), 406).

[2] Jones was ordained in 1734 (Rees, *Protestant Nonconformity*, 405).

[3] For example, in 1782, Jones travelled on foot 400 miles to north Wales, preaching twice daily. In 1789, at the age of 87, he preached 411 times (J. Glyndwr Harris, *Edmund Jones: The Old Prophet* (Pontnewynydd: Ebenezer Church, 1987), 36, 41, 48; Griffith Jones in *The Dictionary of Welsh Bibliography down to 1940* (London: The Honourable Society of Cymmrodorion, 1959), 455).

[4] The only formal education he received was as a young boy from the local curate, Howell Prosser, who kept the village school, teaching mainly grammar and divinity at an elementary level (Solomon Owen Caradoc, *The Leaves of the Tree of Life; or, The Nations Healed by the Gospel of Jesus Christ* (Carmarthen: Samuel Lewis, 1745), v; Rees, *Protestant Nonconformity*, 404).

[5] Jones completed manuscripts for at least two further prospective publications. One comprised sermons on various subjects, including 'The Mistake of God's People, In Not Believing that God Will Give Them a Sufficiency of the Good Things of Life, For Their Support'. The theme proved true in his experience; he sustained a wife and an itinerant ministry on annual donations amounting to as little as £10. The other work is entitled 'Caradoc's Sermons', in which name he also published three works (National Library of Wales, MS 15171B; NLW MS 15170; Rees, *Protestant Nonconformity*, 406).

[6] The Revd Mr Thomas Lewis of Llan-ddew, Breconshire (a personal friend of Jones and a noted preacher) contributed at least seven accounts to Jones's collection (more than any other individual) (see accounts 2, 3, 4, 6, 23, 68 and 71).

[7] Rees, *Protestant Nonconformity*, 407.

[8] Martin Luther, *Table Talk* (1566), trans. William Hazlitt, Founts Classics, Spiritual Direction (London: Fount, 1995), 278.

[9] Interestingly, Christ does not contradict the disciples' belief in the appearance of spirits. Rather, as Calvin notes, he 'distinguisheth a corporall man, from a spirite . . . Christ sayeth that his body is palpable' (John Calvin, *A Harmonie upon Three Evangelists, Matthew, Mark, and Luke, with the Commentary*, trans. E.P. (London: George Bishop, 1584), 790).

[10] Noel Taillepied (1540–89), a Roman Catholic priest and a learned advocate for the existence of spirits, considered that Calvin's refusal to countenance supernatural manifestations was also a consequence of Protestant rejection of other aspects of Roman Catholic doctrine: 'where he [Calvin] declares that all the Fathers and Doctors of the Church have taught concerning the *Limbus Patrum* is just a grandam fable, a nursery tale for babes. All those writers who have drunk of the muddy and stinking waters of the lake of Geneva incline absolutely to deny apparitions and ghosts, and this lie they have brewed out of their superstitious hatred of Prayers of the Dead' (Calvin, *A Harmonie*, 429, 790; Noel Taillepied, *A Treatise on Ghosts* (1588) (London: Fortune Press, [1933]), 5).

[11] Edward Langton, *Supernatural: Spirits, Angels, and Demons, from the Middle Ages to the Present Time* (London: Rider & Co., 1934), 218–36.

[12] John Calvin, *Institutes of the Christian Religion*, trans. Henry Beveridge, 3 vols (Edinburgh: Calvin Translation Society, 1845), I, 120–7.

[13] Merick Casaubon, *Of Credulity and Incredulity in Things Divine and Spiritual* (London: Samuel Lownds, 1670), 171.

[14] Richard Baxter, *The Certainty of the Worlds of Spirits, Fully Evinced by Unquestionable Histories of Apparitions and Witchcrafts* (London: T. Parkhurst, 1691), [7], 14–15.

[15] Joseph Glanvill, *Saducismus Triumphatus* (1661) (London: F. Collins, 1681), 4.

[16] [Anon.], *Apparitions, Supernatural Occurrences, Demonstrative of the Soul's Immortality* (London: J. Barker, 1799), 5.

[17] The extraordinary lengths to which Jones pursued his dispute with this heresy are evident not only in his published works but also in the copious, vitriolic, and pernickety annotations he wrote in the margins of Joseph Mottershead's Deistical *Jesus Christ: A Divine Teacher. A Sermon Preached at Shrewsbury at the Ordination of the Reverend Mr Job Orton; September 18, 1745* (Birmingham: Warren, 1745). Jones's copy is deposited at the British Library, London.

[18] Edmund Jones, *A Relation of Apparitions of Spirits in the Principality of Wales; to which is Added the Remarkable Account of the Apparition in Sunderland* ([no imprint], 1780), iii; Samuel Hibbert, *Sketches of the Philosophy of Apparitions; or, An Attempt to Trace such Illusions to their Physical Causes* (London: Oliver & Boyd; Geo. B. Whittacker, 1825), 14.

[19] [Anon.], *The Possibility of Apparitions* ([no imprint]), 14–15.

[20] Richard Gilpin, *Daemonologia Sacra; or, A Treatise of Satan's Temptations* (Edinburgh: J. Nichol, 1862), 33.

[21] George Sinclair, *Satan's Invisible World Discovered* (Edinburgh: Thomas George Stevenson, 1871), lxix.

[22] 'A Clergyman', *The History of Apparitions, Ghosts, Spirits or Spectres; Consisting of a Variety of Remarkable Stories of Apparitions by People of Undoubted Veracity* (London: J. Simpson, 1762), iii; [Anon.], *Apparitions*, 6. Jones's library includes an edition of John Locke's *Essay Concerning Human Understanding* (1690).

[23] There is no evidence in Jones's published works and diaries that he had either formal affiliation with the Society (he is not mentioned in the Society's membership lists for the second half of the eighteenth century) or informal contact with the London Welsh, who were its founders (R. T. Jenkins and Helen Ramage, *A History of The Honourable Society of Cymmrodorion and of The Gwyneddigion and Cyreigyddion Societies (1751–1951)* (London: The Honourable Society of Cymmrodorion, 1951); Jones, *Relation*, 111).

[24] [Honourable Society of Cymmrodorion], *A Sketch of the History of the Cymmrodorion, Including a Re-print of the Constitutions* (London: T. Richards, 1877), 47.

[25] Giraldus Cambrensis, *The Itinerary through Wales and the Description of Wales* (London: Dent, [1908]), 25, 68–9, 86–9.

[26] An eighteenth-century account of a knocker is given in a letter of 1754, from Lewis Morris to William Morris: 'Last week three men together at our work of Llwynllwyd were ear-witnesses of knockers pumping, driving a wheelbarrow, etc., but there is no pump in the work, nor any within less than a mile of it' (Baxter, *Certainty*, 133; Jonathan Ceredig Davies, *Folk-lore of West and Mid-Wales* (1911) (Felinfach: Llanerch Publishers, 1992), 136–8; John H. Davies (ed.), *The Letters of Lewis, Richard, William and John Morris, of Anglesey*, 2 vols (Aberystwyth: John H. Davies, 1907), I, 321; W. Howells, *Cambrian Superstitions, Comprising Ghosts, Omens, Witchcraft, Traditions, Etc.* (1831), facsimile edition (Felinfach: Llanerch Publishers, 1991), 59–60; T. Gwyn Jones, *Welsh Folklore and Folk-Customs* (London: Methuen & Co., 1930), 40.

[27] Ceredig Davies relates the popular belief that: 'If the light was seen early in the evening a death was to take place soon, but if late it was not to take place for some time', and the tradition (to which Jones also referred) 'that St David, by prayer, obtained the corpse-candle as a sign to the

living of the reality of another world, and according to some people it was confined to the Diocese of St David's, but the fact of it is there are tales of corpse-candles all over Wales' (Baxter, *Certainty*, 131; Robert Burton, *The History of the Principality of Wales* (London: A. Bettesworth & J. Batley, 1730), 133; Ceredig Davies, *Folk-lore*, 202; Howells, *Cambrian Superstitions*, 59–60; Jones, *Relation*, 94–5; Marie Trevelyan, *Folk-Lore and Folk-Stories of Wales* (London: Elliot Stock, 1909), 178).

28 Jones, *Relation*, 82, 86, 89.

29 Baxter, *Certainty*, 138.

30 Trevelyan, *Folk-Lore*, 179.

31 [Anon.], 'Article IV. A Relation of Ghosts and Apparitions which Commonly Appear in the Principality of Wales', [no imprint], 86; Peter Roberts, *The Cambrian Popular Antiquities of Wales* (1815), facsimile edition (Clwyd: County Council, 1994), 169–72.

32 Jones, *Relation*, 93.

33 Jones, *Relation*, 85–8; *A Geographical, Historical, and Religious Account of the Parish of Aberystruth* (Trefeca, 1779), 73–4.

34 In Jones's works there are comparatively few reports of haunting (that is, a repeated manifestation of spirits and ghosts confined to a specific location). Hauntings take place more often in the landscape than in a house (see accounts 1, 5, 87–9, 129). Usually, the apparitions are a spontaneous or unique incidence. Where they do recur, it is only until the task, which the spirit has commissioned the witness to undertake, is completed (Jones, *Relation*, 24–7, 44–5, 76–7; NLW MS 16161B).

35 Jones, *Relation*, 1–2, 19–22, 37, 45, 52–5, 97–104; NLW MS 16161B.

36 Jones, *Relation*, 1–2, 62–8; NLW MS 16161B.

37 Surprisingly, Jones did not know about or else chose not to include the account of a remarkable apparition that took place in the sky over Carmarthen. It was seen by many people simultaneously and comprised groanings, appeals, and cries, and what appeared to be a succession of aerial battles between two armies and two fleets of ships which took place over many hours on two successive days. Some writers claimed that similar prodigies appeared over other parts of Great Britain and several European countries during the seventeenth century. In England, these manifestations may have expressed a collective, social anxiety in response to a century characterized by instability, civil war, and great disasters, notably the Great Plague and the Great Fire of London (Henry Lewys, *The True and Wonderful Relation of the Dreadful Fighting and Groans that were Heard and Seen in the Ayr, on the Fifteenth of this Instant January in Carmarthen, in South Wales* ([London]: W. T. & S. C., 1681)).

38 Jones, *Relation*, 111.

39 Jones was responsible for bringing Harris to preach for the first time in Monmouthshire in 1738. His friendship with Harris was severely strained when, fearing that Methodism would draw Nonconformists away to the Established Church, Jones encouraged societies to re-constitute themselves into Independent churches at Devynock and Neath (Rees, *Protestant Nonconformity*, 336).

40 Glanmor Williams, *The Welsh and their Religion: Historical Essays* (Cardiff: University of Wales Press, 1991), 50.

41 Geraint H. Jenkins, *Protestant Dissenters in Wales 1639–1689*, The Past in Perspective (Cardiff: University of Wales Press, 1992), 2; Edgar Phillips, *Edmund Jones 'The Old Prophet'* (London: Robert Hale, 1959), 11–13.

42 Jonathan Edwards, *The Works of Jonathan Edwards* (1834), 2 vols (Edinburgh: Banner of Truth Trust, 1974), I, 397–8; David Hamilton, *The Inward Testimony of the Spirit of Christ to his Outward Revelation* (London: John Lawrence, 1701), 67–86.

43 Jones, *Relation*, vi, 58.

44 Ibid., 14–15.

45 Conjuring was denounced by the Scriptures (Deuteronomy 18:10–12) and prohibited by both

Protestants and Roman Catholics. It was not a parlour trick but a medieval black-magic ritual which typically involved magic circles and the use of consecrated candles, incense, a rod or wand, a talisman, the drawing of images, special garments, and drumming. Intellectuals, including scientists, philosophers, and (conspicuously, in Jones's accounts) clergymen, practised the art. They evoked and bound demons, usually in deserted places (such as in woods, at crossroads, amid ruins, and by the seashore), in order to reveal secret knowledge or receive a commission to work mischief, retrieve money, or find hidden treasure. Ceredig Davies implies that conjurors had an important and valued role within communities. John Harries (d. 1839), for example, had power over lunatics, could cure diseases in people and cattle, foretell future events, advise people on their future marriage partners, help find missing things, protect people from witches, and exorcise spirits (Ceredig Davies, *Folk-lore*, 252–3, 59; J. H. Davies, *Rhai o Hen Ddewiniaid Cymru* (London: Grellier a'i Fab, 1901); Claire Fanger, *Conjuring Spirits: Texts and Traditions of Medieval Ritual Magic*, Magic in History series (Stroud: Sutton Publishing, 1999), ix–x; Montague Summers, *Witchcraft and Black Magic* (1946) (London: Arrow Books, 1974), 234–5, 248; Keith Thomas, *Religion and the Decline of Magic* (1971) (Harmondsworth: Penguin Books, 1973), 709).

[46] Jones, *Relation*, 17–19, 36, 87–8; Andrew Joynes, *Medieval Ghost Stories: An Anthology of Miracles, Marvels and Prodigies* (Woodbridge: Boydell Press, 2001), 34; NLW MS 16161B.

[47] Ceredig Davies, *Folk-lore*, 152–60.

[48] Jones, *Relation*, 67.

[49] NLW MS 16161B.

[50] Jones, *Relation*, 31–2, 107–8; NLW MS 16161B.

[51] Jones, *Relation*, 8–9, 55–7, 79–82.

[52] Jones, *Geographical*, 9–11, 28, 78; *Relation*, 24–5, 46–7; NLW MS 16161B.

[53] Jones, *Geographical*, 75–6; Jones, *Relation*, 8, 11–12, 23–4, 39–40; NLW MS 16161B.

[54] Jones, *Relation*, 31.

[55] Glanvill, *Saducismus*, 139.

[56] Sinclair, *Satan's Invisible World*, 10–11, 14; Francis Hutchinson, *Historical Essay concerning Witchcraft* (London: R. Knaplock, 1720), 9.

[57] NLW MS 7029A.

[58] For instance, the annual wage for farm servants in Glamorgan in the early 1790s averaged between £5 and £6 and as much as £8, £9 and £10 (David H. Howell, *The Rural Poor in Eighteenth-Century Wales* (Cardiff: University of Wales Press, 2000), 69).

[59] The full cost of printing may have included at least one other payment for printing materials. Two years earlier, Jones 'paid 3 f[lorins] for 6 sheaves of paper, 10 shillings for a ream at Trefeca on the 11 day of the month of March for future printing' (NLW MS 1728).

[60] The 1780 edition contains elements of printing ornament (such as the colophons) similar to those found in his *A Geographical, Historical, and Religious Account of the Parish of Aberystruth*, which the Trefeca press printed a year earlier. However, it appears that Jones intended The Honourable Society of Cymmrodorion to publish the book; his reference (made in the context of his discussion of the Society) to the preparation of 'this kind of work for the Press' suggests this (see note 23). However, the Society may not have wished to associate with Jones's publication due to its fiercely polemical tone, insistence on the unquestionable veracity of the accounts, and theological tub-thumping, which would not have accorded with the Society's more scholarly, dispassionate, and non-partisan principles of investigation.

[61] Evans was not alone or premature in his opinion. The account of apparitions included in *A Geographical, Historical, and Religious Account of the Parish of Aberystruth*, in the opinion of Jones's vindicators, had met with 'weak, inconsiderate and unjust' censure shortly after its publication. Enthusiasts like Jones were easy targets, and shot at often. Typically, *A History of the Ridiculous Extravagancies of Monsieur Oufle* by the French Roman Catholic Abbot Bordelon, published in English at the beginning of the eighteenth century, takes as its subject a whimsical,

credulous, and fictional character (in the tradition of Don Quixote). The work was designed to exemplify and expose the ridiculousness of those who, 'depraved' by reading books on fairies, magic, astrology, apparitions and other superstitious practices, believed everything they read or heard (Abbot Bordelon, *A History of the Ridiculous Extravagancies of Monsieur Oufle* (London: J. Morphew 1711), [ii–iii]; J. Evans, *A Topographical and Historical Description of the County of Monmouth* (London: Sherwood, Neely and Jones, 1810), 102–3; Jones, *Relation*, vii).

[62] Jones, *Geographical*, 75–6.

[63] He was a prolific preacher. In his *History of Protestant Nonconformity in Wales*, Rees included an inventory of the number of times Jones delivered sermons for each of the following years: 1731 (104), 1732 (76), 1739 (240), 1768 (300), 1770 (337), 1773 (511), 1778 (260), 1780 (340), 1789 (405). This fact alone refutes John Evans's cloaked criticism that Jones had 'much leisure time' (Evans, *County of Monmouth*, 102; Rees, *Protestant Nonconformity*, 405–6).

[64] NLW MS 7030A.

[65] NLW MS 16161B.

[66] Owen Evans, 'Edmund Jones – "Yr Hen Broffwyd" – O Bontypool', *Y Geninen* (March, 1905), 17–25; Evan Jones, 'Edmund Jones a'i Amseroedd', *Yr Adolygydd*, 1 (June, 1850) 100–18; 3 (Dec., 1850) 227–301.

[67] Jones, *Geographical*, 104–5.

[68] See T. B., *A Treatise on Specters; or, An History of Apparitions, Oracles, Prophecies, and Predictions* (London: John Streater, 1658); Roberts, *Cambrian Popular Antiquities*, 270–300.

[69] Jones's extant library (84 volumes deposited at the National Library of Wales, Aberystwyth) includes a number of books by divines such as Bernard Sentent, Jeremiah Burroghes, and George Hutcheson on major and minor Old Testament prophets. Typologically, for example, the ark typifies the Church of Christ, Noah is a type of Christ, and Mount Ararat is a pattern of heaven (Edmund Jones, *Two Sermons, First of the Creatures Going into Noah's Ark; Typically Representing the Salvation of God's Elect Church in and by Jesus Christ. Second of the Creatures Going Out of the Ark to Mount Ararat, Typically Representing The Removal of the Church Militant Out of the State of Grace into the State of Glory* (Trefeca: 1781), 54).

[70] Caradoc, *The Leaves of the Tree of Life*, v.

[71] Edmund Jones, *Samson's Hair, An Eminent Representation of the Church of God: in Two Parts. To Which is Added, Two Sermons: First Showing, the Evil Nature and Hurtful Effects of Unbelief. Second, of God's Subduing and Keeping under the Strong Corruptions of His People: and Healing Them* (Trefeca, 1777), 10, 12.

[72] Jones also repeatedly stressed that the operations of the spirits 'in this world' were sometimes mysterious and incomprehensible; their meaning would be fully understood only in eternity (Jones, *Relation*, 78–9; NLW MS 16161B).

[73] John Wood Oman, *The Natural and the Supernatural* (Cambridge: Cambridge University Press, 1931), 72.

[74] Andrew Moreton, *The Secrets of the Invisible World Disclosed; or, An Universal History of Apparitions* (London: J. Clarke, 1729), 54.

[75] Milton Klonsky, *William Blake: The Seer and his Visions* (London: Orbis Publishing, 1977), 10.

[76] This mode of vision seemed 'to have involved an element of hallucination' (Kenneth Clarke, *Blake and Visionary Art* (Glasgow: University of Glasgow Press, 1973), 5).

[77] Cambrensis, *Itinerary*, 55.

[78] Glanvill, *Saducismus*, 35–6.

[79] There are instances, Jones records, where the apparition requires the assistance of human hands to retrieve and dispose of money and other property, which they had hid when alive. This suggests that the apparition either did not possess the requisite materiality to undertake the task itself, or that a human agency was necessary for other reasons (see accounts 2, 3, 41–2, 49) (Jones, *Relation*, v, 1–2, 63–9).

[80] Again, when Ursula Powel's departed sweetheart returned to her: 'She felt his face, as she

thought as cold as a stone' (see account 9). The belief in corporeal apparitions goes back at least to the Middle Ages, when ghosts assumed five distinct forms. The first four forms mentioned below may have assumed material substance: first, the living dead: there is no perceptible difference between the ghost and the person(s) to whom it appears, until it vanishes; secondly, the soul: the ghost takes the form of a small, naked infant, sometimes seen emerging from the mouth of the deceased; thirdly, the phantom: the ghost appears enveloped in a diaphanous shroud; fourthly, the living cadaver: the ghost's 'body' is in a more or less advanced state of decomposition (the *transi* – the skeletal personification of death – is closely related to this type); and, lastly, the invisible: the ghost's presence is vouched for by the text accompanying the image rather than by the image implicitly (ibid., 36, 39–40; NLW MS 16161B; Jean-Claude Schmitt, *Ghosts in the Middle Ages: The Living and the Dead in Medieval Society* (Chicago, London: University of Chicago Press, 1998), 195–219).

[81] The 'Drummer of Tedworth' is an account of audition (rather than an apparition) accompanied by poltergeist activity. The phenomenon was manifest in drumming noises which originated from above the roof of a house. The engraving makes the invisible source of the disturbance comprehensible, envisaging the spirits in the form of a dark, winged satyr banging a drum accompanied by dragon- and serpent-like creatures suspended above the house (Glanvill, *Saducismus*, [iii]; Sinclair, *Satan's Invisible World*, 55–75).

[82] Artists, unlike storytellers and writers, wrestle with the difficulty of conveying an apparition's otherness and discontinuity with the physical world through the stubborn substantiality of their materials. Pictorial illustrations, moreover, necessarily give fixity to the verbal or textual account: they are imaginative interpretations – retellings of the stories, no more true or binding than the mental images we each conjure up when reading apparition accounts. In the nineteenth century, the development of more realistic modes of representation – larger format, steel-plate engraving, and photography – permitted the representation of vaporous and transparent ghosts (accounts of which go back at least to antiquity), and a visual iconography capable of suggesting a material difference between the apparition and the physical world it inhabited.

[83] Jones, *Relation*, 17–18.

[84] John Alderson, *An Essay on Apparitions in which their Appearance is Accounted for by Causes Wholly Independent of Preternatural Agency* (London: Longman, Hurst, Rees, Orme, 1823), 50.

[85] Edmund Burke, *A Philosophical Enquiry into the Origin of our Ideas of the Sublime and Beautiful* (1759), Scolar Press facsimile, 2nd edn. (Menston: Scolar Press, 1970), 99.

[86] Ibid., 102.

[87] Jones, *Geographical*, vii.

[88] The sensation of feeling no clothes on encountering an apparition was a common response (Jones, *Relation*, 3, 37, 78).

[89] Ibid., 6–8.

[90] J. H. Clark, *The History of Monmouthshire* (Usk: County Observer Office [1869]), 32; Jones, *Geographical*, 10–11.

[91] Chorography was the term used in the seventeenth century to denote the description and delineation of countries or districts in a manner that combined aspects of the study of their geography and topography.

[92] Jones, *Geographical*, 19.

[93] Ibid., 50.

[94] William Coxe, *An Historical Tour of Monmouthshire* (London: T. Caldwell & W. Davies, 1801), 245.

[95] Prior to the standardization of orthography 'Aberystruth' was also spelt 'Aberystwith' and 'Aberystwyth' (Evans, *Topographical and Historical Description*, 101; D. P. M. Michael, *The Mapping of Monmouthshire* (Bristol: Regional Publications, 1985), 30).

[96] See: John Thomas Barber, *A Tour throughout South Wales and Monmouthshire: Comprehending a General Survey of the Picturesque Scenery, Remains of Antiquity* (London: J. Nichols, 1803), 270–3; Benjamin Heath Malkin, *The Scenery, Antiquities, and Biography of South Wales, from Materials*

Collected during Two Excursions in the Year 1803 (London: T. N. Longman & O. Rees, 1804), 178; *Black's Picturesque Guide through North and South Wales and Monmouthshire* (Edinburgh: Adam & Charles Black, 1854), 363.

[97] Jones, *Geographical*, 53–4.

[98] No detailed descriptions of the church are extant. It was Gothic, built from local stone with a stone-tiled roof and an embattled tower on the north-west corner. The walls were whitewashed inside and out. On the interior east wall, over the nave, there was a painting, mentioned by Coxe, showing 'a whimsical group carved in wood, and painted; two angels are represented, and between them a clergyman in his robes, holding an enormous trumpet in his hand, as if fatigued with blowing'. Jones also described what was presumably an earlier painting showing the Apostle Peter 'with a key by his side to let the people in Heaven'. In either case, the paintings were the only example of religious art or of the depiction of supernatural entities in the parish (Coxe, *Historical Tour*, 250; Jones, *Geographical*, 51–2; NLW MS 16156B).

[99] Malcom Andrews, *The Search for the Picturesque: Landscape, Aesthetics and Tourism in Britain, 1760–1800* (Aldershot: Scolar Press, 1989), viii.

[100] [Anon.], 'Article IV', 70.

[101] Coxe, *Historical Tour*, 250.

[102] Basil Willey, *The Eighteenth Century: Background* (London: Chatto & Windus, 1940), 4.

[103] Jones, *Geographical*, 31–2.

[104] Ibid., 18; John Speed and Peter Koerius, *Description of Great Britain: Wales and Monmouth* (1627), [33].

[105] Jones, *Geographical*, 34; Wyndam H. Penruddocke, *A Gentleman's Tour through Wales* (London: T. Evans, 1781), 213.

[106] Burton, *History*, 127; Speed, *Description*, [19].

[107] Jones, *Geographical*, 37

[108] NLW MS 7025A.

[109] Newell relates a conversation he had with a Wesleyan Methodist woman about another mysterious inscribed stone, which, she suggested, had a supernatural aura: 'When at Aberystwyth [Ceredigion], I chanced to mention the fall of the Rhydoll to an old lady, who asked me, if I had seen the wonderful stone there? What stone? Why, one on which, as she had heard, there were words written, which no man could read!' (Jones, *Geographical*, 62; R. H. Newell, *Letters on the Scenery of Wales; including a Series of Subjects for the Pencil, with their Stations* (London: Baldwin, Cradock & Joy, 1821), 83).

[110] Jones, *Geographical*, 34–5.

[111] Ibid., 11.

[112] NLW MS 7022A.

[113] Jones, *Relation*, vii.

[114] Matthew Henry, *Matthew Henry's Commentary on the Whole Bible* (Basingstoke: Marshall, Morgan & Scott, 1960), 8.

[115] NLW MS 16161B.

[116] Burke, *Philosophical Enquiry*, 274–5.

[117] Jones, *Relation*, 129.

[118] Edmund Jones, *Two Sermons, First Showing the Misery of Those who are without the Light of Christ; Second Showing the Felicity of Being in the State of the Light of Grace* (Trefeca, 1776), 30.

[119] Here the quality of sound (strangely) clarifies the visual aspect of this account, as it does in the story of the black man: 'he whistled' – an attribute so odd and wholly unexpected, that its mention intensifies both the sense of the apparition and of place. The audible accompaniment to apparitions made an equally startling impression on both the witnesses and Jones. For example, the departure of a spirit is frequently with such a fearful 'noise as if all about [or 'the world'] was going to pieces' (Jones, *Relation*, 40–1, 58, 84; NLW MS 16161B).

[120] In another of Jones's accounts (see account 74), the black man is again in proximity to a holly tree and described as having 'the resemblance of a man but of somewhat odd figure'. In this

account, the 'black man became two men' and is unequivocally identified as a devil. Jones suggests the significance of the holly tree in account 94 (NLW MS 16161B; Andrew MacKenzie, *Apparitions and Ghosts: A Modern Study* (London: Arthur Baker, 1971), 11).

[121] Baxter, *Certainty*, 38; Glanvill, *Saducismus*, 127; Sinclair, *Satan's Invisible World*, 14.

[122] S.O.C., *The Miraculous Increase of Jacob's Flock Opened and Applied from Genesis XXX.25* (London: Edmund Jones; J. Oswald, 1753), 135.

[123] Burke tells the story of a boy, once blind, whose sight was restored. On seeing a 'negro woman', he became frightened – so powerful was the association of black and terror for him (Burke, *Philosophical Enquiry*, 276; S.O.C, *Miraculous Increase*, 135).

[124] The image of the devil in cloven hoofs, horns, and tail is derived from the iconography of the Greek god Pan and the satyrs of Greek myth (Robin Lane Fox, *Pagans and Christians* (New York: Harper & Row, 1988), 7).

[125] NLW MS 16161B.

[126] Jones, *Relation*, 69.

[127] Ibid., 30.

[128] Ibid., 77.

[129] In another history of spirits, there is an account of a man on all fours who went into a hedge, but without rustling its leaves ([Anon.], *Fair and Fatal Warnings; or, Visits from the World of Spirits; Being Concise Relations of the Most Curious and Remarkable Apparitions, Ghosts, Spectres, and Visions* (London: T. & R. Hughes, [n.d.]), 7; Jones, *Relation*, 28).

[130] We do not know whether accounts of spirits crawling on all fours influenced Blake's image. Lister believes he was possibly indebted to the following pictorial antecedents: a contemporary drawing by John Hamilton Mortimer entitled 'Nebuchadnezzar Recovering his Reason', an anonymous engraving of Cicero from 1531 and Dürer's engraving of the 'Penance of St John Chrysostomus' (Raymond Lister, *The Paintings of William Blake* (Cambridge: Cambridge University Press, 1986), [46]).

[131] The analogy, made in the theological realm, between physical corruption and spiritual perversity, held true (so it was believed) in the realm of medicine, too. Some eighteenth-century physicians went as far as to suggest a causal correlation, linking a person's physical deformity and their emotional or psychological deficit: 'There certainly is a Consent between the Body and the Mind; and where Nature erreth in the one, she ventureth in the other; and therefore Deformity may be best considered, in this respect, as a Cause which seldom fails to Effect, and not as a sign . . . deformed persons are commonly [devoid] of natural affections' (William Hay, *Deformity: An Essay* (London: R. & J. Dodsley, 1755), 40–1).

[132] In the same way, witches, 'Johannes Weir, and Edward Jorden in early-seventeenth-century England, argued . . . were not indeed physically and literally possessed by the Devil but were rather suffering from the essentially organic disease, hysteria' (Roy Porter, *A Social History of Madness* (1987) (London: Phoenix Giant, 1999), 13–14, 112).

[133] Jones, *Relation*, 3–5.

[134] Ceredig Davies records that one-year-old infants would be swapped, and the changeling would have 'a very old look about him' (Ceredig Davies, *Folk-lore*, 132; Jones, *Geographical*, 79–80).

[135] Cotton Mather, *The Great Works of Christ in America: Magnalia Christi Americana* (1702), 2 vols (Edinburgh: Banner of Truth Trust, 1979), I, 206; Jones, *Relation*, 9.

[136] Jones, *Relation*, 3.

[137] E. O., 'The Fairies: Their Kindness'; 'Fairies Seen', *Archaeologia Cambrensis*, 5th series, III, 9 (January 1886), 72–3 (72–3).

[138] A century later, severely deformed individuals were exhibited as grotesques, monstrosities, and marvels in freak-shows and travelling fairs. Interestingly, as abnormal physical types became identified as anomalies of the natural world, rather than representatives of the supernatural world, the iconography of certain spirit entities changes. Victorian photographs, putatively showing ghosts, depict apparitions of the dead with entirely normal bodies, incomplete only in respect of the extent of their materialization: they are rendered either transparent or partially

formed, showing just their head or torso. (For a historical description of physical deviance see Martin Howard, *Victorian Grotesque* (London: Jupiter Books, 1977).)

[139] Alderson, *Essay on Apparitions*, 20–1.

[140] James Frederick Ferrier, *An Essay towards a Theory of Apparitions* (London: Warrington, 1813), 119; Hibbert, *Sketches*, 133; W. Newnham, *Essay on Superstition: Being an Inquiry into the Effects of Physical Influence on the Mind* (London: J. Hatchard & Son, 1830), 268–317.

[141] Madeleine Gray, *Images of Piety: The Iconography of Traditional Religion in Late Medieval Wales*, BAR British Series 316 (Oxford: Archaeopress, 2000), 1.

[142] Ceredig Davies relates that at the *gwylnos* (wake-night) it was 'customary to keep vigil over the dead . . . in order to pass the time a good many stories were related about corpse candles and phantom funerals, etc.' (Ceredig Davies, *Folk-lore*, 41).

[143] In the occult symbolism of ancient Egyptian religion, the pyramid is associated with the afterlife and rebirth; astronomical and mystical significance and power are attributed to the structure's dimensions, angles, and ratios. However, in the account of Mr Thomas Williams and Mr Hanbury's experience, Jones invested the white pyramidal form with an idiosyncratic spiritual meaning: 'that it grew narrow upward, and into nothing heavenward (as a pyramid doth in the natural heavens or the air); but was broad downward – backwards from the heaven towards the earth and hell', which suggested its antipathy to God and predilection for the devil (NLW MS 16161B).

[144] Jones, *Relation*, 29.

[145] Ibid., 37.

[146] The phenomenon of a sound 'weakening when nearer [but growing] louder when far away' was also heard in connection with the *cyhyraeth* (see account 14). Ceredig Davies records the popular belief that: 'If the howling was faint, it meant that the pack was close at hand, if loud, the hounds were only hunting at a distance. The hounds were supposed to watch for the souls of notoriously wicked men about to die.' However, one of Jones's accounts refers to the death of a woman, and none of his accounts mention the deceased's moral standing (ibid., 28, 85–6; Ceredig Davies, *Folk-lore*, 213; Trevelyan, *Folk-Lore*, 47).

[147] James, *Relation*, 31–3; Jones, *Geographical*, 80.

[148] Jones, *Relation*, 31, 17–18, 109, 77, 58; NLW MS 16161B.

[149] Jones, *Relation*, 9.

[150] Phillips, *Edmund Jones*, flyleaf.

[151] W. B. Yeats, *The Celtic Twilight: Myth, Fantasy and Folklore* (1893), 4th reprint (Bridport, Dorset: Prism Press, 1999), 86.

[152] An enlightening discussion of the contrasts between the disposition of popular folk religion in Wales and the 'official culture of Protestant Christianity' is provided by Geraint H. Jenkins in his 'Popular beliefs in Wales from the Restoration to Methodism', *Bulletin of the Board of Celtic Studies*, 27, 3 (Nov., 1977), 440–62; see also Nicole Belmont, 'Superstition and Popular Religion in Western Societies', in *Between Belief and Transgression: Structuralist Essays in Religion, History, and Myth*, edited by Pierre Smith and Michael Izard (Chicago, London: University of Chicago Press, 1982), 9–23.

[153]

> Hobgoblin, nor foul Fiend,
> Can daunt his Spirit;
> He knows he at the *end*
> *Shall Life inherit*,
> Then Fancies fly away,
> He'll ne'er fear what Men say,
> But labour Night and Day
> *To be a Pilgrim.*

(John Bunyan, *The Pilgrim's Progress from This World to That which is to Come*, 2nd part (London: A.W. for W. Johnston, 1754), 157).

Notes to A Note on the Text

[1] H. Lewis was the first press established in Newport, Monmouthshire. He was not alone in corrupting Jones's book. The folklorist Wirt Sikes comments that copies of Lewis's edition were 'extremely rare, and writers who have quoted from them have generally been content to do so at second-hand. Keightley, quoting from the "Apparitions", misprints the author's name as "Edward Jones of the Tiarch", and credits the publication to "the latter half of the nineteenth century"' (Ifano Jones, *A History of Printing and Printers in Wales to 1810* (Cardiff: William Lewis, 1925), 240; Wirt Sikes, *British Goblins: Welsh Folk-lore, Fairy Mythology, Legends and Traditions* (London: Sampson Low, Marston, Searle and Rivington, 1880), 104).

[2] Local place-names have altered, sometimes considerably, over the years, reflecting changes in the pronunciation, rationalization of the meaning, and either the partial or the wholesale anglicization of the Welsh forms. Furthermore, there was considerable variation in the spelling of some place-names during the same period. (Jones sometimes spelled the same place-name in several different ways within the editions and holograph of apparition accounts, and used anglicized forms for some places and Welsh forms for others.) I have adopted a pragmatic approach to the orthography, consonant with one of the chief objectives of this edition: to render Jones's work intelligible to a contemporary readership. To this end, I have enabled readers (from inside and outside Wales) to identify the sites of apparition accounts in Jones's book in relation to a map of the country today, as far as possible. (Some place-names, such as those associated with farms and fields, have long since disappeared, together with the landmarks they denoted.) No doubt, Welsh-speaking readers would prefer me to have restored the Welsh forms of anglicized place-names. However, many of the English-speaking Welsh (like me) are equally passionate about retaining the anglicized spelling of the names of their towns and villages, with which they are familiar. Inevitably, my policy will not please everyone (Elwyn Davies (ed.), *Rhestr o Enwau Lleoedd / A Gazetteer of Welsh Place-Names* (Cardiff: University of Wales Press, 1958); G. Ellis, *A List of Welsh Place-Names*, 2 vols (Cardiff: National Museum of Wales, 1968); Melville Richards, *Welsh Administrative and Territorial Units: Medieval and Modern* (Cardiff: University of Wales Press, 1969)).

[3] Part two of the 1780 edition was dedicated to accounts of good spirits and of apparitions in England and comprised the following: 'An Extraordinary Account of Elizabeth Hobson'; 'A Notable Account of a certain Person's Conversation with an evil Spirit to his own ruin, Etc.'; 'Remarks'; 'Of the Heavenly Dream of the Rev. Dr Dodderidge'; 'Of the Devil's attempt to send out a Minister to Preach the Gospel, Etc.'; and 'Of the Apparition to Lord Lyttleton, warning him of his sudden dissolution, Etc.'. Jones included the English examples in order 'to prevent some wrong thoughts that may arise in some English readers, that Wales is a hellish place where so many Apparitions have been seen, and far worse than England'. The account of Elizabeth Hobson had been published previously by John Wesley and later appeared in several compilations by other collectors of apparition accounts in England. Similarly, the accounts concerning Philip Dodderidge and Lord Lyttleton were published earlier and elsewhere (Jones, *Relation*, 105–36).

[4] Jones organized the accounts of apparitions in Wales (which comprise part one of the 1780 edition) into two sections: by parish and by county. Neither section is set out alphabetically. His decision to classify the accounts by location rather than by, say, the type of apparition, reflects one of the author's other preoccupations, namely, the study of Wales's geography.

[5] Williams was a schoolmaster at Pontypridd, Glamorgan. The manuscript was donated to the National Library of Wales, Aberystwyth by Dr and Mrs T. J. M. Gregg of Swansea (NLW MS 16161B; National Library of Wales, *Annual Report, 1957–1958* (Aberystwyth: National Library of Wales, 1958), 23).

[6] For example, Edgar Phillips proposed that the first edition was published in 1767, the second edition in 1780, and the third edition in 1813. Sikes, it seems, was not aware of any edition of

this 'quaint' book by the 'The Prophet Jones' (as Sikes called him), before that of 1813 (Phillips, *Edmund Jones*, 66; Sikes, *British Goblins*, 27).

Notes to *Apparitions of Spirits in Wales*

1 Groat: a denomination of money.
2 Ceredig Davies names the ghost as one Anne Dewy (Ceredig Davies, *Folk-lore*, 156).
3 Ceredig Davies records accounts not only of humans but also of churches being, likewise, transported supernaturally (Ceredig Davies, *Folk-lore*, 149, 175–8).
4 Lake Syfaddan [Llyn Syfaddan]: more commonly known today as Llangorse lake. The lake had a history of supernatural associations and manifestations. Howells described it as a 'dark and extensive lake . . . supposed to carry no more water out than it brought in; do you ask why? know that *Llyn Savadhan* is a curtain o'er a scene, a lesson to man, and *was* the winding sheet of many a fair corse. The silvery strains of the *telyn* (harp) have oft been heard in that spot, and the laughing voice of the fair, with the loud shouts of drunkenness and revelry, have often filled the surrounding air' (Howells, *Cambrian Superstitions*, 100).
5 Piffing: an imitation of various sounds as that made by the swift noise of a bullet travelling through the air.
6 Such lights were often referred to as *tânwedd* (fiery light). Ceredig Davies quotes what he says is an observation on the phenomenon by Edmund Jones: 'When it falls to the ground it sparkleth and lightens. The freeholders and landlords upon whose ground it falls die in a short time after.' However, the extract does not appear in any of Jones's writings on apparitions (Ceredig Davies, *Folk-lore*, 213).
7 For further examples of stone throwing see Ceredig Davies, *Folk-lore*, 150–2.
8 Dissenters and Nonconformists had no ceremony of ecclesiastical exorcism. They attempted to 'lay' ghosts and spirits not with a bell, book and candle, but with prayer and Bible reading. Ceredig Davies relates: 'When a spirit troubled a house in Wales, it was sometimes customary to call together the most godly persons in the parish to hold a prayer meeting.' Griffith Evans provides an account of a haunted house called Penhelyg, near Aberdovey, Merioneth, in 1845. His father stayed at the house, reading his Bible (making notes in preparation for Sunday school lessons). He heard and saw little activity. But, thereafter, the noises ceased. His reading the Bible was believed, by some, to have exorcised the spirit (1845) (Ceredig Davies, *Folk-lore*, 189; Griffith Evans, 'Exorcism in Wales', *Folk-Lore: A Quarterly Review of Myth, Tradition, Institution, and Custom*, III, 2 (1892), 274–7 (274–5)).
9 Sir David (Dafydd) Llwyd was reputed to have also 'had a most wonderful control over the demons'. 'Sir' was commonly used as the title of a priest in pre-Reformation times (Ceredig Davies, *Folk-lore*, 248–52).
10 Thomas Lewis was later the vicar of Llan-ddew (1741–83).
11 Commot: in Wales, a territorial or administrative division usually subordinate to a hundred (Welsh: *cantref*), being a division of land.
12 Williams's transcription includes both 'Rhiw Edwft' and 'Rhiw Gewith' [*sic*: Gewydd], suggesting that the place-name is indecipherable in the original holograph.
13 For further examples of singing heard before a death, see Ceredig Davies, *Folk-lore*, 200–1.
14 Gingle: an obsolete form of jingle.
15 Niggard: parsimonious.
16 Cavil: a captious or frivolous objection.
17 According to Williams, the next line is indecipherable in the original holograph.
18 According to Williams, part of this sentence is indecipherable in the original holograph.
19 Tridoll valley: does not correspond to any area denoted on maps of Glamorganshire made during the eighteenth century.

[20] Marment: probably a variant or misspelling of marmite, being an earthenware cooking vessel.

[21] Gads of the steeller: the meaning is obscure. Gads are spikes, a handle, or a shaft; steeler: the Welsh forms *stilliard* and *stiliers* are derived from the English forms stilliard and steelyard, being a balance or scales consisting of a level with unequal arms.

[22] Trencher: a flat board of wood, square or circular.

[23] *Cawnen*: probably a misspelling and derivation from the Welsh form grawn, meaning corn.

[24] Sikes observed that 'The Welsh fairies are most often dancing together when seen' (Sikes, *British Goblins*, 70).

[25] Bottoms: the meaning is obscure. It might refer to remnants or offcuts of wool.

[26] Mastiff: a large, strong dog with drooping ears and pendulous lips. Dogs were regarded as an incarnation of the devil. Ceredig Davies relates that, in Wales, it was believed that the devil could assume any shape apart from a white sheep (Ceredig Davies, *Folk-lore*, 181; James I, *Daemonologia* (1597), Number 94: The English Experience, facsimile edition (Amsterdam, New York: Da Capo Press, 1969), 19; Trevelyan, *Folk-lore*, 152).

[27] Boul: an obsolete form of 'bowl', being a round vessel.

[28] Jones, *Geographical*, 112–14.

[29] Wirt Sikes expressed some doubt about Jones's interpretation of events: 'Conceding that the Reverend Edmund Jones, the dissenting minister, was an honest gentleman who meant to tell truth, it is still possible that Master Neddy Jones, the lad, could draw a long bow like another boy; and that having seen, possibly, some gypsy group (or possibly nothing whatever) he embellished his tale to excite wonderment, as boys do. Telling a fictitious tale so often that one at last comes to believe it oneself, is a well-known mental phenomenon' (Sikes, *British Goblins*, 110).

[30] The illustration showing the form that the fairies made derives from Jones's 1780 edition of apparition accounts. It was reprinted in the 1813 edition, and represented in Sikes's *British Goblins* (Sikes, 98).

[31] Phantom funeral (Welsh: *toili*), (Ceredig Davies, *Folk-lore*, 193).

[32] It was popularly believed that a changeling could be vanquished by holding a red-hot shovel to its face (Ceredig Davies, *Folk-lore*, 132).

[33] Sikes includes a discussion of the changeling and a retelling of the accounts of Dazzy Walter's and Jennet Francis's experience, although he makes no reference to Jones's book as the source (Sikes, *British Goblins*, 56, 62–3).

[34] Conjurors, like witches, were commonly believed to possess the ability to assume the shapes of animals.

[35] Twyn Gwynllyw: today known as St Woolos.

[36] For further examples of fairy money see Ceredig Davies, *Folk-lore*, 134.

[37] A discussion of the origin and development of the notion of 'The Witch as Hare' can be found in George Ewart Edwards and David Thompson, *The Leaping Hare* (London: Faber & Faber, 1972), 142–77; see also Ceredig Davies, *Folk-lore*, 242–5.

[38] Watch-nights may correspond to wake-nights (the term used in Pembrokeshire), at which strange and mysterious events sometimes took place, including disembodied sounds and phantom removals of the corpse (Ceredig Davies, *Folk-lore*, 44–5).

[39] Bowl and puis: bowl is an obsolete form of ball; the meaning and derivation of puis is unknown.

[40] Dipas, drine, macas: the names are obscure. They may be derived from the following species of venomous snakes: *Dipsadoboa*, *Drysdalia* and *Macrelaps*.

[41] Witnesses dispatched ghosts in the same way (Ceredig Davies, *Folk-lore*, 188).

[42] Rheen or rhine: a large open ditch or drain.

[43] Roller: a rotating cylinder.

[44] Dun: a dull, greyish-brown colour.

[45] Kann (or kan): an obsolete form of can.

[46] Plashy: a plash is a marshy pool.

[47] Pen y ddoi-gae: does not correspond to the name of any mountain denoted on maps of either

Monmouthshire or Breconshire made during the eighteenth century. Possibly, it is a variant spelling of Penygawsai.

[48] The transformation of the apparition of a figure or animal into a ball of light or fire was a relatively common occurrence in spirit narratives, signifying a manifestation of the devil (see account 130) (Ceredig Davies, *Folk-lore*, 154, 180; Trevelyan, *Folk-lore*, 152).

[49] Lanhither and Abergweidd do not correspond to the names of any villages denoted on maps of this parish made during the eighteenth century. Possibly, they are variant Welsh forms of Llanhilleth and Aberbeeg.

[50] Bowl: either bowl-shaped, like a basin, bowl or spoon, or the form of a ball, globe or sphere (see accounts 100, 118, 125); pompion: a large melon or pumpkin. The word occurs in the Welsh translation of the Bible (1588) as an early borrowing from English.

[51] See account 130.

[52] See accounts 14, 15, 16.

[53] See account 57.

[54] Ceredig Davies relates that 'The beautiful old Welsh air "Toriad y Dydd" (Dawn of the Day) is supposed to have been composed by the Fairies, and which they chanted just as the pale light of the east announced the approach of returning day . . . "Can y Tylwyth Teg", or "The Fairies' Song", was well known once in Wales, and these mythical beings were believed to chant it whilst dancing on summer nights' (Ceredig Davies, *Folk-lore*, 107; see also Sikes, *British Goblins*, 98–9).

[55] Cur-dog: a worthless, low-bred and snappy dog; bear-dog: large, strong dog used for bear-baiting in past.

[56] Jetting: spurting or spouting.

[57] Kybidiog and Rhadland do not correspond to any villages denoted on maps of Wales made during the eighteenth century. Possibly, Rhadland is a variant spelling of Rhuddlan, in either Ceredigion or Denbighshire.

[58] According to Williams, the end of the sentence is indecipherable in the original holograph.

[59] The phenomenon was referred to as the *tolaeth*: the sound of supernatural rapping, footsteps, or carriages before death or a funeral (Ceredig Davies, *Folk-lore*, 209).

Notes to Epilogue

[1] This would help determine whether artists, writers, and witnesses derive their images from a common source of ideation, as scholars who seek a psychological explanation for apparitions would argue. To date, little research has been done on these fascinating aspects of the paranormal.

[2] An apparition could conceivably engage in this activity, too, deploying a visual iconography which, while fearsomely transcendent, is nevertheless sufficiently intelligible to the witness's mindset to communicate its nature and purpose unambiguously.

[3] John Wesley's childhood home, Epworth Rectory, was notoriously haunted by knocks, groans, travelling furniture, and rustling gowns during the period 1716–17 (Robert Southey, *The Life of John Wesley* (1820), abridged (London: Hutchinson & Co., 1903), 17–23). Jones appears to have had, at the very least, indirect contact with Wesley. The former's unpublished manuscript, entitled 'Caradoc's Sermons', includes the inscription: 'This has been read + approved by my esteemed friend John Wesley' (Harris, *Edmund Jones*, 51; NLW MS 15170).

[4] Ceredig Davies remarked that: 'The belief in the existence of Fairies in Wales has almost died out, but we still find many people who are more or less superstitious with regard to ghosts, spirits, etc.' Somewhat to the contrary, Sikes believed that 'Among the vulgar in Wales, the belief in fairies is less nearly extinct than casual observers would likely to suppose' (Ceredig Davies, *Folk-lore*, 148; Sikes, *British Goblins*, 2).

5   Besides accounts of apparitions, these works comprised other fields of folklore customs and stories regarding, for example, the weather, birth, courtship, marriage, and death; and seasonal celebrations such as Easter, harvest, and solstice.

6   Sikes, *British Goblins*, 105, 134–5.

7   Sikes regarded the old woman of the mountain as a type of mountain fairy, and cites Jones's accounts of the old hag named Juan White, who roamed Llanhilleth mountain, as an example (see accounts 88–90) (Sikes, *British Goblins*, 13, 20–1, 30–2, 49–52).

8   Ibid., 112.

9   Ceredig Davies, *Folk-lore*, 156, 174, 204, 206, 208, 213; Sikes, *British Goblins*, 49–52, 56, 62–3, 98–9, 104–6, 110–11.

10 In one example (corresponding to Jones's account 125), Howells refers to the informant as Mr Griffith, whereas Jones provides the full name. He also omits the detail (mentioned by Jones) that the light was 'very red', together with any reference to the 'great noise overhead, as if at the top of the house', which Griffith heard a few days subsequently. However, Howells includes information absent from Jones's account, such as his reference to the light, which Griffith 'concluded was one of the Cambrian phenomena'. In another example from *A Relation of Apparitions of Spirits* (see account 124), Jones provides specific information regarding the particular parish in which the audition took place, and the name of the dying man. However, Howells is vague and general, and situates the audition 'in some parts of north Wales when the husband of the house has been quitting for immortality'. Similarly, in the account of a particular audition experienced by D. P., of Llanybyther parish, his wife, and maidservant, Jones describes 'the doleful tone of the *cyhyraeth* ', 'when it came over against the window', as pronouncing the strange words 'woolach, woolach'. Ceredig Davies refers to these same words as a general phenomenon associated with the *cyhyraeth* (Ceredig Davies, *Folk-lore*, 208; Howells, *Cambrian Superstitions*, 61, 65).

11 Ceredig Davies includes one account relating to portentous, spirit lights, which he says appeared in '"Apparitions in Wales" by Rev. Edmund Jones'. However, it is not to be found in either the 1780 and 1813 editions or the holograph manuscript. Possibly this is a case of misattribution: '"Some years ago one Jane Wyat, my wife's sister, being nurse to Baronet Rudd's three children, and his Lady being dead, his housekeeper going late into a chamber where the maidservants lay, saw five of these lights together: while after that chamber being newly plastered, a great grate of coal fire was kindled therein to hasten the drying of it. At night five of the maidservants went there to bed as these were wont, and in the morning were all found dead, and suffocated with the steam of the new-tempered lime and coal." This was at Llangathen, in Carmarthenshire' (Ceredig Davies, *Folk-lore*, 206).

12 Evangelical interest in supernatural visions was paralleled by a renewed enthusiasm for an encounter with apparitions that began over half a century earlier, in somewhat unorthodox circles. In 1848, at a supposedly haunted house in Hydesville, New York, the vigorous movement known as Spiritualism was born. Its claim to make direct communication with the spirit world through rappings and, later, feats of levitation, automatic writing, and paranormal materializations of spirits and objects offered putative evidence of survival after death. The movement spread throughout Europe and Britain, in particular, during the second half of the nineteenth century. By the 1920s, public interest in the movement had waned as science failed to provide any solid basis for its assertions, although, in the years during and shortly after the First World War, its popularity rallied, as large numbers of relatives sought solace for their bereavement at seances. Arthur Conan Doyle (1859–1930) believed in Spiritualism, as well as in fairies. He wrote *The Coming of the Fairies* (1922) in part in response to (what now appear to be obviously faked) photographs of the same, taken in 1917 by two teenage girls in Cottingley, Yorkshire. Photography had, since the 1860s, been requisitioned as a means of recording ghosts invoked at seances and, as importantly, as an instrument of verification. The reputation of the photographic medium for being an objective means of recording invested the proceedings of

the spiritualist medium with a quasi-'scientific' aura. Photographs of ghosts and fairies not only preserved the ephemeral event but also helped to propagate the proof of their existence. With the advent of photography, the (presumed) impartial eye of a camera lens replaced the testimony of honest and reliable witnesses, while the visual record displaced the textual account as the means of authenticating apparitions. Unlike Jones and his Puritan predecessors, twentieth-century Evangelical Christians did not seize upon such evidence of paranormal phenomena to vindicate belief in the afterlife. Instead, they vilified attempts to contact the dead, regarding the practice as diabolical dabbling.

[13] Jones, *Relation*, 108.

[14] Ibid., 78–9; *South Wales Daily News* (3 February 1905), 6.

[15] More paranormal activity was reported during that month than at any time during the two years of the awakening. The daily newspapers carried accounts of not only visions but also numerous sightings of ghosts (*South Wales Daily News* (11 February 1905), 11; (14 February 1905), 5; (21 February 1905), 6).

[16] Similar lights had been seen in the locality 250 years earlier. Thomas Pennant described what were called *tân dyeithr* (angelic strange fires), which moved in the sky over Cardigan Bay. Today, the luminescences are interpreted as an electromagnetic discharge, sometimes known as earth lights. One of the most often sung hymns of the revival was John Henry Newman's (1801–90) 'Lead Kindly Light'. After Jones made her visions public, the sentiment must have assumed an unusual poignancy (*Evening Express* (9 February 1905), 3; *North Wales Chronicle* (28 January 1905), 5; (11 February 1905), 6; (18 February 1905), 9; *South Wales Daily News* (23 February 1905), 6); Paul Devereux, *Earth Lights Revelation: UFOs and Mystery Lightform Phenomena* (London: Blandford, 1989).

[17] Mary Jones also saw a triangle of light with rounded corners, each side measuring five feet in length, filled with diamond lights of considerable brilliance. The triangle is an adaptation of a Renaissance symbol for the Holy Trinity, sometimes shown enclosing an eye, which radiates light to suggest the infinite holiness of God. Her vision substitutes a shining interior for the eye – a subconscious self-censorship determined by the anti-iconic tradition of Calvinism (*Evening Express* (9 February 1905), 3).

Bibliography

MANUSCRIPTS

National Library of Wales:
MS 1728
MS 7022A
MS 7025A
MS 7029A
MS 7030A
MS 15170
MS 15171B
MS 16156B
MS 16161B

NEWSPAPERS

Evening Express
North Wales Chronicle
South Wales Daily News

PRINTED SOURCES

[Anon.], *Apparitions, Supernatural Occurrences, Demonstrative of the Soul's Immortality* (London: J. Barker, 1799).
[Anon.], 'Article IV. A Relation of Ghosts and Apparitions which Commonly Appear in the Principality of Wales' ([no imprint]).
[Anon.], *Fair and Fatal Warnings; or, Visits from the World of Spirits; Being Concise Relations of the Most Curious and Remarkable Apparitions, Ghosts, Spectres, and Visions* (London: T. & R. Hughes, [n.d.]).
[Anon.], *The Possibility of Apparitions* ([no imprint]).
Alderson, John, *An Essay on Apparitions in which their Appearance is Accounted for by Causes Wholly Independent of Preternatural Agency* (London: Longman, Hurst, Rees, Orme, 1823).
Allestree, Richard, *The Causes of the Decay of Christian Piety: Or, An Impartial Investigation of the Ruines of Christian Religion Undermin'd by Unchristian Practice* (London: R. Norton, 1683).
Barber, John Thomas, *A Tour throughout South Wales and Monmouthshire: Comprehending a General Survey of the Picturesque Scenery, Remains of Antiquity* (London: J. Nichols, 1803).

Baxter, Richard, *The Certainty of the Worlds of Spirits, Fully Evinced by Unquestionable Histories of Apparitions and Witchcrafts* (London: T. Parkhurst, 1691).

Bickham, George, *A Curious Antique Collection of Bird's-eye Views of Several Counties in England and Wales* (London: R. Laurice and J. Whittle, 1796).

[Black], *Black's Picturesque Guide through North and South Wales and Monmouthshire* (Edinburgh: Adam & Charles Black, 1854).

Blake, William, *For Children: The Gates of Paradise* (Lambeth: J. Johnson, 1793).

Bordelon, Abbot, *A History of the Ridiculous Extravagancies of Monsieur Oufle* (London: J. Morphew, 1711).

Buck, Samuel, and Buck, Nathaniel, *Buck's Antiquities; Or, Venerable Remains of Above a Hundred Castles in England and Wales* (London: D. Bond, 1774).

Bunyan, John, *The Pilgrim's Progress from This World to That which is to Come*, 2nd part (London: A.W. for W. Johnston, 1754).

Burke, Edmund, *A Philosophical Enquiry into the Origin of our Ideas of the Sublime and Beautiful* (1759), a Scolar Press facsimile, 2nd edn. (Menston: Scolar Press, 1970).

Burton, Robert, *The History of the Principality of Wales* (London: A. Bettesworth & J. Batley, 1730).

Calmet, Augustine, *The Phantom World: The Philosophy of Spirits, Apparitions, Etc.* (London: Richard Bentley, 1850).

Calvin, John, *A Harmonie upon Three Evangelists, Matthew, Mark, and Luke, with the Commentary*, trans. E. P. (London: George Bishop, 1584).

Calvin, John, *Institutes of the Christian Religion*, trans. Henry Beveridge, 3 vols (Edinburgh: Calvin Translation Society, 1845).

Campbell, Archibald, *Some of The Primitive Doctrines Revived: Or the Intermediate or Middle State of Departed Souls* (London: S. Keble & R. Gosling, 1713).

Caradoc, Solomon Owen, *The Leaves of the Tree of Life: or, The Nations Healed by the Gospel of Jesus Christ* (Carmarthen: Samuel Lewis, 1745).

Caradoc, Solomon Owen, *The Evil and Punishment of Not Loving the Lord Jesus: Set Forth in a Sermon Written Upon 1 Cor. xvi. 22* (London: J. Oswald, 1748).

Caradoc, Solomon Owen, *The Miraculous Increase of Jacob's Flock Opened and Applied from Genesis XXX. 25* (London: Edmund Jones; J. Oswald, 1753).

Casaubon, Merick, *Of Credulity and Incredulity in Things Divine and Spiritual* (London: Samuel Lownds, 1670).

Clark, J. H., *The History of Monmouthshire* (Usk: County Observer Office [1869]).

'A Clergyman', *The History of Apparitions, Ghosts, Spirits or Spectres; Consisting of a Variety of Remarkable Stories of Apparitions by People of Undoubted Veracity* (London: J. Simpson, 1762).

Coxe, William, *An Historical Tour of Monmouthshire* (London: T. Cadell & W. Davies, 1801).

Davies, John H. (ed.), *The Letters of Lewis, Richard, William and John Morris, of Anglesey* (Aberystwyth: John H. Davies, 1907).

Davies, Jonathan Ceredig, *Folk-lore of West and Mid-Wales* (1911), facsimile edition (Felinfach: Llanerch Publishers, 1992).

Derham, William, *Physico-Theology: Or a Demonstration of the Being and Attributes of God from his Works of Creation* (London: W. Innys, 1713).

Donovan, Edward, *Descriptive Excursions through South Wales and Monmouthsire in the Year 1804, and the Four Preceding Summers* (1805).

Doyle, Arthur Conan, *The Coming of the Fairies* (London: Hodder & Stoughton, 1922).

Edwards, Jonathan, *The Works of Jonathan Edwards* (1834), 2 vols (Edinburgh: Banner of Truth Trust, 1974).

E.O., 'A Dead Man Appearing to his Mother', *Archaeologia Cambrensis*, 5th series, II, 8 (October 1885), 314.

E.O., 'The Fairies: Their Kindness'; 'Fairies Seen', *Archaeologia Cambrensis*, 5th series, III, 9 (January 1886), 72–3.

Evans, J., *A Topographical and Historical Description of the County of Monmouth* (London: Sherwood, Neely and Jones, 1810).

Evans, Owen, 'Edmund Jones – "Yr Hen Broffwyd" – O Bontypool', *Y Geninin* (March 1905), 17– 25.

Gifford, George, *A Discourse of the Subtill Practises of Devilles* (1587), Number 871: The English Experience, facsimile edition (Amsterdam; Norwood, New Jersey: Walter J. Johnson, Inc., 1977).

Gillies, John, *Memoirs of The Late Reverend George Whitfield, A. M.* (London: T. Williams, Gale & Curtis, & L. B. Seeley, 1811).

Gilpin, Richard, *Daemonologia Sacra; or, A Treatise of Satan's Temptations* (Edinburgh: J. Nichol, 1862).

Giraldus Cambrensis, *The Itinerary through Wales and the Description of Wales* (London: Dent [1908]).

Glanvill, Joseph, *A Blow at Modern Sadducism* (London: E. Coates, 1688).

Glanvill, Joseph, *Saducismus Triumphatus* (1661) (London: F. Collins, 1681).

Guazzo, Francesco-Maria, *Compendium Maleficarum* (1608), edited by Montague Summers, translated by E. A. Ashwin, The Church & Witchcraft series (London: John Rodker, 1929).

Hamilton, David, *The Inward Testimony of the Spirit of Christ to his Outward Revelation* (London: John Lawrence, 1701).

[Harris, Howel], *An Account of the Most Remarkable Particulars Relating to the Present Progress of the Gospel* (London: John Lewes, 1743).

Hay, William, *Deformity: An Essay* (London: R. & J. Dodsley, 1755).

Hibbert, Samuel, *Sketches of the Philosophy of Apparitions; or, An Attempt to Trace such Illusions to their Physical Causes* (London: Oliver & Boyd; Geo. B. Whittacker, 1825).

[Honourable Society of Cymmrodorion], *A Sketch of the History of the Cymmrodorion, Including a Re-print of the Constitutions* (London: T. Richards, 1877).

Howells, W., *Cambrian Superstitions, Comprising Ghosts, Omens, Witchcraft, Traditions, Etc.* (1831), facsimile edition (Felinfach: Llanerch Publishers, 1991).

Hutchinson, Francis, *Historical Essay concerning Witchcraft* (London: R. Knaplock, 1720).

James I, *Daemonologia* (1597), Number 94: The English Experience, facsimile edition (Amsterdam, New York: Da Capo Press, 1969).

Jones, Edmund, *A Geographical, Historical, and Religious Account of the Parish of Aberystruth* (Trefeca, 1779).

Jones, Edmund, *A Relation of Apparitions of Spirits in the Principality of Wales; to which is Added the Remarkable Account of the Apparition in Sunderland* ([no imprint] 1780).

Jones, Edmund, *A Relation of Apparitions of Spirits in the County of Monmouth and the Principality of Wales* (Newport: H. Lewis, 1813).

Jones, Edmund, *Samson's Hair, An Eminent Representation of the Church of God: in Two Parts. To Which is Added, Two Sermons: First Showing, the Evil Nature and Hurtful Effects of Unbelief. Second, of God's Subduing and Keeping under the Strong Corruptions of His People: and Healing Them* (Trefeca, 1777).

Jones, Edmund, *Two Sermons, First of the Creatures Going into Noah's Ark; Typically Representing the Salvation of God's Elect Church in and by Jesus Christ. Second of the Creatures Going Out of The Ark to Mount Ararat, Typically Representing The Removal of the Church Militant Out of the State of Grace into the State of Glory* (Trefeca, 1781).

Jones, Edmund, *Two Sermons, First Showing the Misery of Those who are without the Light of Christ; Second Showing the Felicity of Being in the State of the Light of Grace* (Trefeca, 1776).

Jones, Griffith, *The Dictionary of Welsh Bibliography down to 1940* (London: The Honourable Society of Cymmrodorion, 1959).

Lewys, Henry, *The True and Wonderful Relation of the Dreadful Fighting and Groans that were Heard and Seen in the Ayr, on The Fifteenth of this Instant January in Carmarthen, in South Wales* ([London]: W. T. & S. C., 1681).

Locke, John, *Essay Concerning Human Understanding* (London: Thomas Basset, 1690).

Locke, John, *The Reasonableness of Christianity: As Delivered in the Scriptures* (London: John Churchil, 1695).

Luther, Martin, *Table Talk* (1566), trans. William Hazlitt, Founts Classics, Spiritual Direction (London: Fount, 1995).

Malkin, Benjamin Heath, *The Scenery, Antiquities, and Biography of South Wales, from Materials Collected during Two Excursions in the Year 1803* (London: T. N. Longman & O. Rees, 1804).

Mather, Cotton, *The Great Works of Christ in America: Magnalia Christi Americana* (1702), 2 vols (Edinburgh: Banner of Truth Trust, 1979).

Mather, Cotton, *The Wonders of the Invisible World: Being an Account of the Tryals of Several Witches Lately Executed in New England* (1702) (London: John Russell Smith, 1862).

More, Henry, *An Antidote Against Atheism: Or an Appeal to the Natural Faculties of the Minde of Man* (London, 1653).

Mottershead, Joseph, *Jesus Christ: A Divine Teacher. A Sermon Preached at Shrewsbury at the Ordination of the Reverend Mr Job Orton; September 18, 1745* (Birmingham: Warren, 1745).

Newell, R. H., *Letters on the Scenery of Wales; including a Series of Subjects for the Pencil, with their Stations* (London: Baldwin, Cradock & Joy, 1821).

Newnham, W., *Essay on Superstition: Being an Inquiry into the Effects of Physical Influence on the Mind* (London: J. Hatchard & Son, 1830).

Pennant, Thomas, *A Tour of Wales* (1770), 2nd edn, 2 vols (London: H. Hughes, 1778–81).

Penruddocke, Wyndam H., *A Gentleman's Tour through Wales* (London: T. Evans, 1781).

Penruddocke, Wyndam H., *A Tour Through Monmouthshire and Wales, Made in the Months of June, and July 1774. And in the Months of June, July, August, 1777*, 2nd edn (London: G. Wilkie; Salisbury: E. Easton, 1781).

Quarles, Francis, *Emblemes, Divine and Moral; Together with Hieroglyphicks of the Life of Man* (1635) (London: John Clarke, 1736).

Ray, John, *Wisdom of God Manifested in the Works of the Creation* (London: Samuel Smith, 1691).

R. B., *The Kingdom of Darkness; Or, The History of Daemons, Specters, Witches, Apparitions, Possessions, Disturbances* (London: Nathaniel Crouch, 1688).

Rees, Thomas, *History of Protestant Nonconformity in Wales, from its Rise in 1633 to the Present Time*, 1861, 2nd edn. (London: John Snow, 1883).

Richards, Melville, *Welsh Administrative and Territorial Units: Medieval and Modern* (Cardiff: University of Wales Press, 1969).

Roberts, Peter, *The Cambrian Popular Antiquities of Wales* (1815), facsimile edition (Clwyd: County Council, 1994).

Sikes, Wirt, *British Goblins: Welsh Folk-lore, Fairy Mythology, Legends and Traditions* (London: Sampson Low, Marston, Searle and Rivington, 1880).

Speed, John, and Koerius, Peter, *Description of Great Britain: Wales and Monmouth* ([no imprint], 1627).

Taillepied, Noel, *A Treatise on Ghosts* (1588) (London: Fortune Press, [1933]).

T. B., *A Treatise on Specters; or, An History of Apparitions, Oracles, Prophecies, and Predictions* (London: John Streater, 1658).

Toland, John, *Christianity Not Mysterious: Or a Treatise Showing that there is Nothing in the Gospel Contrary to Reason* (London, 1695).

Williams, David, *The History of Monmouthshire* (London: Baldwin, 1796).

SECONDARY SOURCES

[Anon.], *Yr Hen Bererinion: Sef, Hanes Bywyd Richard Jones, o Lwyngwril; Rhys Dafis (y Glun Blen); ac Edmwnd Jones, o Bontypool* (Liverpool: I. Foulkes, 1880).

[Anon.], *Index Villaris: Or, An Exact Register, Alphabetically Digested, of all the Cities, Market-Towns, Parishes . . . in England and Wales* (London: T. Sawbridge & M. Gillyflower, 1690).

Andrews, Malcom, *The Search for the Picturesque: Landscape Aesthetics and Tourism in Britain 1760–1800* (Aldershot: Scolar Press, 1989).

Belmont, Nicole, 'Superstition and Popular Religion in Western Societies', in *Between Belief and Transgression: Structuralist Essays in Religion, History, and Myth*, edited by Pierre Smith and Michael Izard (Chicago, London: University of Chicago Press, 1982).

Chambers, Arthur, *Our Life After Death. Or, The Teaching of the Bible Concerning the Unseen-World* (London: Charles Taylor, 1896).

Clarke, Kenneth, *Blake and Visionary Art* (Glasgow: University of Glasgow Press, 1973).

Cooke, George Alexander, *Topographical and Statistical Description of the Principality of Wales* (London: C. Cooke, [1810]).

Davies, E. T., *An Ecclesiastical History of Monmouthshire* (Risca, Monmouthshire: Starsons, 1953).

Davies, Elwyn (ed.), *Rhestr o Enwau Lleoedd / A Gazetteer of Welsh Place-Names* (Cardiff: University of Wales Press, 1958).

Davies, John H., *Rhai o Hen Ddewiniaid Cymru* (London: Grellier a'i Fab, 1901).

Davies, T. Witton, *Magic, Divination, and Demonology* (London: James Clarke & Co., [n.d.]).

Devereux, Paul, *Earth Lights Revelation: UFOs and Mystery Lightform Phenomena* (London: Blandford, 1989).

Edwards, George Ewart, and Thompson, David, *The Leaping Hare* (London: Faber & Faber, 1972).

Ellis, G., *A List of Welsh Place-Names*, 2 vols (Cardiff: National Museum of Wales, 1968).

Evans, Griffith, 'Exorcism in Wales', *Folk-Lore: A Quarterly Review of Myth, Tradition, Institution, & Custom*, III, 2 (1892), 274–7.

Fanger, Claire, *Conjuring Spirits: Texts and Traditions of Medieval Ritual Magic*, Magic in History series (Stroud: Sutton Publishing, 1999).

Ferrier, James Frederick, *An Essay Towards a Theory of Apparitions* (London: Warrington, 1813).

Finucane, R. C., *Appearances of the Dead: A Cultural History of Ghosts* (London: Junction Books, 1982).

Fox, Robin Lane, *Pagans and Christians* (New York: Harper & Row, 1988).

Gittleson, Bernard, *Intangible Evidence* (London: Simon & Schuster, 1987).

Gray, Madeleine, *Images of Piety: The Iconography of Traditional Religion in Late Medieval Wales*, BAR British Series 316 (Oxford: Archaeopress, 2000).

Harris, J. Glyndwr, *Edmund Jones: The Old Prophet* (Pontnewynydd: Ebenezer Church, 1987).

Henry, Matthew, *Matthew Henry's Commentary on the Whole Bible* (Basingstoke: Marshall, Morgan & Scott, 1960).

Howard, Martin, *Victorian Grotesque* (London: Jupiter Books, 1977).

Howell, David H., *The Rural Poor in Eighteenth-Century Wales* (Cardiff: University of Wales Press, 2000).

Jenkins, Geraint H., 'Popular beliefs in Wales from the Restoration to Methodism', *Bulletin of the Board of Celtic Studies*, 27, 3 (Nov., 1977), 440–62.

Jenkins, Geraint H., *Protestant Dissenters in Wales 1639–1689*, The Past in Perspective (Cardiff: University of Wales Press, 1992).

Jenkins, R. T., and Ramage, Helen, *A History of The Honourable Society of Cymmrodorion and of The Gwyneddigion and Cymreigyddion Societies (1751–1951)* (London: The Honourable Society of Cymmrodorion, 1951).

Jones, Evan, 'Edmund Jones a'i Amseroedd', *Yr Adolygydd*, 1 (June, 1850) 100–18; 3 (Dec., 1850) 227–301.

Jones, Ifano, *A History of Printing and Printers in Wales to 1810* (Cardiff: William Lewis, 1925).

Jones, T. Gwyn, *Welsh Folklore and Folk-Customs* (London: Methuen & Co., 1930).

Joynes, Andrew, *Medieval Ghost Stories: An Anthology of Miracles, Marvels and Prodigies* (Woodbridge: Boydell Press, 2001).

Klonsky, Milton, *William Blake: The Seer and his Visions* (London: Orbis Publishing, 1977).

Langton, Edward, *Good and Evil Spirits: A Study of the Jewish and Christian Doctrine, its Origin and Development* (London: SPCK, 1942).

Langton, Edward, *Supernatural: Spirits, Angels, and Demons, from the Middle Ages to the Present Time* (London: Rider & Co., 1934).

Lewis, Samuel, *A Topographical Dictionary of Wales* (London: S. Lewis and Co., 1844).

Lister, Raymond, *The Paintings of William Blake* (Cambridge: Cambridge University Press, 1986).

MacKenzie, Andrew, *Apparitions and Ghosts: A Modern Study* (London: Arthur Baker, 1971).

Michael, D. P. M., *The Mapping of Monmouthshire* (Bristol: Regional Publications, 1985).

Moreton, Andrew, *The Secrets of the Invisible World Disclosed; or, An Universal History of Apparitions* (London: J. Clarke, 1729).

Morgan, Thomas, *Handbook of the Origin of Place-Names in Wales and Monmouthshire* (Merthyr Tydfil: H. W. Southey, 1887).

National Library of Wales, *Annual Report, 1957–1958* (Aberystwyth: National Library of Wales, 1958).

Oman, John Wood, *The Natural and the Supernatural* (Cambridge: Cambridge University Press, 1931).

Phillips, Edgar, *Edmund Jones, 'The Old Prophet'* (London: Robert Hale, 1959).

Porter, Roy, *A Social History of Madness* (1987) (London: Phoenix Giant, 1999).

Row, C. A., *The Supernatural in The New Testament: Possible, Credible, and Historical* (London: Frederic Norgate, 1875).

Schmitt, Jean-Claude, *Ghosts in the Middle Ages: The Living and the Dead in Medieval Society* (Chicago, London: University of Chicago Press, 1998).

Sinclair, George, *Satan's Invisible World Discovered* (Edinburgh: Thomas George Stevenson, 1871).

Southey, Robert, *The Life of John Wesley* (1820) abridged (London: Hutchinson & Co., 1903).

Summers, Montague, *Witchcraft and Black Magic* (1946) (London: Arrow Books, 1974).

Thomas, Keith, *Religion and the Decline of Magic* (1971) (Harmondsworth: Penguin Books, 1973).

Trevelyan, Marie, *Folk-Lore and Folk-Stories of Wales* (London: Elliot Stock, 1909).

Tyrrell, G. N. M., *Apparitions: Being the Seventh Frederic W. H. Meyers Memorial Lecture*, 1942 (London: The Society for Psychical Research, [1942]).

W. B. T., *Signs Before Death* (London: William Tegg & Co., 1875).

Willey, Basil, *The Eighteenth Century: Background* (London: Chatto & Windus, 1940).

Williams, Glanmor, *The Welsh and their Religion: Historical Essays* (Cardiff: University of Wales Press, 1991).

Yeats, W. B., *The Celtic Twilight: Myth, Fantasy and Folklore* (1893), 4th reprint (Bridport, Dorset: Prism Press, 1999).

Appendix: Place-names

In the table below, the left-hand column lists Welsh counties, parishes, towns, villages, mountains, lakes, and rivers as they are spelled in this edition. (The Welsh forms of commonly Anglicized place-names are given in parentheses.) The right-hand column lists Jones's usual spelling of the same names in his holograph and in the 1780 edition:

Aber Pengam	Aber Pengam
Aberafan	Aberavan
Aberbeeg (Aber-big)	Aberbeeg
Abergavenny (Y Fenni)	Abergavenny
Abergweidd	Abergweidd
Abertillery (Abertyleri)	Abertileri
Aberystruth	Aberystruth
Anglesey (Môn)	Anglesey
Amlwch	Amlwch
Arail (Arael)	Arail
Bangor	Bangor
Bassaleg (Basaleg)	Bassaleg
Bedwas	Bedwes
Bedwellty (Bedwellte)	Bedwellty
Betws	Bettws
Black Mountain (Mynydd Du)	Black Mountain
Blaen-nant-ddu	Blaen-nant-dee
Blaenwaun	Blaen y Waen
Blaen-y-cwm	Blaene y Koome
Blaen y cynw	Blaen y Knew
Bodfari	Bodvary
Brecon (Aberhonddu)	Brecon
Breconshire (Sir Frycheiniog)	Breconshire
Brynmawr (Bryn-mawr)	Brynmawr
Bwlch y Llwyn	Bwlch y Llwyn
Cae-caled	Kae-kaled
Cae'r cefn	Kae yr Keven
Caerleon (Caerllion)	Caerleon
Caernarvonshire (Sir Gaernarfon)	Caernarvonshire
Caernarvon (Caernarfon)	Carnarvon
Caerwent (Caer-went)	Caerwent
Capel Iwan	Cappel Ewen
Cardiganshire (Ceredigion)	Cardiganshire
Carmarthen (Caerfyrddin)	Carmarthen
Carmarthenshire (Sir Gaerfyrddin)	Carmarthenshire

Cefn Bach	Kevin Bach
Cefn Brith	Kevin brith
Cefnrhychdir	Keven Rhychdir
Cefnrhychdir Uchaf	Keven Rhychdir ucha
Certwyn	Certwyn
Certwyn Machen	Certwyn Machen
Christchurch (Eglwys y Drindod)	Christchurch
Cilrhedyn	Cil rhedin
Clwyd yr Helygen	Clwyd yr Helygen
Coed y paun (Coed-y-paun)	Coed y Pame
Coedycymmer	Coed y Cymmar
Cottesmore	Cot-moor
Crickhowell (Crucywel)	Crichowell
Crumlin (Crymlyn)	Crynlyn
Cwm	Koome
Cwm-celyn	Koome Kelin
Cwmllynfell	Koome Llyfynallt
Cwm y gollen	Koome y gollen
Cydweli (Kidwelly)	Cydweli
Denbigh (Dinbych)	Denbigh
Denbighshire (Sir Ddinbych)	Denbighshire
Ebbw Fawr (Ebwy Fawr)	Ebwy Vawr
Eglwys Ila	Eglwys Ila
Eilian	Elian
Elgy	Elgy
Ffynnon yr Yspryd	Ffynnon yr Yspryd
Gelli-gaer	Kelligare
Gilfach	Gilvach
Glamorganshire (Morgannwg)	Glamorganshire
Glanbrân	Glanbran
Graig y Saeson	Graig y Saeson
Hafod	Havod
Hafod-y-dafol	Havodavel
Harlech	Harlech
Hendy	Hen-dy
Henllan Amgoed	Henllan-Amgoed
Heol Bwlch y Gwynt	Heol bwlch y gwynt
Illtyd (Illtud)	Iltut
Knighton (Trefyclo)	Knighton
Kybidiog	Kybidiog
Lanhither	Lanhither
Laugharne (Talacharn)	Laugharn
Llanarthney (Llanarthne)	Lanarthney
Llanboidy	Lanboydi
Llandeilo Fawr	Landeilo Vawr
Llanddetty (Llanddeti)	Landdetty
Llandovery (Llanymddyfri)	Landovery
Llan-ddew	Llandduw/Landdw
Llanedeyrn	Lanedarn
Llanedy (Llanedi)	Lanedi
Llaneirwg	Llaneurwg

Llanelwedd	Lanelwyd
Llanfigan (Llanfeugan)	Lanvengan
Llanfihangel Llantarnam	Lanihangel Lantarnam
Llangadog	Llangadog
Llangamarch	Langamarch
Llangattock (Llangatwg)	Langattock
Llangennech	Langenich
Llangiwg (Llan-giwg)	Lanquake
Llangurig	Langyrig
Llangyndeyrn	Langyrdeirn
Llangynllo	Langynllo
Llangynwyd Fawr	Langynwyd Vawr
Llanharan	Lanharan
Llanhilleth (Llanhiledd)	Lanhithel
Llanidloes	Lanidlos
Llanllechid	Llanllechyd
Llannon	Lannon
Llantrisant	Llantrisant
Llanwinio	Lanwnio
Llanybyther (Llanybydder)	Lan y Byther
Llanychlwydog	Lanvercb-llawddog
Llidiart	Llwydart
Llynwent	Llynwent
Llywel	Lliwel
Machen	Machen
Machen cymmer	Machen cwmwr
Magor (Magwyr)	Magor
Merioneth (Meirionnydd)	Merioneth
Merionethshire (Sir Feirionnydd)	Merionethshire
Merthyr	Merthyr
Merthyr Tydfil (Merthyr Tudful)	Martyr Tidvil
Milfraen	Milvre
Monmouth (Trefynwy)	Monmouth
Monmouthshire (Sir Fynwy)	Monmouthshire
Montgomeryshire (Sir Drefaldwyn)	Montgomeryshire
Mynach	Menich
Mynyddislwyn	Monithislion
Neath (Castell-nedd)	Neath
Neuadd	Neuath
Newport (Casnewydd-ar-Wysg)	Newport
Pant	Pante
Pantmelyn	Pant melin
Pant-teg	Pant-Teag
Pant y madog	Pant y Madog
Pembrokeshire (Sir Benfro)	Pembrokeshire
Pen rhiw traine	Pen rhiw traine
Pen y ddoi-gae	Pen y ddoi-gae
Pen y Lasgarn	Pen y Lasgarn
Pen-Bre (Pen-bre)	Pen-fre
Penllwyn	Pen y Llwyn
Penmaen (Pen-maen)	Penmain

Pentre-bach	Pentre Bach
Pont Evan Llywarch	Pont Evan Lliwarch
Pont Newynydd (Pontnewynydd)	Newynith bridge
Pontvaen	Pont-Vaen
Pontymister	Pont y meister
Pontypool (Pont-y-pŵl)	Pont y Pool
Pontypridd	Pont y pryth
Pwll y Gasseg	Pwll y Gasseg
Radnorshire (Sir Faesyfed)	Radnorshire
Rhadland	Rhadland
Rhayader Gwy (Rhaeadr Gwy)	Rhaiadr Gwy
Rhiw Edwst	Rhiw Edwft
Rhiw-newynydd	Rhiwnewith
Risca (Rhisga)	Risca
Rumney (Rhymni)	Rumney
Sirhowy (Sirhywi)	Syrowy
St David's (Tyddewi)	St Davids
St Mellons (Llaneirwg)	St Melens
Swansea (Abertawe)	Swansea
Syfaddan (Llangorse Lake)	Savavan
Taf Fechan	Tave Vechan
Tafarn-y-garreg	Tavarn y Garreg
Talachddu (Talach-ddu)	Dolachddu
Tarren y Trwyn	Tarren y Trwyn
Tillery (Tyleri)	Tillery
Towy (Tywi)	Tawey
Tredavid	Tre-Davith
Trefach	Trevach
Trelech	Trelech
Tretower (Tretŵr)	Tretower
Trevethin	Trevethin
Trewyn	Trwyn
Tridoll	Tridoll
Trostra (Trostre)	Trofdra
Twyn Gwynllyw	Twyn Gwnlliw
Tŷ gwyn	Ty Gwyn
Tŷ Llan y Dwr	Ty Llan y Dwr
Tŷ Llwyn	Ty yn y Llwyn
Tŷ'r Ffynon	Ty 'r ffynon
Tŷ'n-y-fyd	Ty yn y Fid
Tŷ'r Polin	Ty 'r Polin
Wrexham (Wrecsam)	Wrexham
Wye (Gwy)	Wye
Ynis Erwith	Ynis Erwith
Ynys-Cenin	Ynis-Cenin
Ysbyty Ystwyth	Yspythi-Ystwyth
Ysgubor y Grug Llwyn	Yskibor y Gruglwyn
Ysgubor y Llan	Ysgybor y lann
Ystrad Dyvodog (Ystradyfodwg)	Ystrad Devodoc
Ystradgynlais	Ystrad-gynlas
Y Weirglodd Fawr Dafalog	Y Weirglod Vawr Davalog

Index

Italic denotes a reference to an illustration

PROMINENT PEOPLE

TYPES OF APPARITION